CONTRIBUTIONS TO ECONOMIC ANALYSIS

Volume 123

NORTH-HOLLAND PUBLISHING COMPANY
AMSTERDAM · NEW YORK · OXFORD

STUDIES IN THE ECONOMICS OF SEARCH

Editors

S. A. LIPPMAN

J. J. McCALL

UCLA

1979

NORTH-HOLLAND PUBLISHING COMPANY

AMSTERDAM · NEW YORK · OXFORD

Library of Congress Catalog Card Number 78-26150
ISBN 0-444-85222-0

Publishers:

NORTH-HOLLAND PUBLISHING COMPANY
AMSTERDAM · NEW YORK · OXFORD

Sole distributors for the U.S.A. and Canada:

ELSEVIER NORTH-HOLLAND, INC.
52 VANDERBILT AVENUE
NEW YORK, N.Y. 10017

Library of Congress Cataloging in Publication Data
Main entry under title:

Studies in the economics of search.

(Contributions to economic analysis ; 123)
1. Labor supply--Addresses, essays, lectures.
2. Employment (Economic theory)--Addresses, essays, lectures. I. Lippman, Steven A. II. McCall, John Joseph, 1933- III. Series
HD5706.S83 331.1'26 78-26150
ISBN 0-444-85222-0

PRINTED IN THE NETHERLANDS

Introduction to the series

This series consists of a number of hitherto unpublished studies, which are introduced by the editors in the belief that they represent fresh contributions to economic science.

The term *economic analysis* as used in the title of the series has been adopted because it covers both the activities of the theoretical economist and the research worker.

Although the analytical methods used by the various contributors are not the same, they are nevertheless conditioned by the common origin of their studies, namely theoretical problems encountered in practical research. Since for this reason, business cycle research and national accounting, research work on behalf of economic policy, and problems of planning are the main sources of the subjects dealt with, they necessarily determine the manner of approach adopted by the authors. Their methods tend to be "practical" in the sense of not being too far remote from application to actual economic conditions. In addition they are quantitative rather than qualitative.

It is the hope of the editors that the publication of these studies will help to stimulate the exchange of scientific information and to reinforce international cooperation in the field of economics.

The Editors

IN MEMORY OF

JEFFREY R. HALL

Contents

CHAPTER 1

Introduction

STEVEN A. LIPPMAN and JOHN J. McCALL

University of California, Los Angeles

In the neoclassical theory of consumption and production, the information accumulation that occurs prior to most transactions is rarely discussed and never analyzed. Much of the burgeoning literature on the economics of information is aimed at amending these oversights. This is especially true in the recent work on the economics of search. Indeed, the acquisition of information is exactly what search theory is all about. The major actors in this theory are firms and consumers. They perform no set play, but instead must improvise in response to the random challenges of their audience. The performance—the sequence of improvisations—improves as the actors learn more about the audience. From this perspective, search theory is simply sequential decision making under uncertainty. Therefore, it is clear that search theory rather than being a special topic of economic inquiry is an essential ingredient of any economic model of individual behavior under uncertainty.

The essays in this volume are devoted to extending search theory and testing some of its empirical implications. The motivation for the theoretical work is to derive testable implications that will impinge upon extant notions or tell us something new about economic behavior. Consequently, we consider the purely theoretical work presented in this volume as a necessary prelude to serious empirical work.

Each of the essays views search as a basic characteristic of economic markets. Any theory that ignores search by either assuming that firms and consumers are perfectly informed or that the cost of information is zero labors under severe handicaps. Commonplace occurrences like different prices for identical goods, advertising, queuing, and persistent positive levels of unemployed resources will be invisible in such a deterministic portrait of the economic landscape. As we will see, search theory provides a ready explanation of these events.

In this introduction we first present a brief description of the point of departure for each of the subsequent essays—the standard search model. The reason for this presentation is two-fold. First, some readers may be unfamiliar with this model and secondly, it is a simple device for pinpointing the contribution of each essay. This is done by indicating exactly where each author has modified and extended the elementary model.

After describing the elementary paradigm we then summarize each essay. These summaries are, of course, quite incomplete. Their function is to provide the reader with a brief and impartial tour guide—a *Guide Michelin* sans stars.

1. The standard search model

For the most part the standard model of search has been presented in a labor market setting. We keep with this tradition and consider an individual who is looking for a job. Each period he pays a fixed amount c and receives exactly one job offer. The cost includes all out of pocket expenses like advertising and transportation that are incurred each time a job offer is received. He may continue his search as long as he wishes (i.e., the model has an infinite time horizon), and there is no discounting. In this model we will see that there is no difference between sampling with and without recall. In the former case the searcher retains the best offer received thus far, whereas in the latter all rejected offers are immediately withdrawn. When a job offer is accepted the searcher becomes permanently attached to that job. He is not allowed to quit and he cannot be discharged by his employer.

Now the searcher's skills are invariant, but prospective employers do not necessarily value them equally. Thus different employers may submit different offers to the searcher. This distribution of job offers is the basic source of uncertainty in the job search model. Each offer is assumed to be a random variable with cumulative distribution function F. The parameters of F are known by the searchers and F is immutable.

Another key assumption is risk neutrality on the part of all job searchers. Thus their objective is to maximize expected income net of search costs. This maximization is achieved by classifying all possible job offers into two mutually exclusive classes: acceptable and unacceptable. The job offer that separates these two classes is called the reservation wage.

The amount of search depends on the distribution of wages that the individual knows his services can command in the labor market and on c, the opportunity cost of searching. If the searcher knows that his skills are highly valued, he will reject offers that fall short of his expectations and remain unemployed. On the other hand, if the cost of search is high, the searcher will reduce the (expected) period of search unemployment.

Under the foregoing set of assumptions, it has been shown[1] that the optimal policy is characterized by a single critical number, the reservation wage, such that all offers below the reservation wage belong to the unacceptable class and all those above belong to the acceptable class. Policies with this simple structure are said to have the reservation wage property. The reservation wage is calculated so that the marginal cost of obtaining exactly one more job offer is equal to the expected marginal return of one more offer. In this infinite horizon model the reservation wage is constant over time and bears an inverse relation to the cost of search—the higher the search cost, the lower the reservation wage, and the stochastically shorter the period of search unemployment.

To be more precise, let g_y be the expected gain from search when using a policy with reservation wage y. Also denote by N_y the number of offers until an acceptable offer arrives. Clearly N_y is a geometric random variable with parameter $p \equiv 1-F(y)$ and $E(N_y)=1/p$. Then with the proviso that $1-F(y)>0$, g_y satisfies

$$g_y = -c/(1-F(y)) + \int_y^\infty x\mathrm{d}F(x)/(1-F(y)), \tag{1}$$

where the first term on the right hand side represents the expected cost incurred when the reservation is set equal to y and the second term is simply the conditional expected value of an offer given that it is at least y. Rearrangement of (1) gives

$$c = \int_y^\infty (x-g_y)\mathrm{d}F(x). \tag{2}$$

Setting the derivative of g with respect to y equal to zero gives ($F'(y) \equiv f(y)$)

$$g_y' = \left\{-cf(y) - yf(y)(1-F(y)) + f(y)\int_y^\infty x\mathrm{d}F(x)\right\}/(1-F(y))^2 = 0.$$

[1]For references see Lippman and McCall, "The Economics of Job Search: A Survey (Parts I and II)", *Economic Inquiry*, 14 (1976), 155–189 and 347–368.

It follows that

$$c=\int_{y}^{\infty}(x-y)\mathrm{d}F(x)=H(y), \tag{3}$$

so that if ξ is the optimal reservation wage then $g_\xi=\xi$ and

$$c=\int_{\xi}^{\infty}(x-\xi)\mathrm{d}F(x). \tag{4}$$

Notice that H is a convex, nonnegative, strictly decreasing function which approaches zero as y goes to infinity. Consequently, ξ is the unique solution of (3). (If $c>E(X_1)$, then $\xi\equiv 0$.)

An alternative and heuristic line of reasoning implies that ξ is the unique wage for which the searcher is indifferent between accepting ξ and continuing. If he continues it will be optimal to stop with the next observation as the wage available will then be at least ξ. Thus, ξ should satisfy

$$\xi=E\max(\xi,X_1)-c, \tag{5}$$

as the left hand side is what he receives upon accepting the offer of ξ and the right hand side is the expected return of taking one more observation. It is easy to verify that (5) is equivalent to (4).

Equation (4) has a simple economic interpretation: the critical value ξ associated with the optimal stopping rule is chosen to equate c, the marginal cost of obtaining one more job offer, with $H(\xi)$, the expected marginal return from one more observation. Thus it suffices for the job searcher to behave myopically; namely, he need only compare his return from accepting employment with the expected return from exactly one more observation.

It is important to distinguish between the reservation wage property and the myopic property: the former tells us which offers are acceptable, specifically those exceeding ξ, whereas the latter provides us with a simple method for calculating ξ. Summing up, the structure of the optimal policy is such that it is characterized by a single number, referred to as the reservation wage. In addition, this number is obtained by comparing the value of stopping not with the value of continuing on (perhaps for a long time) in an "optimal" manner but rather with the value of taking exactly one more observation. Furthermore, the expected return from following the optimal policy is precisely equal to the reservation wage (i.e., $g_\xi=\xi$).

This then is the standard search model. We will briefly indicate how this model is extended and/or its implications tested by the studies in this volume.

As we noted quits are not allowed by the standard model. Obviously, quits are important labor market phenomena and cannot be ignored. Wilde extends the standard model to include quits. He accomplishes this by assuming that job offers have both pecuniary and nonpecuniary attributes. The pecuniary attribute is known prior to acceptance, whereas the nonpecuniary attribute is discovered only after the job has been accepted. If the value of the nonpecuniary attribute lies below some critical value, Wilde shows that it is optimal for the employee to quit and seek employment elsewhere.

In the standard model, the job offer distribution is given exogenously. Kormendi presents a general model of exchange in which the offer distribution is determined endogenously. He demonstrates that this distribution does not have all of its mass concentrated on a single price provided searchers are heterogeneous *and* never achieve complete information about prices. Wharton's paper addresses the same issue and presents conditions under which the job search process converges to a competitive equilibrium. He does this using a Markov chain analysis.

The criterion function of the standard model is to maximize expected income. This is appropriate when searchers are risk neutral *and* income is a suitable proxy for consumption. Danforth examines both of these conditions by assuming risk aversion and maximization of the expected utility of consumption. Hall, Lippman and McCall study a model in which risk aversion is permitted with searchers continuing to maximize the expected utility of income.

The standard model assumes that the utility function depends only on income. In keeping with the neoclassical theory of labor supply, Burdett relaxes this assumption by letting utility depend on both income and leisure. Burdett also lets searchers vary their intensity of search and engage in on-the-job search. Neither of these was permissible in the standard model.

One of the predictions of the standard model is that the presence of unemployment insurance should increase both the duration of search and post-unemployment wages. The first implication follows from the negative relationship between the cost of search and its expected duration, whereas the second implication is a consequence of a constant and higher reservation wage. In an example Classen demonstrates that the second "consequence" may not hold in the appropriate version of the standard model.

She tests these and finds that unemployment income does increase reservation wages and the duration of search, but does not increase post-unemployment wages. She argues that the infinite horizon model should be replaced by a finite horizon model in which the finite duration of unemployment insurance payments is also explicitly recognized.

Kiefer and Neumann develop methods for estimating both the reservation wage and the wage offer distribution from incomplete data. In most empirical studies, the reservation wage is not observed and the offer distribution is truncated (i.e., only the accepted wages are observed). Their methods are designed for precisely these situations. This new econometric methodology is illustrated using a sample of workers who were permanently discharged.

Stuart shows how the search methodology can be used to explain behavior in both labor and nonlabor markets. He constructs a location model in which search plays a prominent role. Previous location models ignored the responses of sellers to search sensitive buyers. This force causes sellers to locate near one another. Using a search theoretic analysis, Stuart presents a convincing rationale for the location decisions that give rise to agglomerative entities like shopping centers and supermarkets.

2. Summaries

In his paper on "Search and the Spatial Organization of Trading", Charles Stuart uses search theory to explain the spatial clustering of sellers. For the most part previous work on this topic ignores the role of imperfect information and concludes that demand-based forces are disagglomerative. Stuart demonstrates that this conclusion may be reversed when information is imperfect and buyers are allowed to search. In analyzing this situation he isolates two opposing forces. The first, in accord with traditional locational analysis, induces sellers to eschew any competition that might reduce market shares. The second causes sellers to locate near competitors in order to attract search conscious buyers.

A finite horizon search model with no recall is applied to a market with S sellers. The buyer is assumed to purchase one unit of a good whose quality (an independent identically distributed random variable) differs among sellers according to a known cumulative distribution function. Stuart shows that the buyer's expected utility increases with increased sellers, decreased search costs, increased heterogeneity, and increased number of goods.

Using this model he considers two markets, one in which there are many sellers located in a distant marketplace and another in which there are a few sellers located in a nearby marketplace. He shows that:

> the differential attractiveness to a buyer of marketplaces with relatively many sellers increases with (1) decreases in the general level of per unit search and/or travel costs, (2) increases in the perceived heterogeneity of offers of the good(s) to be purchased, and (3) increases in the sizes of shopping lists.

With these results in hand Stuart then turns to a formal analysis of agglomeration. He distinguishes between two types of agglomeration. The first considers sellers of the same good while the second focuses on sellers of different goods. In the second case he finds that there is an unambiguous increase in the demand faced by seller i as the number of other sellers of other noncompeting goods increases. Here the addition of sellers enhances the attractiveness of the market to buyers without diminishing the market share of seller i. On the other hand, in the first case an increase in sellers of the same good produces two effects. Demand increases because of the increased attractiveness of the marketplace to buyers and demand declines due to the presence of competitive sellers. Agglomeration occurs when the attractive effect dominates. This will be true when the relative increase in buyers is greater than the relative increase in sellers of the same good.

Stuart uses his model to explain supermarkets and shopping centers. They are methods by which sellers attempt to capture the attraction externality associated with greater heterogeneity and lower search and travel costs.

In the standard model of job search there is no provision for quits and jobs are described by a single attribute, the wage rate. The paper "An Information-Theoretic Approach to Job Quits", by Louis Wilde presents a model in which jobs are characterized by two attributes, a wage that is observed before the job is accepted and a specific attribute that is revealed only after the job is accepted. In contrast with the standard model, the searcher's acceptance of a job is conditional (i.e., he will continue to work if the specific characteristic is above some critical value, otherwise he will quit and look for another job).

Other models have considered jobs with multiple attributes where the searcher knows all the attributes before he accepts an offer. The standard search model has also been modified to include on-the-job search thereby explaining quits. Wilde shows how quits can be explained by imperfect information about job attributes. He does this by analyzing a model in which jobs have two attributes: one general, the wage rate (w), and one specific, say y. It is demonstrated that the optimal policy for this problem is sequential and characterized by a reservation wage and a critical value function of the specific attribute, $y^*(w)$. If the wage offer w exceeds the reservation wage it is accepted provisionally. Offers less than the reservation wage are rejected. After working for one period at a provisionally acceptable job, the specific attribute is observed. If it exceeds $y^*(w)$, the worker makes a permanent commitment to this job; if it is less than $y^*(w)$, the worker quits and looks for another job. Using this model Wilde proves that there is a non-zero probability of quitting provided the reservation wage is positive.

Finally, the effects of increasing the time to learn the value of the specific characteristic are studied. First, the searcher is worse off the greater the learning time. Also as the learning time increases there is a concomitant increase in the reservation wage. This means that when evaluation of the specific characteristic becomes more costly, it behoves the searcher to spend more time acquiring a high wage offer. Furthermore, the critical value of the specific job characteristic declines as the learning time increases (i.e., once a job is provisionally accepted the probability of quitting declines with learning time).

Most of the previous theories of search have modelled individual search behavior. In his paper, “Dispersed Transactions Prices in a Model of Decentralized Pure Exchange”, Roger Kormendi presents a market model of search. As the title indicates he develops a model of decentralized pure exchange. Now in the modelling of individual search behavior it is assumed that agents randomly sample from a *given* distribution of prices. The sampling is costly and the amount of search varies inversely with the cost of generating observations. But how can we be sure that the market equilibrium will be characterized by a nondegenerate distribution of prices? This is Kormendi’s basic question.

To answer it he studies an exchange economy in which there are two nonstorable goods: X and Y. There is a continuum of agents endowed only with X and a continuum endowed only with Y. The assumption that distinguishes his model from the classical competitive model is the requirement that agents desiring a trade must contact other agents to obtain information about trading opportunities. After calculating his offer price, each agent randomly contacts agents on the other side of the market until he encounters an agent with an overlapping offer or he completes R contacts without an overlapping offer. In the first case trade takes place at a price that is the weighted average of the two offer prices. If no overlap occurs in R contacts, the agent consumes his endowment. The offer price is calculated so as to maximize expected utility. This is accomplished when the marginal gain associated with the increased expected utility given an overlap is balanced by the marginal loss emanating from the reduced probability of obtaining an overlapping price.

Using this model he shows that there will be price dispersion when two conditions are satisfied. First, agents must have limited information about prices (i.e., $R < \infty$). Secondly, agents must be heterogeneous. Heterogeneity alone is not sufficient to guarantee a nondegenerate equilibrium price distribution. If agents are allowed to contact other agents without limit (i.e., $R = \infty$), then the equilibrium price distribution can have all of its mass concentrated at a single point.

Kormendi also studies the resource allocation properties of a dispersed price equilibrium. He finds that "in equilibrium, holding risk aversion constant, those Y-endowed agents who place a higher value on X *relative to* Y have a higher probability of getting X allocated towards them through trade". The same is true when X and Y are interchanged. "Therefore, though pure Pareto optimality does not characterize the allocation of resources, we have a 'quasi-optimality' result which tells us that resources flow with higher probability to higher valued uses, holding risk aversion constant."

In the classical competitive model risk aversion does not influence the allocation of resources. In Kormendi's model, resource allocation does depend on risk aversion. The greater the risk aversion the greater is the frequency of trade *and* the higher are the prices paid. Thus once again we see goods flowing with higher probability to uses with higher values.

The chapter "The Theory of Search and Equilibrium in a Non-auctioneered Market", written by Joseph Wharton develops a model of search that is used to investigate the properties of market equilibrium. While the model is quite general and applicable to any economic market, it is presented in a labor market setting. The market is composed of a finite number of firms. Each firm employs households and the hiring decision is reconsidered each week. New hires are obtained from the pool of searching households. The firm's offer is derived from its known value of the marginal product (VMP) function. Households are told each week how much they will earn if they do not change firms. They also know the distribution of offers at other firms. Each household can sample from this distribution by paying a fee for each observation. Recall is permitted and households are assumed to be myopic in that their decision making is based on a one week look ahead.

Wharton demonstrates that this model of market adjustment is a finite state Markov chain. The state of the market each week is completely determined by the number of households employed at each firm and each firm's wage offer.

An important subset of states is those for which each firm's wage offer lies on his *VMP* curve. These are called stationary wage states. Within this subset there is assumed to be a unique competitive equilibrium in which "the allocation of households across firms is such that the *VMP*s, and thus wage offers, are all *equal*".

Wharton stipulates that searchers may receive only a finite number of offers. This condition is satisfied by assuming first (Version A) that the costs of successive observations increase until search doesn't pay and secondly (Version B) by placing a bound on the number of searches:

> The first theorem considers Version A and exhibits a bound on the cost of the *first* observation. If across all households this bound is not exceeded, then with probability one the market will reach the competitive equilibrium state with certainty in some finite (but perhaps unbounded) number of periods and remain there. For Version B, a similar constraint is placed on the observation cost and the size of *N* [a bound on the total time available for search], and convergence to competitive equilibrium is similarly demonstrated.

His third theorem shows that multiple equilibria are also possible when search costs are sufficiently large. In this circumstance, one of these equilibria will be achieved in a finite number of periods.

The major contribution of John Danforth's paper, "On the Role of Consumption and Decreasing Absolute Risk Aversion in the Theory of Job Search", is a reformulation of the job search model to include optimal consumption behavior. In the standard search model, the job seeker is assumed to maximize expected discounted income net of search costs. Danforth assumes that the job searcher maximizes the expected utility of lifetime consumption. The resulting model of search is more general since it entails fewer restrictions on preferences. In this more general setting, Danforth assumes that the utility of consumption is additively separable and possesses decreasing absolute risk aversion. The model is analyzed for both finite and infinite horizons.

In the finite horizon environment it is assumed that an individual's satisfaction is determined by his lifetime path of single-period consumption. The ordering of these paths is given by a von Neumann–Morgenstern separable utility function with decreasing absolute risk aversion. A wage offer (an independent identically distributed random variable with known cumulative distribution function) occurs each period, at a fixed cost, and may be accepted or rejected (without recall). The individual has assets and labor income both of which are spent on consumption. He may borrow and lend at a constant interest rate. Total indebtedness at the end of the last period may not exceed a fixed upper bound. Danforth shows that the optimal search policy has the reservation wage property, where the reservation wage depends on the asset level and the time remaining. This reservation wage need not be unique *and* the unemployed worker may display risk preference for certain levels of wealth. "Thus, while the individual would never think of accepting an actuarially unfair gamble so as to alter his assets when employed, he might be anxious to do so when unemployed."

Given these assumptions, the reservation wage is shown to be an increasing function of asset holdings. Furthermore, the expected duration of search is also increasing in asset holdings. Finally, it is demonstrated that the expected discounted returns from job search is also an increasing function of asset holdings.

Danforth then addresses the same problem in an infinite horizon milieu. He does this to capture the pure effect of asset holdings on the reservation wage. It is difficult to do this in a finite horizon model where reservation wages decline as the horizon draws near. First he shows that when the personal time preference exceeds the interest rate, the job searcher's assets diminish over time. This in turn implies that the reservation wages decline with time. Thus even when the offer distribution is stationary and known to the searcher (i.e., adaptive policies are not needed, and there is no limit on the length of search), the reservation wage may still decline.

In "Expected Utility Maximizing Search," Hall, Lippman and McCall assume that job searchers maximize expected utility. This contrasts with the expected income maximization that is usually assumed in job search models.

They begin by studying expected utility maximization when search is conducted with recall. When at most i offers are to be received, it is shown that the reservation wage increases with i. Furthermore, if one searcher is more risk averse (larger absolute risk aversion) than another, then his reservation wage is smaller. They also prove that with decreasing absolute risk aversion the reservation wage increases with wealth. These results are as congenial as they are unsurprising. What are surprising and disturbing are the facts that: (a) the optimal strategy need not be myopic, (b) a reservation wage may not exist, (c) the reservation wage need not increase as the offer distribution becomes more risky, and (d) unfair gambles may be accepted. The authors explain (a) by noting that the acceptance set may have "gaps". The explanation of (b) lies in the fact that

> when searching with recall, the best offer received to date serves as a form of insurance against unsuccessful search in the future. If the searcher has a reasonably good wage offer to which he can return, then the loss in utility from unsuccessful continued search is limited. If, however, the maximum wage offer to date is poor, then searching for one more period and failing to get a better offer might entail a large loss of utility. A high wage offer, in effect, raises the searcher's wealth to the point that he can afford to be more selective.

The reservation wage property can be recaptured by introducing the notion of "true wealth" (see Theorem 3).

They then analyze expected utility maximization when search is performed without recall. They show that a reservation wage does exist and is no larger than the smallest acceptable wage when recall is permitted. As in the case of recall, if one searcher is more risk averse than another, his reservation wage is smaller. Similarly, given decreasing absolute risk aversion, the reservation wage increases as the searcher acquires more wealth. Finally, it is observed that once again the myopic policy may not be optimal.

The essay "Search, Leisure and Individual Labor Supply" by Kenneth Burdett integrates job search with the traditional theory of labor supply. The choice between work and leisure is determined when the individual only has imperfect information about the wage rate. In classical labor supply theory, the fraction of time devoted to work is decided by individuals having perfect information about wage rates. In this perfect information environment, the optimal strategy is to allocate time between work and leisure so that the marginal utility of leisure divided by the marginal utility of income equals the wage rate. The wage rate then can be varied to generate the individual's labor supply function. In the traditional labor supply model workers refuse to work at a particular wage rate because of their stronger preference for leisure. In the job search models, wages are rejected because the searcher's expected income can be increased by acquiring additional job offers. In Burdett's paper the worker is assumed to maximize expected lifetime utility where utility depends on both leisure and income. Furthermore, workers are able to vary the intensity of search. That is, the probability of receiving a job offer during a period of search can be increased by reducing leisure and searching more. No recall is permitted in his infinite horizon search model and there are no direct search costs.

The paper has two parts. In the first, the optimal search and leisure decisions are obtained for unemployed workers. In the second, work, search and leisure decisions are calculated for employed workers. It is shown that for an unemployed worker receiving unemployment insurance for the first τ periods of unemployment, the optimal policy has the following form. During the first τ periods of unemployment the reservation wage declines and the intensity of search increases. That is, as the searcher approaches the end of the unemployment insurance subsidy, he becomes less selective (reduced reservation wage) and consumes less leisure (increased search intensity). The proportion of time spent on search is chosen so that the marginal utility of leisure equals the marginal return from search.

The model for employed workers assumes that a worker employed at wage rate w must work at least α per cent of the time. Thus each period the worker must decide how to allocate his time among working, searching for another job, and consuming leisure. Let h, s, and l be proportion of time spent on each of these activities. Then $h>\alpha$ and $h+s+l=1$. The worker chooses those values of work, search and leisure that maximize expected lifetime utility. No costs are incurred when an individual changes jobs. Burdett proves that when this problem has an interior solution, "a worker will choose leisure and work times such that the ratio of the marginal utilities of income and leisure equals the wage rate w. Further, the worker selects a search time such that the marginal utility of leisure equals the expected marginal gain to search time."

Burdett then demonstrates that there is a unique number z such that an individual will participate in on-the-job search if and only if his wage rate is less than z.

Much of the job search literature is theoretical in nature and has little direct contact with economic phenomena. In order to comprehend complex behavioral relationships it is sometimes necessary to withdraw from the hurly burly. Nevertheless, if a theory is to avoid desication, it must eventually make contact with the empirical phenomena. Empirical research has lagged behind the theoretical work on the economics of search because many of the variables in the job search models are difficult to observe. Probably the most important of these is the reservation wage itself. Normally, information about this crucial variable is not available. In their paper, "Estimation of Wage Offer Distributions and Reservation Wages", Kiefer and Neumann develop a methodology for estimating from incomplete data both the reservation wage and the wage offer distribution. Information on the *accepted* wage offers is the incomplete data used to estimate the wage offer distribution. Estimates of the reservation wage can also be derived from these same data provided certain identification conditions are satisfied. They apply this methodology to a sample of workers who were permanently dismissed from their jobs during the period 1969–1973. Over half of this sample received unemployment benefits.

In order to identify the reservation wage, they assume that an individual's prior job tenure and his previous wage affect the wage offer distribution but not the cost of search. Their empirical analysis suggests that reservation wages rather than actual wages are sticky over the business cycle. Thus changes in observed wages do not fully reflect changes in market wage offers. Of course they recognize that by letting the reservation wage decline as search proceeds, this conclusion might be weakened.

The paper by Kathleen Classen "Unemployment Insurance and Job Search" demonstrates the usefulness of job search models in assessing the response of unemployed workers to alternative unemployment insurance schemes. According to the job search models, these unemployed workers choose a search strategy to maximize expected utility. Classen shows how these strategies are altered by the presence of unemployment insurance. Since the unemployment payments reduce the costs of unemployment, search models predict that they will increase the duration of unemployment. The empirical validity of this proposition is a direct measure of the relevance of search theory. Furthermore if there is a positive relation between unemployment insurance and the duration of unemployment, then unemployment rates must be adjusted before they can yield any information about the health of the economy.

Classen utilizes a dynamic programming model to illustrate the relationship of unemployment insurance to expected post employment wages and duration of unemployment. She concludes that an increase in unemployment insurance does increase duration but need not increase expected post-employment wages. The search model used in this illustration has a finite time horizon and incorporates the fact that unemployment insurance is available only for a fixed number of periods. These are the reasons why the reservation wage declines with time. Classen also specifies other conditions that lead to a declining reservation wage. These include risk aversion, wealth effects, bankruptcy, systematic search, adaptation to an unknown offer distribution and variable intensity of search. The last has the most significance for her study. An increase in unemployment insurance causes a decline in the intensity of search and an increase in duration. The effect of reduced intensity on post employment earnings is ambiguous.

In the empirical part of the paper Classen uses unemployment insurance data from Arizona and Pennsylvania. After a sophisticated econometric analysis of these data Classen concludes that there is

> strong evidence that an increase in the weekly benefit amount leads to an increase in the average duration of unemployment. Thus, when benefits are liberalized, as they have been recently, the resulting increase in the unemployment rate should not be interpreted as a sign that the economy is suffering from some ailment that can easily be cured by aggregate demand policies.

CHAPTER 2

Search and the spatial organization of trading

CHARLES STUART*

University of Western Ontario and University of Lund, Sweden

1. Introduction

In this paper it will be argued that a spatial clustering of sellers—"agglomeration"—can result from desires of buyers to search in marketplaces where there are relatively many sellers. The contention is that buyers prefer to shop in marketplaces with many sellers. Thus the addition of a new seller to a marketplace might increase the drawing power of the marketplace sufficiently to increase the demands faced by the sellers already there. In such cases, agglomerational forces are transmitted via the demands faced by sellers.

This view of agglomeration differs sharply from the tradition in location theory where demand-based forces have been disagglomerative. For instance, Chamberlin [2, p. 62] observed that a seller's location constitutes a form of product differentiation and that spatially separated sellers can thus be regarded as "spatial monopolists". In criticizing Hotelling's [9] earlier work on agglomeration, Chamberlin maintained [2, pp. 260–263] that if a buying population is evenly spread out along a line then profit-maximizing sellers will locate so as to be evenly dispersed throughout the population. This dispersion arises because buyers are assumed to purchase from the sellers from which the sum of price and travel costs are minimal, so that each seller's demand is greatest when he maximizes the distance between himself and the nearest seller on each side (neglecting endpoints).

*I am indebted to Brian Ellickson, Roger Kormendi, Axel Leijonhufvud, Steven Lippman, John McCall, Ingemar Ståhl, and Lars Söderström for comments on an earlier version of this paper, and to the Bank of Sweden Tercentenary Fund for financial support.

Hotelling [9] was the first writer to systematically devote attention to agglomeration. He showed that two identical sellers who must choose locations along a homogeneously populated, one-dimensional continuum of buyers will locate next to each other at the center of the population. This comes about as each seller attempts to "capture" buyers by offering them a lower sum of price and travel costs. Since each seller captures all buyers on his "tail" of the population and must share buyers between himself and his competitor, a profit-maximizing, competitive locational equilibrium is one in which each seller "maximizes his tail", that is, one where both sellers agglomerate at the center of the population.

While Hotelling's work is logically correct for the case of two sellers, his behavioral assumption that buyers focus solely on the known sums of purchase price and travel costs from different sellers leads—via the demands faced by sellers—to disagglomeration in an n-seller setting. This is the thrust of market-area analysis as developed by Fetter [6], Christaller [3], Lösch [13], Greenhut [7] and Mills and Lav [15].[1] Market-area models differ from Hotelling's only in that there are many sellers and a two-dimensional homogeneous buying population; the behavioral specifications are the same. Market-area analysis recognizes that isolated sellers have exploitable monopolistic power. Under free entry, potential sellers will continue to enter and set up shop as spatial monopolists until a monopolistic competitive equilibrium is achieved. In equilibrium, the plain of buyers will be partitioned into space-filling hexagonal market areas with a seller located in the center of each hexagon who captures all buyers in his market area.[2]

The common theme in these models is that if buyers have perfect price and quality information for the (single) good they wish to purchase then demand-based locational forces will be disagglomerative. What we will do here is to show that this result need not hold if information is imperfect and buyers wish to search.[3] Such an approach has been hinted at by Chamberlin:

> It is obviously for the convenience of buyers that *different* products be sold in proximity to each other, and herein lies the explanation for

[1]The Christaller–Lösch–Mills–Lav variant of market area analysis is sometimes referred to as "central place theory". Note that the Mills and Lav article contains a flaw which has been corrected by Stern [19] and Bollobàs and Stern [1].

[2]Each good possesses its own set of hexagons. When different hexagonsets overlap then larger and smaller hexagons may have, at times, common centers called "central places".

[3]Agglomerational forces can also arise on the supply side if, say, delivery costs are lower for agglomerated retailers. We will not consider supply-side explanations here.

> much of the concentration actually found in retail trading. The simplest form of such concentration is the individual shop itself, which, by offering a variety of merchandise, enable the buyer (a) to economize on time by making many purchases under one roof, and (b) to 'shop', i.e., to make comparisons of price and quality before purchasing. [2, p. 262]

By examining the effects of buyers' marketplace choice decisions on the demands faced by sellers in different marketplaces, it will be possible to discern two countervailing locational forces.[4] As in the traditional market-area models, a seller will find it profitable to avoid competition which *dilutes* (i.e., reduces) his marketplace-share. On the other hand, a seller who does locate as a spatial monopolist might have a hard time *attracting* search-conscious buyers in the first place. The following question will be considered: when might we expect such "attraction effects" to outweigh "dilution effects"? Put differently, when will a seller prefer that a competitor sets up shop next door instead of across town, and when will agglomeration occur? Implicit in the phrasing of these questions is the notion that attraction and dilution effects are externalities. It is thus also natural to ask if there are any institutions which have arisen as internalization devices for such externalities. We will argue that the existence of stores can be interpreted in just this way; the store "works" by capturing the spillover benefits of offering more than one model (brand) of one good.

The approach of the paper will be to use existing search-theoretic tools to construct a model of optimal buyer search and marketplace choice.[5] Search takes place because various models of a good have different characteristics (in the sense of Lancaster [11]) and are thus valued differently by different buyers.[6] After computing optimal search strategies for each marketplace, the buyer decides which marketplace to shop in. As far

[4]We distinguish between markets and marketplaces. By a *market* we will mean a group of individuals wishing to trade a given good, while a *marketplace* will denote a more or less well-defined geographical area containing a given number of spatially fixed sellers.

[5]Nelson [17] distinguishes between "search goods" and "experience goods" and advances the hypothesis that agglomeration is associated more with the former than the latter. In his scheme, information about search goods is obtained via search and information about experience goods is obtained via experimenting with different models (brands) until a "best" model is determined. The analysis here is more fundamental than Nelson's as it addresses the question: what makes a good a search good? We will thus be looking at the "search sensitivity" of different goods; that is, how senstive buyers' marketplace choice decisions are to the number of sellers of a good in different marketplaces.

[6]This formulation simplifies the analysis by abstracting from price search. Presumably, buyers' desires to search for low prices could also lead to agglomeration. Such a motive likely underlies the highly agglomerated nature of marketplaces for shares of stock and deliveries of wheat, coffee, etc.

as a buyer is concerned, the relevant features of a marketplace are the number of sellers it contains, the costs of travelling to and searching in it, and the (perceived) distribution of offers available in it. The analysis proceeds by tracing the effects of changes in these marketplace parameters on buyers' marketplace-choice decisions and thus on the demands faced by sellers.

The reader should be warned that the analysis does not take place in a full equilibrium setting. Indeed, the model does not even describe a partial equilibrium situation where sellers' price-setting and good-offering behavior is endogenous. It abstracts from this in that buyers are simply assumed to believe that the distribution of offers from any marketplace is given and nondegenerate. There are two justifications for this "partial" treatment. First, there exists at present, to my knowledge, no model of price formation in a market with search which is sufficiently malleable to be subjected to the sorts of comparative static exercises (such as to changes in the number of sellers) which we would wish to perform.[7] And second, even if sellers were allowed to set, or change, the prices at which they sold, the attraction and dilution effects which we focus on here would still exist.

In the next section we formulate the search model and examine its implications for buyers' marketplace choice. Section 3 contains a discussion of the existence and magnitudes of attraction and dilution effects, and in Section 4 we consider internalization schemes for these two locational externalities.

2. Consumer search and marketplace choice

2.1. Search

We now examine the optimal search problem faced by a representative buyer who wishes to purchase a single unit of a good. Prior to sampling, the buyer does not know the net utility to himself, u^s, of the model offered by the sth seller, $s = 1,\ldots,S$, of the good. Instead, the buyer subjectively believes that the utilities from trading with each of the S sellers are identically distributed, stochastically independent, non-negative random

[7]For an attempt to explain search-induced agglomeration in an equilibrium framework, see Eaton and Lipsey [5]. These authors impose the constraint that individuals must sample from exactly two stores prior to purchasing a homogeneous good. Since all stores set the same price, it is hard to justify search in their model.

variables with nondegenerate, cumulative distribution function F. The smallest closed interval such that $F(\bar{a})=0$ and $F(\bar{b})=1$—that is, the support of F—is $[a,b]$ with $a \geqslant 0$, $b < \infty$.

To examine the effects of changes in the heterogeneity of offers (i.e., in the variability of characteristics of offered models) on buyer search, we assume that (pure) increases in heterogeneity can be represented by increasing the spread of the perceived distribution of utilities while holding its mean constant. To do so, we adopt a strengthened form of Rothschild and Stiglitz' [18] concept of a mean-preserving spread whereby the distribution G will be termed more heterogeneous than F when:

$$\int^{y} [G(u)-F(u)]\mathrm{d}u=0 \quad \text{if} \quad G(y)=F(y)=1 \tag{1a}$$

$$\int^{y} [G(u)-F(u)]\mathrm{d}u>0 \quad \text{if} \quad G(y)>0 \quad \text{and} \quad F(y)<1. \tag{1b}$$

As a convention, omitted lower or upper limits of integration will mean that integration proceeds from the lower limit or to the upper limit of the support of the distribution. Condition (1a) guarantees that the mean is preserved and (1b) implies that G has more weight in the tails than F. Subtracting (1b) from (1a) yields:

$$\int_{y} [G(u)-F(u)]\mathrm{d}u<0 \quad \text{if} \quad G(y)>0 \quad \text{and} \quad F(y)<1. \tag{1c}$$

The buyer must expend search cost $c > 0$ to (randomly) obtain each seller's offer. It is assumed that c is low enough so that it pays to search—this will be further quantified below. There is no recall of past (rejected) offers and the buyer may not search any seller twice.[8]

We can now characterize the buyer's expected utility maximizing search behavior.[9] Assume first that he has chosen a marketplace and has sampled

[8]"No recall" is a convenience which simplifies the analysis. It is not particularly reasonable in the context of search within marketplaces. One of the main advantages to a buyer of many-seller maketplaces is the opportunity to return to previously sampled sellers at a low cost. However, analogues of Lemmas 1–5 can be shown to hold given costless recall of past offers using the logic of Lippman and McCall [12, pp. 167–169].

[9]The type of search problem described here was first formulated by MacQueen and Miller [14]. For a general treatment, see De Groot [4]. Results similar to Lemmas 1–5 here can be found elsewhere; see e.g. Kohn and Shavell [10]. Nachman [16], Lippman and McCall [12], and Hall, Lippman and McCall [8] deal with more general problems of utility maximizing search.

a seller, receiving an offer u. By backward induction, he should accept that offer if it exceeds the maximal expected utility attainable by continuing net of the cost of continuing. Otherwise, it is optimal to continue sampling offers. Letting V_k denote the maximal expected utility when there are $k<S$ sellers left to sample ("in the kth stage") and defining

$$y_k \equiv -c + V_{k-1}, \tag{2}$$

the optimal strategy in the kth stage is to accept u if $u > y_k$ and reject u and continue search if $u \leqslant y_k$. We adopt the convention that if the utility offer in the kth stage exactly equals y_k then the buyer continues searching.

The maximal expected utility at k is then

$$\begin{aligned} V_k &= (1-F(y_k))E[U \mid u > y_k] + F(y_k)y_k \\ &= \int_{y_k} [u - y_k]\mathrm{d}F(u) + y_k = b - \int_{y_k} F(u)\mathrm{d}u, \end{aligned} \tag{3}$$

where the last step uses integration by parts. For the Sth stage, no sampling has yet taken place so

$$V_S = -c + V_{S-1} \equiv y_S. \tag{4}$$

The buyer's optimal behavior thus depends on what may be expected to happen in later stages (i.e., in stages with fewer sellers left to be sampled). The process is anchored by the fact that in the last stage the buyer must purchase, so his expected utility here will be

$$V_1 = \int u\,\mathrm{d}F(u) = b - \int F(u)\mathrm{d}u. \tag{5}$$

Obviously, for marketplaces with one seller of the good in question, expected utility once in the marketplace is V_1.

Finally, the stipulation that the buyer finds it advantageous to search can be expressed as

$$V_2 > V_1. \tag{6}$$

This will be assumed throughout. It is equivalent to the statement that $F(y_2) > 0$; that is, if there are two sellers who can be sampled, there is a positive probability that one of their offers will be less than the net expected return from sampling the other.

An immediate implication of (6) and a simple induction argument on (2) and (3) is:

Lemma 1. The optimal search process satisfies $y_k < y_{k+1}$ and $V_{k-1} < V_k$.

We can now derive several comparative statics results on the returns to optimal search. We examine the effects of changes in the number of sellers of the good, in search costs, and in the nature of the distribution of utilities.

Lemma 2. An increase in the number of sellers of the good increases the expected utility of optimal search.

Proof. This follows from Lemma 1 when $k = S$. QED

Lemma 3. An increase in the search cost decreases the expected utility of optimal search.

Proof. Let $c > \bar{c}$ and let $\bar{y}_k$ and $\bar{V}_k$ be given by (2) to (5) when search costs are $\bar{c}$. Then $y_2 < \bar{y}_2 \Rightarrow V_2 < \bar{V}_2 \Rightarrow y_3 < \bar{y}_3 \Rightarrow \ldots \Rightarrow y_S < \bar{y}_S$ and the proposition holds. QED

Lemma 4. A translation of F to the right increases the expected utility of optimal search.

Proof. Let $\bar{F}(u+t) = F(u)$. From (5),

$$V_1 = b - \int_a^b F(u)\,\mathrm{d}u = b - \int_{a+t}^{b+t} \bar{F}(u)\,\mathrm{d}u < b + t_1 - \int_{a+t}^{b+t}$$

$\bar{F}(u)\mathrm{d}u = \bar{V}_1$. If $V_{k-1} < V_k$ then $y_k < y_{k+1}$ and a similar argument on (3) establishes the proposition. QED

Lemma 5. An increase in the heterogeneity of offers increases the expected utility of optimal search.

Proof. Let F and G be as in (1a, b, c); variables are labelled with F and G when appropriate. For (1b) to hold, $b^F \leqslant b^G$. Since the means of F and G are identical, $y_2^F = y_2^G$. Thus from (1c), (3), (2), and (4), $V_2^F < V_2^G \Rightarrow y_3^F < y_3^G \Rightarrow V_3^F < V_3^G \Rightarrow \ldots \Rightarrow y_S^F < y_S^G$, establishing the proposition. QED

It is also of interest to know when searching buyers will be most prone to choose marketplaces where there are many sellers; the answer to this "second order" question should tell us "where to look" for agglomeration.

First, the gains to having additional search opportunities increase if the cost of search falls.

Lemma 6.

$$\frac{\mathrm{d}(V_S - V_{S-1})}{\mathrm{d}c} < 0.$$

Proof. This holds with k replacing S for $k=2$ by Lemma 3 and the fact that V_1 is constant. Otherwise $\mathrm{d}(V_k - V_{k-1})/\mathrm{d}c = F(y_k)(\mathrm{d}y_k/\mathrm{d}c) - F(y_{k-1})(\mathrm{d}y_{k-1}/\mathrm{d}c)$. Since $F(y_k) > F(y_{k-1})$ and $\mathrm{d}y_k/\mathrm{d}c = (\mathrm{d}V_{k-1}/\mathrm{d}c) - 1$, then $\mathrm{d}(V_k - V_{k-1})/\mathrm{d}c < 0$ if $\mathrm{d}(V_{k-1} - V_{k-2})/\mathrm{d}c < 0$ and the proposition holds *a fortiori* for $k = S$. QED

Another proposition which should hold is that increases in heterogeneity increase the gains to additional search opportunities. I have been unable to show this for general distributions, but it is easy to find situations where it is true. Among them are:

Lemma 7. $V_S^G - V_S^F$ is increasing in S when G represents greater heterogeneity than F if (i) G and F are uniform or (ii) c is sufficiently high and S sufficiently low so that $G(y_S^G) > F(y_S^G)$ and if there is a point z such that $G(u) \geqslant F(u)$ for $u < z$ and $G(u) \geqslant F(u)$ for $u > z$.

Proof. We need only show that $V_k^G - V_k^F > V_{k-1}^G - V_{k-1}^F$ or, equivalently, from (3), that

$$\int_{y_{k-1}^G}^{y_k^G} G(u)\mathrm{d}u > \int_{y_{k-1}^F}^{y_k^F} F(u)\mathrm{d}u.$$

If F is uniform on $[a^F, b^F]$ then a uniform G will satisfy conditions (1) only if G is on $[a^F - x, b^F + x]$ for $x > 0$. Substituting into the integral above and solving, our condition is $(y_k^G)^2 - (y_{k-1}^G)^2 > (y_k^F)^2 - (y_{k-1}^F)^2$. For $k=2$ we have $y_{k-1}^F = y_{k-1}^G$ and the statement holds by Lemma 5. If $V_{k-1}^G - V_{k-1}^F > V_{k-2}^G - V_{k-2}^F$ then (2) yields $y_k^G - y_{k-1}^G > y_k^F - y_{k-1}^F$ and since $y_k^G > y_k^F$ and $y_{k-1}^G > y_{k-1}^F$ our condition holds for k.

In the second case, the hypotheses (ii) insure that $G(u)$ exceeds $F(u)$ for all points less than y_S^G. For $k=2$, Lemma 5, (2), and (1) imply $\int^{y_2^G} G(u)\mathrm{d}u > \int^{y_2^F} G(u)\mathrm{d}u > \int^{y_2^F} F(u)\mathrm{d}u$. If $V_{k-1}^G - V_{k-1}^F > V_{k-2}^G - V_{k-2}^F$ then $y_k^G - y_{k-1}^G$

$>y_k^F - y_{k-1}^F$ and as $y_k^G > y_k^F$ and $y_{k-1}^G > y_{k-1}^F$, the integral form of the statement to be shown also holds for k. QED

It should be clear that increases in c and/or decreases in S will decrease y_S^G and thus make the condition $G(y_S^G) > F(y_S^G)$ more likely.

2.2 *Marketplace choice*

The results above specify how a buyer's maximal expected utility under search for a single good varies with the parameters of the search process. In choosing a marketplace in which to search, the buyer must take into account the effects of such factors on the outcomes of search for each good he wishes to purchase and for each marketplace, as well as the costs of travelling to each marketplace. To analyze this, we make the following assumptions: (i) The buyer wishes to purchase n goods. (ii) Each seller offers only one model of one good for sale and the buyer's search processes for different goods are thus independent. (iii) The buyer has the same search cost for each good. (iv) The buyer must pay utility cost c_o^m to travel to marketplace m, where m is a finite index of marketplaces. (v) The buyer may pick only one marketplace in which to shop. Letting $V^{i,m}$ denote the maximal subjective utility attainable by our buyer for good i in marketplace m, the marketplace choice decision can thus be stated as "pick the m which maximizes the sum of $-c_o^m + \Sigma_{i=1}^n V^{i,m}$", where $V^{j,m} = 0$ if good j is not available in marketplace m.[10]

By applying our comparative statics results on optimal search to this objective function it is possible to derive a number of properties of optimal marketplace choice. It will prove useful in this section to picture the buyer as having two marketplaces which he can choose to visit, a local one, m, with low travel costs and a more distant one, m', with greater travel costs. As in traditional location theory, if all else is equal (i.e., $V^{i,m} = V^{i,m'}$, all $i = 1, \ldots, n$), the fact that $c_o^m < c_o^{m'}$ is decisive and the local marketplace is chosen. If there is a change in the more distant marketplace in the sense

[10] We are assuming that the buyer knows the characteristics of each marketplace. In Nelson's [17] terminology, marketplaces may be experience goods in that a buyer might have to experiment with different marketplaces to find the one which is best. Inclusion of uncertainty as to the characteristics of different marketplaces may strengthen the tendency toward agglomeration in the model. For instance, if a buyer knew only the total number of sellers of all goods together in each marketplace but didn't know what goods were offered where, then larger marketplaces would have the advantage of yielding higher probabilities of actually finding specific goods.

that (for goods $1,\ldots,n$):

(1) its number of sellers of some good increases; or
(2) its search costs are reduced; or
(3) it offers better deals for some good; or
(4) its selections (heterogeneity) of some good increase; or
(5) it offers more goods;

then by Lemmas 2–5, the utility sum for the more distant marketplace will increase and the travel cost differential may be overcome so that the more distant marketplace is chosen for shopping. This is summarized in:

Proposition 1. The attractiveness of a marketplace to a buyer increases with: (1) increases in the number of sellers of each good it contains; (2) decreases in its level of search costs and/or travel costs; (3) increases in the general (perceived) utility level of its offers; (4) increases in the (perceived) heterogeneity of its offers of each good; and (5) increases in the number of goods offered in it.

It is the first effect—that a marketplace's attractiveness increases with size (size will refer to number of sellers henceforth)—which may lead to agglomeration. In order to predict when agglomeration should arise, it is also of interest to know when this size effect will be large. Assume that the local marketplace (m) has less sellers of each good than the more distant marketplace (m'), but that they are otherwise identical except that, as above, $c_o^m < c_o^{m'}$.

Then clearly $\Sigma_{i=1}^n V^{i,m} < \Sigma_{i=1}^n V^{i,m'}$ and we ask: when will search in the larger marketplace be sufficiently more favorable than search in the smaller marketplace that the travel cost differential is overcome and the larger marketplace is chosen? First, this will happen if the travel cost differential itself is small. Put differently, larger marketplaces are relatively more advantageous the lower the general level of travel costs. Similarly, the more goods on the buyer's shopping list, the greater the difference between $\Sigma_{i=1}^n V^{i,m}$ and $\Sigma_{i=1}^n V^{i,m'}$ and the more likely it is that the larger marketplace will be chosen. Another result, from Lemma 6, is that the gain from shopping in the larger of two marketplaces increases as the (common) cost of sampling falls. Finally, Lemma 7 implies that increases in the perceived heterogeneity of offers of one or several goods also increase the differential benefit of shopping in the larger marketplace. Summing up:

Proposition 2. The differential attractiveness to a buyer of marketplaces with relatively many sellers increases with: (1) decreases in the general level of per unit search and/or travel costs; (2) increases in the perceived heterogeneity of offers of the good(s) to be purchased; and (3) increases in the sizes of shopping lists.

3. Agglomeration

We postulate that the demand (quantity), q^i, faced by a single seller of good i in a given marketplace (marketplace superscripts will be deleted from here on) depends positively on the number of shoppers in the marketplace and negatively on the number of competitors in the marketplace. The last effect reflects the notion that more competing sellers of a good implies a smaller portion of the total marketplace demand for the good for each seller; this is the analogue in our fixed-price model of the desire to exploit a monopolistic market position in traditional location theories. To capture this, we assume that each seller expects to get an average share of the total marketplace demand. If H buyers choose to shop in the marketplace and there are S^i sellers of good i located there, then

$$q^i = H/S^i. \tag{7}$$

It remains to introduce a coterie of buyers and specify how H is determined. We assume in the remainder of this section that all buyers behave like the single buyer of the last section. Further, all buyers have the same search cost, c, for each good and each marketplace. All buyers also have the same perceptions about the distribution of utilities of a good in all marketplaces where the good is sold. (Note that this does not imply that all buyers have the same utility rankings of different models.) Buyers do differ, however, in their travel costs to different marketplaces. These assumptions correspond closely to the assumptions of traditional location theory where a "homogeneous plane of identical buyers with travel costs an increasing function of distance" is postulated. The difference between the model here and the traditional models is that our model admits the possibility of buyer search.

These assumptions together with the results of the last section allow us to write H as a function of the number of sellers of each good in the marketplace, the cost of search, and the perceived distribution of utilities of each good. Since the only property of these distributions which we are interested in here is their heterogeneity, we let v^i denote the (common) perceived heterogeneity or variability of good i and write

$$H = H(S^1,\ldots,S^n,c,v^1,\ldots,v^n,C_0), \tag{8}$$

where C_0 is a vector of all buyers' travel costs to *all* marketplaces. Neglecting the discreteness of H and S^i, Proposition 1 then implies that $\partial H/\partial S^i > 0$ while Proposition 2 leads us to conclude that $\partial^2 H/\partial S^i \partial c < 0$ (greater search costs decrease the relative benefits of larger marketplaces) and $\partial^2 H/\partial S^i \partial v^i > 0$ (greater heterogeneity increases the benefits of additional sampling opportunities).

Our argument for agglomeration is that the demand faced by a seller of good i can increase if the number of sellers located in his marketplace increases. There are two ways in which this number of sellers can increase; either the number of sellers of good i can increase or the number of sellers of some other good, $j \neq i$, can increase. If clustering occurs in the first case, it is essentially because agglomerated marketplaces economize on total search costs. In the second case, clustering would instead economize on the costs of travelling to different sellers to purchase different goods. This will become clearer when we examine these situations in more detail. Since the first case is the more interesting and has not been treated in traditional location theory, we consider it first.

3.1. Search-induced agglomeration of sellers of the same good

Differentiating (7) and (8) yields

$$\frac{\mathrm{d}q^i}{\mathrm{d}S^i} = \frac{1}{S^i}\left[\frac{\partial H}{\partial S^i} - \frac{H}{S^i}\right], \tag{9}$$

which cannot be signed in general as $\partial H/\partial S^i > 0$ and $H/S^i > 0$. The first of these represents the partial increase in demand due to the increase in the attractiveness of the marketplace to buyers following the increase in the number of competing sellers, and the second term accounts for the partial effect of the dilution of the seller's marketplace share caused by the presence of the new competitor.

A tendency toward clustering should arise when the attraction effect of an increase in the number of competing sellers outweighs the dilution effect so that $\mathrm{d}q^i/\mathrm{d}S^i > 0$. From (9), this will occur when the elasticity of H with respect to S is greater than 1. Our previous analysis of buyer marketplace-choice gave no direct results on when this elasticity will exceed one, but Proposition 2 suggests that $(\partial H/\partial S^i)(S^i/H)$ is most likely to exceed one when travel and/or search costs are low and for goods which (buyers perceive to) have great heterogeneity. That is, under these three circumstances, buyers will be especially sensitive to marketplace size in choosing where to shop.

The effect of travel costs on clustering of similar sellers is easiest to see. Consider the polar case where the vector C_0 of all buyers' travel costs is zero. Then it is obvious that all buyers will choose to shop in the marketplace containing the most sellers, and consequently we would expect all sellers to cluster together in one marketplace, or to go out of business. On the other hand, suppose travel costs are positive and consider the effect of decreasing them all by the same proportion. This causes travel cost *differentials* between marketplaces to fall and will lead some buyers to shift from small (local) marketplaces to larger (more distant) ones. These notions can be expressed in terms of the elasticity $(\partial H/\partial S^i)(S^i/H)$. For simplicity, take two marketplaces of the same size located along a continuum of buyers such that each attracts the same number of buyers. The magnitude of $\partial H/\partial S^i$ is a decreasing function of the general level travel costs by Proposition 2; that is, decreased travel cost differentials make buyers more sensitive to marketplace size. Thus the elasticity of H with respect to the number of competing sellers of a good in a marketplace and hence the tendency toward agglomeration in the trading of the good will decrease with the general level of travel costs.

Almost identical arguments can be constructed for the effects of search costs and the heterogeneity of the good on clustering. By Proposition 2, either a decrease in the cost of search or an increase in the heterogeneity of the good will increase buyers' sensitivity to marketplace size $(\partial H/\partial S^i)$. Again considering two identical marketplaces (with the same numbers of buyers and sellers), the elasticity $(\partial H/\partial S^i)(S^i/H)$ will rise. This in turn increases the likelihood that a one seller increase in the size of one of the marketplaces will bring about a more than proportional increase in the number of buyers electing to shop there.

This analysis suggests that agglomeration should be most prevalent in the trading of heterogeneous goods under conditions of low search costs and travel costs. Casual empiricism bears this out. Many consumer durables are (perceived to be) heterogeneous and sellers of them are often found located near to each other in central shopping districts—as is the case with jewellers, photo stores, optical retailers, furniture, and clothing—or in more specialized shopping areas. Probably the best example of the latter is the clustering of car sellers in many cities. This clustering often takes place at other than the most "attractive" locations in central retailing areas, presumably because car dealerships are land intensive.

Rough, formal support for these notions is available. Nelson [17, pp. 323–324] cities a study in which Van Handel [20] used the average percentage of a city's total sales of a good which took place in the central business district as a measure of clustering in the sales of the good. Van Handel estimated that 61 per cent of all sales of clothing took place in CBDs. The percentages for furniture and appliances were 48 per cent and 36 per cent, respectively. On the other end of the scale, only 5 per cent of all sales of food and 16 per cent of all liquor sales occurred in central business districts.

The search-theoretic underpinnings of the central business district (or for that matter of any specialized shopping area) are of some interest. Such areas specialize largely in the sale of goods for which buyers find search particularly advantageous; that is goods where heterogeneity is great compared to the costs of searching and travelling to large marketplaces. The existence of these marketplaces is efficient in the sense that they promote search by providing buyers with ample sampling opportunities and in effect reduce information costs in the trading of "search sensitive" goods. If the sellers of these goods were not clustered together but were instead evenly distributed over space, one to a marketplace, then buyers would either have to travel long (costly) distances between sellers in order to search or would have to forego the advantages of search.

The forces which lead to this specialized agglomeration of sellers of search sensitive goods in central retailing districts might be summarized as follows. Not only will sellers of such goods prefer to have competing sellers located nearby but they will also wish to locate in a place which is easily accessible to buyers. Both of these conditions—the presence of competition and low travel costs for buyers—are extant in the central retailing district. In the spirit of von Thünen [21], land rents in such areas will be high. This serves to guarantee that activities such as manufacturing, private residences, or "excessive" retailing of nonsearch sensitive goods will not take place in the district; consequently, the district is reserved for the sales of search sensitive goods. Similarly, the district may grow as sellers of search sensitive goods out-compete other activities at the edge of the district.

Another theoretical aspect of marketplaces containing a number of sellers of the same good is that the forces of attraction and dilution should operate to maintain the heterogeneity of offers of the good at a "high" level. Consider two sellers who wish to locate in such a marketplace. The first wishes to offer a model which would effectively increase the overall heterogeneity of offers in the marketplace and the second wishes to offer a model which would not. (A rough example might be a marketplace for new cars containing a Ford dealer, a Chevrolet dealer, and a Volkswagen dealer, and where the first potential entrant is a Toyota dealer and the second sells Fords.) Suppose there is space for only one more seller in the marketplace and the potential entrant who is willing to pay the highest rent moves in. Since the entry of the first seller would generate a greater attraction effect (by Proposition 2 in the form $\partial^2 H/\partial S\,\partial v^i > 0$), then the first seller would also face a greater demand himself if he entered and he will be able to out-compete the second seller for the locale.[11]

In summary, our analysis suggests that the clustering of sellers who offer different models of a heterogeneous good can come about as a result of buyers' marketplace choice decisions. These marketplace choice decisions essentially express a demand on the part of buyers for a locational configuration which permits search.

3.2. *Agglomeration of sellers of different goods*

What happens to the demand faced by a seller of good i if the number of sellers of good $j \neq i$ located in his marketplace increases? Differentiation on (7) and (8) yields

$$\frac{\mathrm{d}q^i}{\mathrm{d}S^j} = \frac{1}{S^i}\frac{\partial H}{\partial S^j}, \tag{10}$$

which is unambiguously positive. That is, an increase in the number of noncompeting sellers in the marketplace will make the marketplace more attractive to buyers but will not cause any dilution of the marketplace share of our seller. There will thus generally exist a positive, demand-based, agglomerational bias in the trading of different goods which are often purchased together. Note the theoretical basis of this sort of agglomeration—of unlike sellers—differs fundamentally from the view of agglomeration of several sellers of the same good given above in that it reflects the notion that buyers may decide to purchase several goods during the same shopping trip in order to economize (mainly) on the costs

[11]This bias in favor of the first seller will be heightened if the second seller offers essentially the same model as an existing seller so that the two are forced to compete with each other for buyers who value that model highly. That is, differential dilution effects may also operate against the entry of sellers who do not increase the heterogeneity of offers. Such differential dilution effects were assumed away in the formulation of demand in equation (7).

of travelling to different sellers to purchase goods *without searching*. Travel costs do not have the same overriding importance in the single-good-agglomeration case. Such a total-travel-cost reduction motive forms the behavioral basis for the theories of Christaller [3] and Lösch [13] wherein agglomeration of dissimilar sellers occurs at "central places". These traditional theories thus seem to have implicitly taken account of attraction effects among unlike sellers while at the same time recognizing only dilution effects among like sellers.

4. Internalization of attraction externalities

The increase in marketplace attractiveness caused by the movement of a new seller to a marketplace is a positive externality which falls on existing sellers. Similar externalities would result if one seller in the marketplace somehow caused travel or search costs in the marketplace to fall. This raises the question: how might sellers internalize such externalities? Two phenomena which can be interpreted as internalization devices are stores and shopping centers. To the extent that these are successful at internalizing spillover attraction benefits, they will drive out sellers offering a single model of a single good.

A store can be regarded as a complete (agglomerated) marketplace for a single good or class of goods. Spillover benefits among the models of the good, or among the different goods, are captured by the owner. The attractiveness of the store to buyers can be increased by offering a wider selection of models or of different goods, and by keeping search and travel costs low by providing sales personnel, wide aisles, parking facilities, etc. The profit-maximizing size of a store, in terms of models and goods offered, depends crucially on the magnitude of the attraction externalities which would be generated by increased offerings. We thus expect stores to exist under much the same circumstances as those which led to agglomerated marketplaces in the last section; that is, stores should specialize in the sales of heterogeneous goods such as furniture and clothing, or they should specialize in the sales of mixes of goods which are often purchased together, such as groceries.

To the extent that stores are too small to internalize all attraction externalities, other selling forms such as shopping centers should arise. The institutional make-up of the shopping center is particularly interesting. When an entrepreneur purchases a plot of land, erects the center on it, and rents out locales to sellers, it will be in his interest as a profit-maximizer to internalize attraction effects. That is, it will be in his interest to find the set of sellers who can benefit the most differentially from a location in the center and then skim off in rents the excess profits due to location. Again, this set will contain either many sellers of a heterogeneous good (e.g., shopping centers which contain many clothing stores) and/or sellers of goods which are often purchased together (e.g., a bank and a supermarket).

References

[1] Bollobàs, B. and Stern, N., "The optimal structure of market areas", *Journal of Economic Theory*, April 1972.

[2] Chamberlin, E., *The Theory of Monopolistic Competition*, Harvard University Press, Cambridge, Mass., 1950 (first edn., 1927).

[3] Christaller, W., *Die Zentralen Orte in Suddeutschland*, Jena, 1933.

[4] DeGroot, M. H., *Optimal Statistical Decisions*, McGraw-Hill, New York, 1970.

[5] Eaton, B. C., and Lipsey, R. G., "Comparison shopping and clusters of homogeneous firms", Discussion Paper No. 226, Institute for Economic Research, Queen's University, May 1976.

[6] Fetter, F., "The economic law of market areas", *Quarterly Journal of Economics*, 1924.

[7] Greenhut, M., "The size and shape of the market area of the firm", *Southern Economic Journal*, July 1952.

[8] Hall, J. R., Lippman, S. A., and McCall, J. J., "Expected utility maximizing job search", see this volume, pages 133–155.

[9] Hotelling, H., "Stability and competition", *Economic Journal*, (1929).

[10] Kohn, M. G., and Shavell, S., "The theory of search", *Journal of Economic Theory*, 9 (1974), 93–124.

[11] Lancaster, K., "A new approach to consumer theory", *Journal of Political Economy*, 74 (1966), 132–157.

[12] Lippman, S. A., and McCall, J. J., "The economics of job search: a survey", *Economic Inquiry*, 14 (1976), 155–189.

[13] Lösch, A., *The Economics of Location*, Yale University Press, Yale, 1954 (German edn. 1944).

[14] MacQueen, J., and Miller, R., "Optimal persistence policies", *Operations Research*, 1960.

[15] Mills, E., and Lav, M., "A model of market areas with free entry", *Journal of Political Economy*, June 1964.

[16] Nachman, D. C., "On risk aversion and optimal stopping", unpublished paper, Northwestern University, 1972.

[17] Nelson, P., "Information and consumer behavior", *Journal of Political Economy*, 78 (1970), 311–329.

[18] Rothschild, M., and Stiglitz, J., "Increasing risk I: a definition", *Journal of Economic Theory*, 2 (1970), 225–243.

[19] Stern, N., "The optimal size of market areas", *Journal of Economic Theory*, April 1972.

[20] Van Handel, R., "Uncertainty and retail location patterns", unpublished paper, State University of New York, Binghamton, 1969.

[21] von Thünen, J., *Der Isolierte Staat in Beziehung auf Landwirtschaft und Nationalökonomie*, (1826).

CHAPTER 3

An information-theoretic approach to job quits

LOUIS L. WILDE*

California Institute of Technology

1. Introduction

Models of job search under imperfect information have become a commonplace in the economics literature.[1] The fundamental problem is the following. An unemployed worker desires to work but he does not know the characteristics of jobs at different firms. He can, however, observe various aspects of jobs by investing resources in "search" activity. Typical assumptions used in modeling this process are that jobs are identical except for wage and that the worker desires to maximize expected income net of search costs. In this case, assuming an infinite horizon and no discounting, it is easy to show that the optimal policy is to search sequentially and set a reservation wage, ξ, according to

$$c = \int_{\xi}^{\infty} (w-\xi) f(w)\,\mathrm{d}w, \tag{1}$$

where c is the unit cost of search and f is the market distribution of wage offers. The decision rule is to accept the first offer which exceeds ξ. Even in this simple setting, a number of useful predictions stem from (1).[2] In

*I would like to thank Robert Forsythe and Steve Salop for helpful discussions of this material. Anonymous referees and the editors of this volume also provided extremely useful comments. A preliminary version of this paper was presented at the 1977 summer meeting of the Econometric Society in Ottawa, Canada.

[1]The literature on the economics of information in general, and on job search in particular, has become enormous. A recent survey of the latter is provided by Lippman and McCall [5].

[2]This sequential version of the search problem is analyzed in McCall [8]. A concise summary of its implications is provided in Rothschild [16]. Although Rothschild's discussion is set in the product market, his model is easily translated into the labor market.

particular, ξ is inversely related to c so that workers with higher search costs set lower reservation wages, expect to search less to find an acceptable job, and expect lower net incomes.

This primitive search model has been extended and generalized in many directions. But two issues are of interest here. The first concerns modifications in the optimal search strategy introduced when jobs are described by more than a single characteristic, the second concerns the role of search theory in explaining the existence and nature of job quits as an equilibrium phenomenon.

The first issue has been studied by Rosen [14], for example, in the context of tied-sales in product markets. His results suggest that as long as all the relevant characteristics of a job can be observed prior to any on-the-job experience, then the nature of the search strategy is not altered in any fundamental way—the reservation wage is replaced by a reservation frontier which defines the trade-off between minimally acceptable bundles of characteristics. However, this conclusion is no longer valid if some of the characteristics of jobs are "specific" in the sense that they cannot be observed without actually working on the job.

A second problem with the basic search model defined above is that it doesn't allow for the possibility of quits. Clearly, in that world, if a searching worker finds a job offer which exceeds his reservation wage, then he accepts it and never quits. The implicit assumption in most search models is that the cost of searching while employed is so high as to preclude any on-the-job search. Burdett [3] provides a recent exception to this rule.[3]

Burdett allows the worker several possible modes of activity; he can search while unemployed, search and work, or work and not search at all (of course, the worker can also not work and not search, but this is uninteresting). If the cost of search while working is not too high relative to the cost of search while unemployed, then it pays the worker to set two reservation wages, $\xi_1 < \xi_2$, such that jobs offering wages less than ξ_1 are rejected, jobs with wages between ξ_1 and ξ_2 are accepted with search

[3]For a similar approach to job quits, see Lippman and McCall [5, pp. 179–181]. Also, since the completion of this work, I have become aware of two related papers. The first is a comment by George Borjas and Matthew Goldberg [2]. They attempt an extension of the basic search model which allows jobs to be described by multiple characteristics, some of which cannot be observed until after the job is taken. However, they do not integrate the possibility of quits into their model. Naturally in this case, given suitable assumptions regarding the market distribution of characteristics, the fundamental aspects of the simple search model are not altered. The second paper is by Dale Mortensen [9]. He models worker turnover based on *stochastic* learning of job characteristics, but does not distinguish between specific and general information or explicitly incorporate search into his model.

continuing, and jobs offering wages above ξ_2 are accepted with search activity ceasing altogether.

Burdett's formulation of the search problem introduces the possibility of quits in a framework of imperfect information and, assuming workers have finite lifetimes, his results are theoretically consistent with the empirical observation that quit rates are inversely related to both job tenure and age. These kinds of results are important because they provide a foundation for the existence of quits as an equilibrium phenomenon,[4] and highlight the importance of imperfect information in explaining labor market activity.

An alternative to Burdett's model is to assume that some characteristics of jobs are specific; that is, they cannot be observed without actually working the job.[5] The process of learning about such characteristics will be called evaluation. Characteristics which can be observed directly (upon paying some search cost) will be called general characteristics and those which require on-the-job experience will be called specific characteristics.[6] In light of Rosen [14], a single general characteristic will suffice. Suppose there are n specific characteristics, $y_1,\ldots,y_n$, and suppose further that these

[4]There are several explanations for the existence of quits. In the classical competitive model, voluntary separations are viewed as a response to disequilibrium states of net advantage across jobs. In equilibrium, the principle of equalizing differences holds that net advantage across all jobs will be the same, so that no worker ever has an incentive to quit. Human capital theory, as expounded by Becker [1], does not explain the existence of quits, but it does suggest that quit rates should be inversely related to age and job tenure. For an application of human capital theory which does explain the existence of some quits as part of an optimal worker strategy see Rosen [13]. Burdett's model provides an alternative to these explanations based upon the concept of on-the-job search. As another information-theoretic alternative, the current analysis formalizes Pencavel's [11] observation that "the taking on of a job for a trial period may be the optimum method for an individual to discover whether that employment suits him".

[5]For a more complete discussion of specific and general information see Wilde [17]. Note, however, that the definition of specific characteristic precludes the possibility of a firm informing potential employees of the exact nature of job's nonwage characteristics before the worker accepts employment.

[6]The term "evaluation" which is used herein to describe the process of learning about specific characteristics is borrowed from MacQueen [6]. MacQueen's model is not set in the labor market and while his "possibilities" are described by multiple characteristics, each of the characteristics can be observed by paying a search cost. The connection is that if the outcome of the first characteristic observed is poor enough, the searcher might choose not to observe the second characteristic at all, preferring to draw a new "possibility" for evaluation. But MacQueen, like Borjas and Goldberg, does not incorporate "turnover" into his model. Also, the distinction between specific and general information is similar to the distinction Nelson [10] made between "search" goods and "experience" goods. However, Nelson's definitions are too strong. He defines search goods as goods for which *only* general characteristics matter and experience goods are defined as those for which *only* specific characteristics matter. As the model in section 2 will suggest, these definitions are polar cases and Nelson's analysis can be extended to intermediate examples.

must be evaluated sequentially. If the sequence of evaluation is optimal in an appropriate sense (roughly, the characteristics are observed sequentially in order of importance) then quit rates decline with job tenure since good observations on early y_i's (where a good observation is one that does *not* induce the worker to quit) will reduce the likelihood that subsequent observations of other specific characteristics will result in a quit.[7] This reduction in the probability of quitting reflects a true accumulation of knowledge.[8]

The next section of this paper presents a formal model of search and evaluation where there is just one general characteristic, the wage rate (w), and one specific characteristic (y) associated with jobs. It is established first that the worker's problem is well-defined, that an optimal policy exists and is unique, and that it is described by a sequential strategy. Next it is shown that under reasonable conditions the optimal strategy is to set a reservation wage, ξ, and search sequentially until a wage which beats the reservation wage is located. After working the job for one period, the specific characteristic associated with the (already known) wage is observed and the quit decision is made. Associated with the specific characteristic is a reservation function, $y^*(w)$, which defines acceptable ranges of y and ranges of y for which it is optimal to quit and search again.

In section 3 it is established that as long as the reservation wage is positive then there is a positive probability of quitting after taking a job. Section 4 considers changes in the optimal strategy when the period of specificity (the time it takes to evaluate the specific characteristic) changes. A concluding section summarizes the results and suggests some problems for further research.

Although this paper presents a theory of the existence of quits which is consistent (at least) with casual observation, it should be emphasized that it refutes neither the theoretical influence of human capital on the quit rate, nor other theories of the existence of quits. For example, it is clear

[7]It turns out that if the order of evaluation of specific characteristics is fixed exogenously, then quit rates need not decline with job tenure. This is because the worker may be forced to evaluate irrelevant characteristics early in his work experience. If the worker is allowed to set the order of evaluation as part of an optimal strategy, then one would expect quit rates to be inversely related to job tenure.

[8]This notion is discussed in Pencavel [11] who quotes Reynolds [12]:

> "Voluntary mobility is essentially a form of job-shopping by workers... workers have great difficulty in judging the attractiveness of a job by talking it over in the company's employment office. The only way to judge it accurately is to work on it for awhile. After a few weeks or months of work, one can tell whether the job is worth keeping. This explains why quits are most frequent during the first few months of service and diminish rapidly after that point."

that on-the-job search is important in explaining some quits, regardless of the existence of specific characteristics; Matilla [7] has estimated that approximately 60 per cent of those who quit already have jobs lined up. But the decision to initiate search while employed may arise from several sources; it may be part of an optimal search strategy (see Burdett [3] or Lippman and McCall [5]), it may reflect a career switch point between jobs offering different rates of accumulation of human capital (see Rosen [13]), or it may be due to a poor outcome in the evaluation of some specific characteristic (see Pencavel [11]). While this paper considers only search while unemployed, relatively straightforward extensions would incorporate cases where employed workers initiate on-the-job search as a result of poor observations of some specific characteristic.

2. A model of search and evaluation

2.1. Basic assumptions

Underlying this model is the notion that unemployed workers seek jobs but are imperfectly informed as to the characteristics of available jobs. Jobs vary with respect to both wage and some nonwage characteristic. While ignorant of specific packages of the wage and nonwage characteristic offered by specific firms, workers can invest in information. The formal structure of this process is defined by the following six assumptions.

Assumption 1. Each job is described by a pair (w,y) where w is wage and y is some nonwage characteristic which *cannot* be observed without working on-the-job for one period; w is observed by direct sampling.

Assumption 2. The market distribution of W and Y is defined by a joint p.d.f. $\phi(w,y)$. Assume ϕ is positive on R^2_+. Let $f(w)$ and $g(y)$ be the marginal p.d.f. of W and the marginal p.d.f. of Y, respectively, and define $g(y|w)$ as the conditional p.d.f. of Y given $W=w$.

Assumption 3. Let $u(w,y)$ be the per period utility of working a job which pays wage w and possesses nonwage characteristic y. Assume u is differentiable and nondecreasing in each argument. Assume further that u is bounded.

Assumption 4. The cost of drawing an observation from ϕ is $c \geqslant 0$. Only one firm can be sampled per period, and the worker cannot sample and work simultaneously. Assume c is measured in the same units as $u(w,y)$ with $E[u(W,Y)] > c$.

Assumption 5. The worker's objective is to maximize his discounted stream of utility, net of search costs.

Assumption 6. The worker knows ϕ with certainty, sampling is without recall, the horizon is infinite, and the discount rate is β, $0<\beta<1$.

2.2. *The searcher's problem*

Given the six assumptions of section 2.1, it is clear that the form of the optimal strategy will be sequential. The searching worker's problem is therefore the following. He knows ϕ. By paying c he can draw an observation, say (w_0,y_0), but he only sees w_0. Information concerning y_0 is limited to knowledge of the conditional distribution of Y given w_0. After observing w_0, the worker can either accept the job or sample again; he cannot both accept the job and draw another observation. If he accepts the job he receives $u(w_0,y_0)$ for as many periods as he stays. But the worker will not discover that y_0 is the true value of Y until he has worked for one period. If w_0 is high, he may accept the job assuming y_0 to be the average according to $g(y|w_0)$, only to discover by the end of the first period of employment that y_0 is very low, for example. If it is low enough, the worker may quit the job and sample again. Consequently, for some values of W it may pay to take the job, knowing ahead of time that the probability of quitting is nonzero. The optimal policy is thus a kind of sequential-lexicographic process whereby the decision whether to take the job or not is based on critical values of W and the decision whether to stay or quit, obviously conditional on having accepted the job, is based on critical values of Y.

In the absence of any constraints on the distribution of W and Y there is no *à priori* relationship between an observed wage and the expected per period utility from accepting a job paying that wage. In fact, if high wages are strongly correlated with low nonwage characteristics, it might pay to reject high wage offers in favor of low wage offers.[9] In the body of this

[9]This model is clearly a "partial partial-equilibrium" model, to use Rothschild's term. As such it must suffer the same criticism Rothschild [15] leveled against early models of job search: the model takes the distribution ϕ as given.

paper enough structure will be imposed on ϕ to guarantee that not only are high wages strictly preferred to low (prior to the observation of the nonwage characteristic) but, in addition, the reservation wage will be unique. In this case the optimal strategy is characterized at each stage of the process by a number, ξ, and a function, $y^*(w)$, as follows:

(a) if $w<\xi$, then sample again
(b) if $w\geqslant\xi$, then take the job for one period and: (i) quit and sample again if $y<y^*(w)$, (ii) keep the job if $y\geqslant y^*(w)$. (2)

2.3. The functional equation

The searcher's objective is to maximize his discounted stream of utility net of search costs. Define $v(w)$ as the expected value of the discounted stream of utility, net of search costs, generated by pursuing an optimal policy from the current period on when w has just been observed. Let V be the expected value of $v(w)$ taken with respect to the marginal distribution of w. Then

$$\begin{aligned} v(w) &= -c+\beta\max\left\{V;\int_0^\infty\left[u(w,y)+\beta\max\left\{\frac{u(w,y)}{1-\beta},V\right\}\right]g(y|w)\,\mathrm{d}y\right\} \\ &= -c+\beta\max\left\{V;\ E[u(w,Y)]\right. \\ &\qquad \left.+\beta\left[VG(y^*(w)|w)+\int_{y^*(w)}^{\infty}\frac{u(w,y)}{1-\beta}g(y|w)\,\mathrm{d}y\right]\right\} \end{aligned} \tag{3}$$

where $G(y|w)$ is the c.d.f. associated with $g(y|w)$, $y^*(w)$ is defined by

$$\frac{u(w,y^*(w))}{1-\beta}\equiv V,\text{[10]} \tag{4}$$

and

$$V=\int_0^\infty v(w)f(w)\,\mathrm{d}w. \tag{5}$$

[10]It is possible that for some w, $u(w,0)/(1-\beta)>V$. In this case we define $y^*(w)=0$. Hence $y^*(w)=0$ implies $u(w,y^*(w))/(1-\beta)>V$.

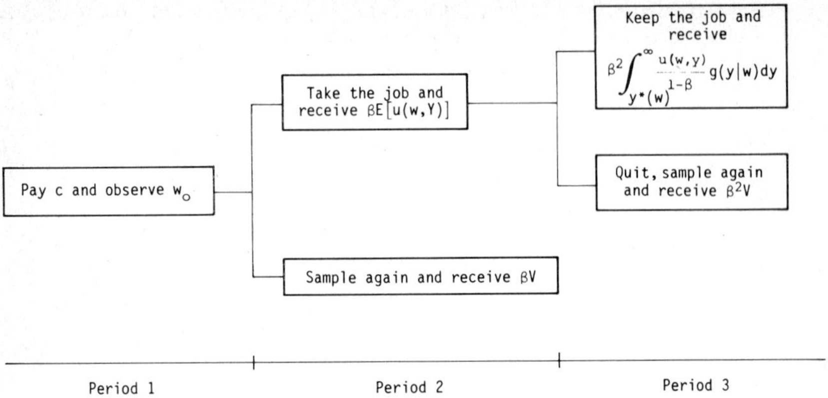

Figure 3.1. The decision process.

The decision process formalized in (3) is illustrated in figure 3.1. Note that $y^*(w)$ is that value of the nonwage characteristic which leaves the worker indifferent between keeping a job paying wage w and quitting to search. As a matter of notational convenience, define the expected utility of taking a job at wage w to be

$$T(w) \equiv E[u(w,Y)] + \beta\left\{ VG(y^*(w)|w) + \int_{y^*(w)}^{\infty} \frac{u(w,y)}{1-\beta} g(y|w)\,dy \right\}. \quad (6)$$

The value of a job offering wage w is the sum of the expected utility this period plus the discounted expected utility from the next period on into the future. This latter quantity is equal to the expected value of search times the probability of quitting plus the expected value of keeping the job times the probability of not quitting. The effect of assuming y to be a specific characteristic is reflected in the second term in (6). That is, the expected value of keeping the job conditional on $y \geqslant y^*(w)$ is not $v(w)$; there is learning which is specific in the sense that it is lost when the worker quits to search.

The immediate problem is to show (3) has a solution. This result is straightforward and follows from Assumptions 1–6.

Theorem 1. There exists a unique, continuous, bounded solution to the functional equation (3). The proof is presented in Appendix 1.

Given a unique solution to (3), V can be taken as a constant. The reservation wage, ξ, is defined by

$$V=T(\xi)=E[u(\xi,Y)]+\beta\left\{VG(y^*(\xi)|\xi)+\int_{y^*(\xi)}^{\infty}\frac{u(\xi,y)}{1-\beta}g(y|\xi)\,\mathrm{d}y\right\}. \quad (7)$$

As it stands, there is no guarantee that ξ is unique. There may be intervals of acceptable wages separated by intervals of unacceptable wages, or it may be that all wages or no wages are acceptable. The next lemma and theorem establish conditions under which: (i) ξ is unique, and (ii) high wage offers are preferred systematically to low wage offers. The approach is to find a sufficient condition for $\partial T(w)/\partial w>0$. In this case either all wage offers are acceptable ($\xi=0$) or there is a unique $\xi>0$ such that $w<\xi$ is rejected but $w\geqslant\xi$ is accepted. The sufficient condition for $\partial T(w)/\partial w>0$ puts restrictions on the conditional distributions $g(\cdot|w)$ and implicitly on ϕ.

Consider an unemployed worker who draws an observation of w_0. He is concerned with the unknown characteristic associated with w_0, but only to the extent that it effects the total utility of the job. That is, he is not concerned with the conditional distribution $g(\cdot|w_0)$ *per se*. Rather, his decision whether to accept w_0 or to reject it is based upon the conditional distribution of utility which is induced by $g(\cdot|w_0)$ through $u(w_0,y)$. Define a random variable Z as the per period utility of a job paying some known wage and possessing unknown characteristic y. Let $\Psi_w(z)$ be the c.d.f. of Z when wage w has been observed. Then a sufficient condition for $\partial T(w)/\partial w>0$ is that $\Psi_w(z)$ be stochastically increasing in w. Thus:

Assumption 7. $\partial\Psi_w(z)/\partial w<0$ for all $w\geqslant 0$.

It is easy to see that Assumption 7 generates a kind of monotonicity with respect to a worker's evaluation of wage offers. The only way a high wage offer could be rejected in favor of a lower wage offer is if the worker believes that the high wage is associated with such a low value of Y that the net *utility* of the high wage job is less than that of the low wage job. Assumption 7 rules out such possibilities.[11] The next lemma formalizes this argument.

[11]Assumption 7 is satisfied, for example, when W and Y are independent. It is also satisfied when the conditional distributions $g(\cdot|w)$ are stochastically increasing in w. However, this last condition implies that higher wages are on average associated with higher values of the nonwage characteristic. Not only is this strong, the classical concept of equalizing differences suggests that in equilibrium it probably isn't true (see n.9).

Lemma 1. Under Assumptions 1–7, $\partial T(w)/\partial w > 0$ for all $w \geqslant 0$.

Proof. From (6), integrating $T(w)$ by parts and differentiating with respect to w yields

$$\partial T(w)/\partial w = -\int_{-\infty}^{\bar{z}(w)} \partial \Psi_w(z)/\partial w \, dz - \left(\frac{\beta}{1-\beta}\right) \int_{V(1-\beta)}^{\bar{z}(w)} \partial \Psi_w(z)/\partial w \, dz, \tag{8}$$

where $\bar{z}(w) = \lim_{y\to\infty} u(w,y)$. Thus $\partial \Psi_w(z)/\partial w < 0$ implies $\partial T(w)/\partial w > 0$.
QED

Theorem 2. Under Assumptions 1–7, either $T(w) \geqslant V$ for all $w \geqslant 0$ in which case $\xi = 0$, or there exists a unique $\xi > 0$ such that $T(\xi) = V$. Moreover, $y^*(w)$ is decreasing in w.

Proof. First note that $\lim_{w\to\infty} T(w) > V$ since otherwise $v(w) = -c + \beta V$ for all $w \geqslant 0$. In this case $V = -c/(1-\beta)$ which contradicts the assumption that $E[u(W,Y)] > c$. Since $T(\cdot)$ is increasing (see Lemma 1), the first part of the theorem follows by rewriting (3) as $V(w) = -c + \beta \max\{V, T(w)\}$. Because $\partial u(w,y)/\partial y > 0$ and $\phi > 0$, inspection of (4) reveals that $dy^*(w)/dw < 0$.
QED

Since $\partial T(w)/\partial w > 0$, it must be that wage offers below ξ are rejected and wage offers above ξ are accepted for at least one period. Thus, to the extent that optimal behavior after accepting any given job is buried in $T(w)$, the optimal policy in this problem is analogous to the optimal policy in a simple search model. The primary difference is the additional reservation function, $y^*(w)$, associated with the nonwage characteristic. Figure 3.2 illustrates ξ and $y^*(w)$.

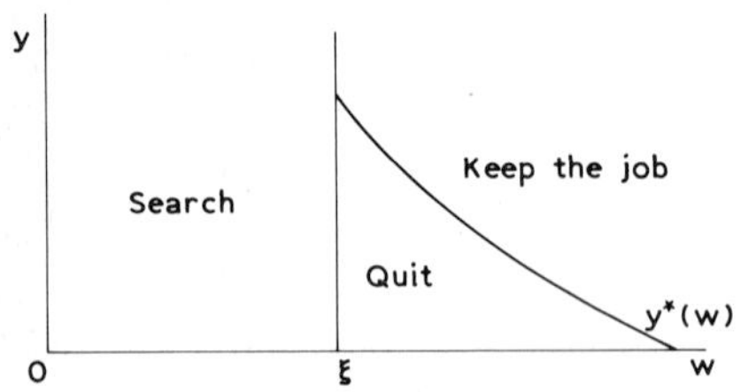

Figure 3.2. ξ and $y^*(w)$.

2.4. The optimal strategy

Using (6), the functional equation (3) can be written

$$v(w) = -c + \beta \max\{T(w), V\} \tag{9}$$

Noting that $w < \xi$ implies $T(w) < V$ and $w \geqslant \xi$ implies $T(w) \geqslant V$, and taking the expectation of $v(w)$ with respect to the marginal p.d.f. of w, gives

$$V = -c + \beta\left\{ VF(\xi) + \int_{\xi}^{\infty} T(w) f(w)\,\mathrm{d}w \right\}, \tag{10}$$

where F is the c.d.f. associated with f. Rearranging (10) and using the relations $T(\xi) = V$ and $u(\xi, y^*(\xi)) = V(1-\beta)$ yields

$$c + u(\xi, y^*(\xi)) = \beta \int_{\xi}^{\infty} [T(w) - T(\xi)] f(w)\,\mathrm{d}w. \tag{11}$$

While this expression is not independent of V, it describes the logic of the optimal strategy in familiar terms. The value of taking a job at w and ξ is given by $T(w)$ and $T(\xi)$, respectively. The marginal cost of a unit of search is the direct cost c plus the opportunity cost $u(\xi, y^*(\xi))$ of shifting back the entire stream of utility one period when ξ has been observed (note that the opportunity cost is *not* $E[(\xi, Y)]$ but, rather, it is the value of working for one period when both margins of indifference, ξ and $y^*(\xi)$, are reached). The right-hand side of (11) is the discounted expected return to a unit of additional search when the current offer is ξ (and there is recall).

In the general model a key comparative statics result concerns changes in c. The result is not surprising, but it will be useful later for comparison purposes.

Theorem 3. The reservation wage decreases with c; that is, $\mathrm{d}\xi/\mathrm{d}c < 0$.

Proof. By definition $V = T(\xi, V)$. Taking the total derivative,

$$\frac{\mathrm{d}\xi}{\mathrm{d}c} = \frac{\partial V}{\partial c}\left[1 - \frac{\partial T}{\partial c}\right] \Big/ \frac{\partial T}{\partial w}.$$

Now $\partial V/\partial c < 0$ and $\partial T/\partial V = \beta G(y^*(w)|w)$. Since $\partial T/\partial w > 0$. This implies $\mathrm{d}\xi/\mathrm{d}c < 0$. QED

Of course, since an increase in c implies V falls, it must also be the case that as c rises, $y^*(w)$ falls for any given w; so investment in both search and evaluation fall as c rises. The probability that a given wage is accepted is $[1-F(\xi)]$. The probability that a given (w,y) pair is acceptable conditional on $w \geqslant \xi$ is

$$[1-F(\xi)]^{-1} \int_{\xi}^{\infty} [1-G(y^*(w)|w)] f(w)\,\mathrm{d}w. \tag{12}$$

As c rises $[1-F(\xi)]$ and $[1-G(y^*(w)|w)]$ both increase. Thus, while it is true that *ex post* the quit rate falls, we cannot be sure that *ex ante* the expected probability of a quit falls as c rises.

3. The quit rate

The purpose of this section is to establish some relationships between acceptable wages and acceptable values of the nonwage characteristic. In particular, it will be shown that as long as the reservation wage is interior to the distribution of wage offers, then the probability of quitting is strictly positive.

Theorem 4. If $\xi > 0$, then $y^*(\xi) > 0$.

Proof. Assume the opposite; let $y^*(\xi) = 0$. Then by the definition of $y^*(\xi)$ given in (4) and footnote 10, we have

$$V \leqslant \frac{u(\xi, 0)}{1-\beta}. \tag{13}$$

But $V = T(\xi)$, so when $y^*(\xi) = 0$,

$$V = T(\xi) = \frac{E[u(\xi, Y)]}{1-\beta}. \tag{14}$$

Equations (13) and (14) imply $u(\xi,0) \geqslant E[u(\xi, Y)]$, which is a contradiction since u is increasing and $g(y|\xi)$ is positive on $[0,\infty)$. Therefore $y^*(\xi) > 0$.
QED

This theorem establishes that the nonwage characteristic is never irrelevant when it pays to differentiate firms by wage. As long as ξ is strictly greater than 0 then at ξ, and in a neighborhood of it, it pays to reject some jobs on the basis of the nonwage characteristic. Thus after observing y, the probability of a quit $G(y^*(w)|w)$ is strictly positive for wages near the reservation wage. While this is a strong result (it proves the existence of quits as part of an optimal job-shopping strategy) it does not say that $y^*(w)>0$ for all wages greater than ξ. For a high enough wage offer it may pay to accept any level of y, in which case the probability of a quit at that wage is zero.

It should also be pointed out that $\xi=0$ does *not* imply $y^*(w)=0$ for all $w\geqslant 0$. That is, even if all wage offers are acceptable, some levels of the nonwage characteristic may be rejected. To see this consider the following example. Assume $\xi=0$ and $T(0)=V$. Then $y^*(0)>0$. The argument proving this is similar to the proof of Theorem 4; by assuming $y^*(0)=0$ one can reach a contradiction.

Finally, note that Theorem 4 does not rely on Assumption 7. Even if there are multiple values of w such that $T(w)=V$, it remains true that at each of them (and in the proper neighborhood of each) the probability of a quit is nonzero.

4. Variable evaluation time

The model analyzed in this paper concerns investment in two kinds of information, general and specific. The cost of investment in general information is c, the direct cost of search. The cost of investment in specific information is the opportunity cost of working for one period at a low $u(w,y)$ level. An increase in the cost of general information is simply an increase in c. An increase in the cost of specific information is equivalent to forcing the worker to work for more than one period before observing y. The purpose of this section is to incorporate such a modification into the basic model and then investigate the effects of changes in the cost of investment in specific information.

The modification is fairly straightforward. As before, the length of time it takes to generate an offer via search is one period, but now suppose it takes s of these periods to evaluate the unobservable characteristic y. In general, the worker would "learn" about the true value of Y during this initial stage of work (observing various random variables and forming expectations about their distributions), but we abstract from this process by fixing the evaluation period and assuming the worker receives

$E[u(w, Y)]$ during each of the first s periods.[12] Hence the only formal change in the model is that upon taking a job at wage w the worker now expects to receive $E[u(w, Y)]$ for s periods, after which he makes a decision with respect to quitting or retaining the job.[13]

In the remainder of this section, the variables of the model will be indexed by the time subscripts or superscripts to reflect the period of specificity. Assumptions 1–7 will again be assumed to hold where Assumption 1 is modified to allow for evaluation periods greater than 1. Under these circumstances $y_s^*(w, V^s)$ is still defined by (4) and ξ_s is unique with wages below ξ_s rejected and wages greater than or equal to ξ_s accepted. The optimal return is now defined by

$$V^s(w) = -c + \beta \max\{T_s(w), V^s\}, \tag{15}$$

where in this case the value of taking a job at wage w is

$$T_s(w) = E[u(w, Y)]B(s) + \beta^s \left\{ V^s G[y_s^*(w)|w] + \int_{y_s^*(w)}^{\infty} \frac{u(w,y)}{1-\beta} g(y|w)\,dy \right\} \tag{16}$$

and $B(s) = \Sigma_{i=1}^{s} \beta^{i-1}$. The first step in analyzing the effects of an increase in s is to show $V^s > V^{s+1}$. That is, as the period of specificity increases, the expected utility of optimal search falls.

Lemma 2. For each $s \geqslant 1, V^s > V^{s+1}$.

Proof. Let ξ_{s+1} and $y_{s+1}^*(w)$ be optimal when evaluation takes $s+1$ periods and let V^{s+1} be the expected value of search when these strategies are used in the $(s+1)$-period problem. Consider the following new problem: Suppose that the first job which is accepted has a nonwage characteristic which can be evaluated in s periods but *all* subsequent jobs require

[12]Alternatively, one might wish to think of s as the length of an initial contract (a "probationary" period). In this case Y might be observed after one period, but the quit decision postponed for s periods.

[13]Of course it is only $E[u(w, Y)]$ which matters to the worker when he decides (before observing Y) whether or not to accept a job offering wage w. Moreover, what he actually receives during the first s periods of employment is qualitatively irrelevant to the quit decision. For example, one variation on this model is to assume W is the wage received during an "apprentice" phase and Y is the subsequent raise received at the end of s periods. Then $E[u(w, Y)] = u(w)$ during apprenticeship and $u(w,y) = u(w+y)$ after promotion.

$s+1$ periods to evaluate the nonwage characteristic. Thus if the first job which is accepted results in a quit, the value of optimal search from then on out is V^{s+1}. Define the value of taking a job under these circumstances as $\hat{T}_{s+1}(w, V^{s+1})$. Then

$$\hat{T}_{s+1}(w, V^{s+1}) = E[u(w, Y)]B(s) + \beta^s \left\{ V^{s+1}G[y^*_{s+1}(w)|w] + \int_{y^*_{s+1}(w)}^{\infty} \frac{u(w,y)}{1-\beta} g(y|w)\,\mathrm{d}y \right\}.$$

The definition of $T_{s+1}(w, V^{s+1})$ given in (16) and the definition of $y^*_{s+1}(w)$ yield

$$\hat{T}_{s+1}(w, V^{s+1}) - T_{s+1}(w, V^{s+1}) \geqslant 0. \tag{17}$$

Define $U^1(w)$ as the expected value of an observation of wage w under the above conditions. Then

$$U^1(w) = -c + \beta \max\{ V^{s+1}, \hat{T}_{s+1}(w, V^{s+1})\}.$$

Let $\bar{U}^1$ be the expected value of $U^1(w)$ with respect to the marginal p.d.f. of wages, $f(w)$. Then (17) implies $\bar{U}^1 \geqslant V^{s+1}$. Repeat the above procedure using $\bar{U}^1$ as the value of search but maintaining use of the strategies ξ_{s+1} and $y^*_{s+1}(w)$. That is, define $\hat{T}_{s+1}(w, \bar{U}^1)$ as the value of taking a job at wage w when the first *two* jobs can be evaluated in s periods but *all* subsequent jobs take $s+1$ periods to evaluate. It is trivial that $\hat{T}_{s+1}(w, \bar{U}^1) > \hat{T}_{s+1}(w, V^{s+1})$. Next define $U^2(w)$ and $\bar{U}^2$ analogously to $U^1(w)$ and $\bar{U}^1$. Then $\bar{U}^2 \geqslant \bar{U}^1$. Repeating the process generates a sequence $\bar{U}^1 \leqslant \bar{U}^2 \leqslant \ldots \leqslant \bar{U}^n \leqslant \ldots$. The limit of this sequence represents the case in which *all* evaluations take precisely s periods and the search strategy is characterized by ξ_{s+1} and $y^*_{s+1}(w)$. Clearly this leads to an expected utility of search which is less than V^s. Thus $\{\bar{U}^i\}_{i+1}^{\infty}$ is nondecreasing and bounded above by V^s. Define $U^* = \lim_{n\to\infty} \bar{U}^n$ then

$$V^{s+1} < \lim_{n\to\infty} \bar{U}^n = U^* \leqslant V^s.$$

Strict inequality derives from the uniqueness of ξ_s and ξ_{s+1}. QED

Lemma 3. For each $s \geqslant 1$, $\partial T_s(w)/\partial w$ is positive and increasing in s.

Proof. Integrating by parts in (16), using $\Psi_w(z)$ as defined in section 2.3, and differentiating,

$$\partial T_s(w)/\partial w = -\left(\frac{1}{1-\beta}\right)\int_{-\infty}^{\bar{z}(w)} \partial\Psi_w(z)/\partial w \,\mathrm{d}z - \left(\frac{\beta^s}{1-\beta}\right)\int_{-\infty}^{V^s(1-\beta)} \partial\Psi_w(z)/\partial w \,\mathrm{d}z, \tag{18}$$

where again $\bar{z}(w)=\lim_{y\to\infty}u(w,y)$. Since $\partial\Psi_z(w)/\partial w<0, \partial T_s(w)/\partial w>0$. Moreover, as s increases, both β^s and $V^s(1-\beta)$ fall, implying the second term in (18) gets smaller. Hence $\partial T_s(w)/\partial w<\partial T_{s+1}(w)/\partial w$. QED

Armed with Lemmas 2 and 3, we are prepared to show that the reservation wage rises with s.

Theorem 5. For each $s\geqslant 1$, $\xi_{s+1}\geqslant\xi_s$ with strict inequality if $\xi_s>0$.

Proof. Assume the opposite; that is, let $\xi_s>\xi_{s+1}$. In this case it must be that

$$T_s(w)-T_{s+1}(w)<V^s-V^{s+1} \tag{19}$$

for all $w\geqslant\xi_{s+1}$. This follows from the fact that when $\xi_s>\xi_{s+1}$ then $T_s(w)-T_{s+1}(w)$ is maximal at ξ_{s+1} over $w\geqslant\xi_{s+1}$. But $\xi_s\geqslant\xi_{s+1}$ implies this is less than or equal to V^s-V^{s+1}. With $\partial T_t(w)/\partial w$ increasing in t, the difference $T_s(w)-T_{s+1}(w)$ can only get smaller than V^s-V^{s+1} as w increases above ξ_{s+1}.

Equation (19) implies $T_s(w)-V^s<T_{s+1}(w)-V^{s+1}$ for all $w\geqslant\xi_{s+1}$. Using (15) as in section 2.4 generates

$$c+V^t(1-\beta)=\beta\int_{\xi_t}^{\infty}[T_t(w)-V^t]f(w)\,\mathrm{d}w. \tag{20}$$

Consider what happens in (20) as t goes from s to $s+1$. V^t falls but $[T_t(w)-V^t]$ rises. Thus ξ_t must rise unless $\xi_s=0=\xi_{s+1}$, implying $\xi_{s+1}\geqslant\xi_s$. This contradicts the original assumption that $\xi_{s+1}<\xi_s$. Thus it must be that $\xi_{s+1}\geqslant\xi_s$. The strict inequality obviously holds when $\xi_s>0$. QED

Theorem 6. For all $w\geqslant 0$, $y_s^*(w)\geqslant y_{s+1}^*(w)$ with strict inequality if $y_s^*(w)>0$.

Proof. By definition $u(w,y_t^*(w))/(1-\beta)=V^t$. But V^t falls as t rises. With w fixed this implies $y_t^*(w)$ is falling as t rises. QED

The implication of Theorems 5 and 6 is that as s rises (the cost of evaluation increases) there is a shift away from evaluation toward search. Moreover, there is an unambiguous fall in the *ex ante* expected probability of a quit when s increases. This is in contrast to the case when c increases. There, while both search and evaluation decrease as w^* and $y^*(w)$ fall,[14] we cannot guarantee a fall in the *ex ante* expected quit rate as c rises.

5. Summary and conclusion

The analysis in this paper has uncovered two strong results. The first is that while an increase in direct search costs decreases both search and evaluation, an increase in the costs of evaluation (a rise in s) causes a shift away from evaluation and towards search. The second strong result is that as long as wage offers matter (i.e., as long as there exists at least one ξ interior to the distribution of potential wage offers), then the quit rate is strictly positive (in a probabilistic sense).

These results forcefully illustrated the importance of distinguishing between general and specific information. In future research, this distinction will be applied to consumer behavior in product markets as well as other problems in labor economics. For example, the same sort of analysis can be used to explain firm's firing behavior; the initially observed characteristics of employees also become known after a certain period of employment.

Appendix 1

This appendix outlines a proof of Theorem 1.

Theorem 1. There exists a unique, continuous, bounded solution to the functional equation (3).

Proof. Since $u(w,y)$ is continuous and bounded on R_+^2 and β satisfies $0<\beta<1$, a straightforward application of Denardo [4] suffices to establish Theorem 1.

[14]Again, the spirit of Theorems 5 and 6 is preserved even if Assumption 7 is dropped. If we define $A_s \equiv \{w|T_s(w) \geqslant V^s\}$ as the "acceptance set," then Theorem 5 becomes $\text{Prob}\{w \in A_s\} \leqslant \text{Prob}\{w \in A_{s+1}\}$ and Theorem 6 holds as stated.

A more traditional approach is to define a sequence of truncated problems by the functional equations

$$v^N(w) = -c + \beta \max\left\{ V^{N-1}; \int_0^\infty \left[u(w,y)\right] + \beta \max\left\{u(w,y)B(N-1), V^{N-2}\right\} g(y|w)\,\mathrm{d}y \right\},$$

where $B(N-1) = \sum_{n=1}^{N-1} \beta^{n-1}$, V^N is the expected value of $v^N(w)$ according to $f(w)$, and $N \geqslant 2$. Otherwise $v^1(w) = -c$ and $v^0(w) = 0$. Standard arguments show that there exists $V(w)$ defined on $[0, \infty)$ such that $\{v^N\}$ converges uniformly to v, v is the unique solution to (3), and is continuous and bounded on $[0, \infty)$. QED

References

[1] Becker, G., *Human Capital*, (2d edn.), Columbia University Press, New York, 1975.
[2] Borjas, G., and Goldberg, M., "The economics of job search: a comment," unpublished manuscript, October 1976.
[3] Burdett, K., "On the job search and quit rates," unpublished manuscript, University of Essex, 1975.
[4] Denardo, E., "Contraction mappings in the theory underlying dynamic programming," *SIAM Review*, 9 (1967), 165–177.
[5] Lippman, S. A., and McCall, J. J., "The economics of job search: a survey," *Economic Inquiry*, 14 (1976), 155–189.
[6] MacQueen, J., "Optimal policies for a class of search and evaluation problems," *Management Science*, 10 (1964), 746–59.
[7] Mattila, P., "Job quitting and frictional unemployment," *American Economic Review*, 64 (1974), 255–240.
[8] McCall, J. J., "Economics of information and job search," *Quarterly Journal of Economics*, 84 (1970), 113–126.
[9] Mortensen, D. T., "The turnover implications of learning about attributes on the job," unpublished paper, Northwestern University, 1975.
[10] Nelson, P., "Information and consumer behavior," *Journal of Political Economy*, 78 (1970), 311–329.
[11] Pencavel, J., "Wages, specific training, and labor turnover in US manufacturing industries,:" *International Economic Review*, 13 (1972), 53–64.
[12] Reynolds, L., *The Structure of Labor Markets*, Harper, New York, 1951.
[13] Rosen, S., "Learning and experience in the labor market," *Journal of Human Resources*, 7 (1972), 326–342.
[14] Rosen, S., "Advertising, information and product differentiation," unpublished, University of Rochester, 1976.
[15] Rothschild, M., "Models of market organization with imperfect information: a survey," *Journal of Political Economy*, 81 (1973), 1283–1308.
[16] Rothschild, M., "Searching for the lowest price when the distribution of prices is unknown," *Journal of Political Economy*, 82 (1974), 689–712.
[17] Wilde, L., "Search as investment in human capital," unpublished, California Institute of Technology, 1976.

CHAPTER 4

Dispersed transactions prices in a model of decentralized pure exchange

ROGER C. KORMENDI*

University of Chicago

1. Introduction

The standard approach to modelling the process of exchange starts by introducing, either implicitly or explicitly, the concept of a central market authority. By now, the major shortcomings of this approach are very well known. In particular, the important question of how individual agent behavior determines the terms at which actual trade takes place is not answered.

The standard price formation mechanism summarized in the "Law of indifference" and the "Law of supply and demand" derives from a story implicit in the works of early writers that can be considered to be an informal model of a *decentralized* pure exchange process.[1] The crucial assumption is that full information about the prices at which the other agents in the market are willing to trade is (costlessly) available to all agents in the market. Armed with this information, agents *compete* for the most attractive trading opportunities at each instant in time. If this competitive bidding process involves no constraints (resource, time, etc.) trade takes place at a single market-clearing price.

Once we leave the realm of a "perfect market", however, we are on much less solid ground about the nature of price formation and the exchange process. There is a long standing but rather vague notion that once one introduces the fact that gathering information about trading

*I wish to thank Kenneth Burdett, Robert Clower, Glen Gotz, Richard Higgins, Jack Hirshleifer, John McCall, Steven Lippman, George Neumann, Josè Schienkman, Gary Skoog and Charles Stuart for helpful comments and discussions.

[1]See Jevons [14], Walras [28] and Marshall [18].

opportunities involves a real cost to agents, the arbitrage induced by such activity will be attenuated, and hence trading at dispersed prices will occur. To move closer to an understanding of the implications of attenuated information gathering activity on price formation and the allocation of resources in a market, a model that incorporates explicitly such activity and derives individual agent behavior as regards price formation and trade is required.

A class of models has recently been developed that can be adapted to the task: search models. There are two related areas of research with respect to these models. By far the greatest amount of work has been in modelling individual agent search behavior.[2] The other less-travelled area, and the one of direct concern for us, has been modelling *markets*.[3]

In models of individual agent behavior, it has been assumed that in the context of an environment with dispersed prices an agent can be perceived as sampling randomly from a given distribution of prices. The individual is assumed to know the distribution, but only in sampling does he gain information about, and thus access to, specific trading opportunities. Furthermore, the information is available to him only at a cost—a cost associated with sampling (i.e., searching). An expected result of this formulation is that agents search less the greater the associated costs. As a first step toward modelling a market, this is an important result. It suggests that agent behavior in the context of an environment of dispersed prices may in turn have a property—attenuated search over trading opportunities —that in a full market setting would serve to generate that same environment. This, of course, is an important consistency condition for any market model.

[2]The seminal paper was by Stigler [25]. For a very comprehensive survey see Lippman and McCall [16].

[3]Rothschild [23] reports on some papers written in the early 1970s that made initial efforts at modelling markets under imperfect information. Mortensen [19] and Telser [27] have developed in unpublished papers what they call models of "decentralized markets". They achieve this decentralization by dividing up a market into many *submarkets*, each of which has a single market-clearing price achieved by, say, a "local auctioneer". Ionnides [13] constructs a model of an ongoing market with dispersed prices due to participants "flowing through" the market with finite lives. His results turn on two elements: (1) an "age distribution" of agents in the market; and (2) a negative relationship between sellers' prices and their "age". Ionnides' model is very interesting, but one can show that the equilibrium is not necessarily characterized by dispersed prices. Butters [6] introduces a model in which firms are price setters who disseminate price information through costly advertising messages to passive consumers. Dispersed prices in Butters' model are characterized by a positive relationship between the price a firm gets and its advertising/sales ratio. Though his results are suggestive, it seems clear that they depend crucially upon the passivity of consumers.

In the sections that follow, we will develop a model of decentralized pure exchange. The reason for using a pure exchange setting is that in many ways it is the most basic economic setting. We will address ourselves to two main questions. First, are there conditions under which dispersed transactions prices will characterize the market equilibrium? Second, what are some properties of the allocation of resources in a dispersed price equilibrium? With respect to the first question, we will show that price dispersion turns on two basic facts: (1) agents have limited capacity to generate information; and (2) agents are heterogeneous with respect to their defining characteristics. With respect to the second question, we will show that the agents with relatively more intense tastes for a good, and agents who are relatively more risk averse pay on average the higher prices, but thereby succeed in trading more frequently. Thus, even when information generating capacity of agents is limited, the result of decentralized allocation of resources has the goods flowing with higher probability to those who place a relatively higher value on consummating trade for that good.

The answers to these two questions reveal the essential character of dispersed transactions prices. In a dispersed price equilibrium, there exists a tradeoff between gains from trade and probability of trading, with agents choosing their optimum "price–probability" pair from the opportunity set defined by the market equilibrium. Where they choose to locate depends upon their relative tastes for the goods and their risk aversion. Limited capacity of agents to gather information generates the stochastic tradeoff between price and probability of trading, and this is supported by the heterogeneity of agents.

2. Setting up the model

Consider the market setting in which there are two nonstorable private goods, X and Y. Suppose further that no physical transformation possibilities exist (i.e., pure exchange of the two goods between agents is the only economic activity). Let there be a continuum of agents who are endowed with good X only, and a continuum who are endowed with good Y only. From this departure point, if one were to assume price-taking behavior on the part of agents and include an auctioneer to set and adjust prices and control exchange at the market-clearing price, one would have the standard model of a competitive market. Instead, we will assume that agents who desire to trade must engage in contacting activity (i.e., they must initiate meetings with other agents) in order to obtain information about trading opportunities and consummate trade. We will also assume that agents have limited capacity to gather and process such information.

When trade between two agents occurs, we assume that exactly one unit of X is transferred from the X-endowed agent to the Y-endowed agent. This assumption serves to simplify the notion of a "trading opportunity" so that it can be parameterized by the number of units of Y that are traded for the one unit of X (i.e., the price of X).

Each agent is assumed to have a utility function, $U(x,y)$, that is concave and increasing in each argument. In general, utility functions as well as endowments vary across agents. Thus, for each X-endowed agent there exists some quantity $y \geqslant 0$ satisfying the equation

$$U(x',0) = U(x'-1,y), \tag{1}$$

where $x' \geqslant 1$ is the agent's endowed quantity of X. The solution to (1) can be interpreted as the minimum acceptable terms at which an X-endowed agent would voluntarily trade (i.e., supply one unit of X in an exchange). We will call that minimum value the "threshold supply price", t_s, of the X-endowed agent. Similarly, the quantity y that solves the equation

$$U(0,y') = U(1,y'-y), \tag{2}$$

where y' is the agent's endowed quantity of Y, can be regarded as the maximum acceptable terms at which that Y-endowed agent would voluntarily trade (i.e., the "threshold demand price", t_d, of the Y-endowed agent).

In this market setting an agent engages in what we have called contacting activity in order to generate information about specific trading opportunities. Contacting activity in the period in question is assumed to have the following structure:

Assumption 1. Contacting takes place after the receipt of endowments (which is assumed to begin the period) and before actual consumption (which is assumed to end the period).

Assumption 2. All contacts between agents are pairwise involving one X-endowed agent and one Y-endowed agent.

Assumption 3. Contacting takes place in "rounds"; in a given round each agent can engage in at most one contact.

Assumption 4. In any given round, the X-endowed agents are paired randomly with the Y-endowed agents.

Assumption 5. A fixed finite number R of rounds occur during the period.

Clearly, if contacting is to generate any information about trading opportunities and lead ultimately to trade, some information about willingness to trade must be exchanged in a contact. We adopt the following assumptions:

Assumption 6. In a contact, both agents simultaneously tell each other their "offer price". The offer supply price s of an X-endowed agent communicates his willingness to trade away one unit of X if he contacts an agent willing to give him s or more units of Y in exchange. The offer demand price d of a Y-endowed agent communicates his willingness to trade away d or fewer units of Y if he contacts an agent willing to give him one unit of X in exchange.

Assumption 7. Each agent sets his offer price prior to his first contact and does not change it for the duration of his contacting activity.

From Assumption 6 we infer that trade will take place in a contact if and only if offer prices overlap (i.e., $d \geqslant s$). Thus, we add the assumption:

Assumption 8. If $d > s$, the actual transaction price is $p = \alpha s + (1-\alpha)d$, where $0 \leqslant \alpha \leqslant 1$, and α is constant over all transactions and known to all agents.

The structure of contacting activity is one of the crucial elements of the information structure of the model. Thus, we will discuss briefly the motivation behind the specific assumptions we have adopted.

Assumption 1 serves the purpose of abstracting from the strategic considerations that would be involved if some agents could start their contacting activity while others have yet to receive their endowments. Assumption 2 rules out multilateral contacts in order to keep the environment "competitive" rather than "cooperative". Assumption 3 precludes the possibility of agents who contact at different speeds. Assumption 4 reflects the fact that we do not want to model agents as having agent-specific information. Assumption 5 is perhaps the most important of our assumptions on contacting activity. Limiting the number of contacts any agent may engage in represents our method of modeling agents with limited capacity to generate information. Assumption 6 restricts the information flows in a contact and rules out "recontracting". That is, when offer prices overlap, agents do not make their commitment to trade contingent upon not finding a preferred partner in future rounds of contacting. Assumption 6 also rules out the possibility of "haggling"—altering offer prices within a contact in the event that there is no initial overlap. Assumption 7 serves to simplify the decision problem of the agents in the model by abstracting from any revision in the offer price within the period under consideration. By assuming a constant α over all transactions known to all agents (Assumption 8), we abstract from "bargaining"—the activity of deciding on the transactions price once an overlap has been determined—by making it a costless activity the outcome of which is known *a priori* to all agents. Clearly, haggling, bargaining, recontracting, and offer price revision are important phenomena, but they would introduce complications unnecessary at this time.

As we have set up the model so far, there is only one decision each agent is assumed to make: where to set his offer price. Once he sets his offer price, the agent randomly contacts agents on the other side of the market over rounds until: (1) he contacts an agent with an overlapping offer; or (2) he has contacted R agents without encountering an overlapping offer. In the first case, the agent is assumed to cease his contacting and consummate trade at the price $p=\alpha d+(1-\alpha)s$. In the second case, the agent simply consumes his endowment.

In either case, an agent has some gain in utility associated with each possible outcome. It will be convenient in what follows to work with an indirect utility function that relates the parameter of the possible outcomes in the market (i.e., the transactions price p), to the gain in utility. Assume for simplicity that all agents have constant risk aversion with respect to market risk. Then the gain in utility for an X-endowed agent $u(p)=U(x'-1,p)-U(x',0)$, can be written as:

$$u(p)=-kA(x')+p, \qquad \rho=0,$$

$$u(p)=-kA(x')+\frac{(1-e^{-\rho p})}{(1-e^{-\rho})}, \qquad \rho>0, \tag{3}$$

where $A(x')$ is a continuous decreasing function that we assume to be the same across agents.[4] We assume, however, that the parameters k and ρ as well as x' vary across agents. We interpret k as a global parameter of tastes for X relative to Y, and ρ as the parameter of risk aversion.

From (3) we can see that the vector of parameters (x',k,ρ) completely defines an X-endowed agent. Consequently, the threshold supply price, $t_s(x',k,\rho)$ (i.e., the price for which $u(p)=0$), is given by

$$t_s(x',k,\rho) = -\frac{\ln[1-kA(x')(1-e^{-\rho})]}{\rho}. \tag{4}$$

Since $A(x')$ is a continuous decreasing function, $t_s(x',k,\rho)$ is continuous, decreasing in x' and ρ, increasing in k, and has $\lim_{\rho\to 0} t_s = kA(x')$.

For a Y-endowed agent, $u(p) = U(1,y'-p) - U(0,y')$, is given by[5]

$$\begin{aligned} u(p) &= ky' - p, \qquad \rho = 0, \\ u(p) &= k - \frac{(e^{\rho p}-1)}{(e^{\rho y'}-1)}, \qquad \rho > 0. \end{aligned} \tag{5}$$

The vector (y',k,ρ) completely defines a Y-endowed agent. Hence, for any agent we can solve (5) for $t_d(y',k,\rho)$:

$$t_d(y',k,\rho) = \frac{\ln[1+k(e^{\rho y'}-1)]}{\rho}. \tag{6}$$

Clearly, $t_d(y',k,\rho)$ is continuous, increasing in y',k, and ρ, and has $\lim_{\rho\to 0} t_d = ky'$.

[4]Market risk in this setting concerns the quantity of Y that will be obtained for one unit of X. Thus, constant risk aversion implies the following utility function:

$$\begin{aligned} U(x,y) &= ka(x) + y, \qquad \rho = 0, \\ U(x,y) &= ka(x) + \frac{(1-e^{-\rho y})}{(1-e^{-\rho})}, \qquad \rho > 0, \end{aligned}$$

where $a(x)$ is a concave increasing function. From the above, (3) follows, where $A(x') = a(x') - a(x'-1)$. The assumption of constant risk aversion is not crucial to any of the results of this paper. It is merely the most convenient way to rank agents by their risk aversion.

[5]Starting with $U(x,y)$ in footnote 4, (5) follows.

3. The offer price decision

In the market setting described in the previous section the only decision an agent has to make is where to set his offer price. Clearly, the offer price set by an agent reflects his beliefs as to his opportunities for trade with other agents in the market. In our market environment, whom an agent contacts in any given round is from his point of view simply a random draw from the set of agents on the other side of the market. Hence, the relevant objective environment for an agent as regards his offer price decision is simply the sequence of distributions of offer prices he faces over the rounds of contacting. Denote the objective sequences of cumulative distributions of offer supply and demand prices by $\langle F_r \rangle$ and $\langle G_r \rangle$, respectively. Throughout this paper, we will be assuming that agents' beliefs are correct in that they know the objective environment facing them. For an X-endowed agent this entails knowing $\langle G_r \rangle$; for a Y-endowed agent $\langle F_r \rangle$.[6]

As an X-endowed agent considers setting higher offer supply prices, he increases his expected utility conditional upon an overlap, but he reduces the probability of actually finding an overlapping demand price. Denote by $V_1(s)$ the expected gain in utility associated with the first round contact of an X-endowed agent who faces G_1 and sets his offer supply price at s. This gain can be expressed as:

$$V_1(s) = \int_s^{\infty} u(p)\,\mathrm{d}G_1(d), \tag{7}$$

where $p = \alpha d + (1-\alpha)s$. The essential tradeoff involved is that a higher offer supply price achieves increased gains when trading with agents within the margin but loses potential trading partners at the margin.

In the context of a setting that involves more than one round of contacting, however, the loss of trading partners at the margin is not a total loss; but it means that the agent must go to the second round with a higher probability where opportunities are not as good.[7] Given an offer price of s, the probability of failing to trade in round 1—and thereby going into round 2—is $G(s)$. Thus, the expected gain in utility associated with a

[6]For an interpretation of this model as a dynamic period model with learning behavior, see Kormendi [15].

[7]This follows from the simple fact that an agent is only one of many agents competing for the trading opportunities on the other side of the market. Therefore, the best opportunities will be the first ones to go. This implies that the relationship between G_r and G_{r+1} must have the property that $G_{r+1}(d) > G_r(d)$ all d. See Appendix 1 for elaboration.

round 2 contact, from the perspective of the initial decision on s, is:

$$V_2(s)=G_1(s)\int_s^{\infty} u(p)\mathrm{d}G_2(d). \tag{8}$$

Continuing the logic, a series of expected gains as seen from the perspective of the initial decision on S can be constructed. Letting $G_0(s)\equiv 1$, the gain in any round $r=1,2,\ldots, R$, is simply:

$$V_r(s)=\left[\prod_{i=0}^{r-1} G_i(s)\right]\int_s^{\infty} u(p)\mathrm{d}G_r(d). \tag{9}$$

Finally, for an X-endowed agent facing $\langle G_r\rangle$ the total gain associated with setting an offer price s is given by the equation:

$$V(s)=\sum_{r=1}^{R} V_r(s)=\sum_{r=1}^{R}\left[\prod_{i=0}^{r-1} G_i(s)\right]\left[\int_s^{\infty} u(p)\mathrm{d}G_r(d)\right]. \tag{10}$$

We assume that the agent sets s to maximize $V(s)$ and that V has only one local maximum, given an agent's x',k, and ρ.[8] Note that it is clear that an agent will never set $s<t_s$, since he would lose by trading at any price $p<t_s$. Consider, however, the price $p^*=\inf\{d;G_1(d)=1\}$, which we can assume is finite. For those agents with $t_s>p^*$, we simply assume that their offer price is their threshold price.

For a Y-endowed agent, the total expected gains from selecting d is:

$$W(d)=\sum_{r=1}^{R}\left[\prod_{i=0}^{r-1}(1-F_i(d))\right]\left[\int_0^{d} u(p)\mathrm{d}F_r(s)\right]. \tag{11}$$

We assume that the agent sets d to maximize $W(d)$ and that this d is uniquely determined given the agent's y',k, and ρ. It is clear that no agent would ever set $d>t_d$, since he would lose by trading at prices $p>t_d$. We will assume, however, that those agents with $t_d<p_*=\sup\{s:F_1(s)=0\}$ simply set their offer demand price $d=t_d$.

We now present two propositions that will be useful in some of the results to be developed later.

[8]Clearly, whether or not V has a unique local maximum depends upon the properties of $\langle G_r\rangle$. The main results of this paper, those on equilibrium price dispersion, are not affected by this assumption. Only Propositions 1 and 2 and some of the discussion in section 7 are affected. In Kormendi [15], conditions that guarantee uniqueness are presented.

Proposition 1. The offer supply (demand) price of an X-endowed (Y-endowed) agent varies positively with his threshold supply (demand) price.

Proof. See Appendix 2.

Corollary 1. The offer supply (demand) price of an X-endowed (Y-endowed) agent varies negatively (positively) with his endowment, x' (y'), and positively with his "global tastes for X", (i.e., k).

The sense of Proposition 1 (and Corollary 1) is simply that for an X-endowed agent an increase in t_s (increase in k, decrease in x') reflects an increase in the X-endowed agent's tastes for X relative to Y. With such an increase in relative tastes towards X, one would expect that the X-endowed agent would desire to trade away X only at relatively more attractive terms (i.e., at higher prices). He achieves this, of course, by raising his offer supply price. Similarly for a Y-endowed agent.

Proposition 2. The offer supply (demand) price of an X-endowed (Y-endowed) agent varies negatively (positively) with ρ, the measure of his risk aversion.

Proof. See Appendix 2.

The intuition of Proposition 2 is that by lowering his offer supply price, an X-endowed agent raises his probability of consummating trade but sacrifices expected gains from trade. Increasing an X-endowed agent's risk aversion makes him more willing to sacrifice expected net gains for the reduced risk of not trading and hence lowers his offer supply price. Similarly for a Y-endowed agent.

4. The market environment

Starting from the initial round, in which the distributions of offers set by agents in the market are F_1 and G_1 and agents are paired randomly, we wish to be able to derive the corresponding sequences of distributions $\langle F_r \rangle$ and $\langle G_r \rangle$ which we indicated earlier to be the relevant objective environment facing agents in our market setting. Doing so requires a precise definition of a "random pairing" of X-endowed agents with Y-endowed agents.

Definition 1. Let F and G be distributions of supply and demand offer prices defined on $[\underline{p},\bar{p}]$. A *pairing* of X-endowed agents with Y-endowed agents is said to be *random* if for *any* $[s_1,s_2]\subseteq[\underline{p},\bar{p}]$, where $s_2>s_1$, and *any* $[d_1,d_2]\subseteq[\underline{p},\bar{p}]$, where $d_2>d_1$, the following hold true:

(i) the proportion of X-endowed agents in $[s_1, s_2]$ who are paired with Y-endowed agents in $[d_1,d_2]$ is $G(d_2)-G(d_1)$, and

(ii) the proportion of Y-endowed agents in $[d_1,d_2]$ who are paired with X-endowed agents in $[s_1,s_2]$ is $F(s_2)-F(s_1)$.

From this definition it is possible to show that from any pair of initial distributions (F_1,G_1) the corresponding sequences $\langle F_r\rangle$ and $\langle G_r\rangle$ can be derived. This is done in Appendix 1. Thus, to describe the market environment, it is sufficient to refer to the pair of offer price distributions (F_1,G_1) (or simply (F,G), dropping the subscripts).

5. Equilibrium

Let us consider now what determines the actual distributions of offer prices, F and G. Clearly, the distribution F of offer supply prices depends upon the joint cumulative distribution of preferences and endowments across X-endowed agents, or, alternatively, upon the joint cumulative distribution of t_s and ρ.[9] Similarly, G depends upon the joint distribution of t_d and ρ across Y-endowed agents. We will denote these joint cumulative distributions by $\Phi(t_s,\rho)$ and $\Gamma(t_d,\rho)$, respectively.

Given an environment $E\equiv(F,G)$, equations (A.6), (A.7) and (A.8) in Appendix 1 define a mapping from E into $(\langle F_r\rangle,\langle G_r\rangle)$. Equations (10) and (11), which represent the offer price decision for X-endowed and Y-endowed agents, define mappings from (t_s,ρ,E) into an s and from (t_d,ρ,E) into a d, respectively. Denote these mappings as $s(t_s,\rho,E)$ and $d(t_d,\rho,E)$, respectively. Finally, given the postulated distributions $\Phi(t_s,\rho)$ and $\Gamma(t_d,\rho)$, we can construct the mapping from (s,d) and (Φ,Γ) into (F,G) defined by the pair of equations:

$$F(s(t_s,\rho,E))=\Phi(t_s,\rho),$$
$$G(d(t_d,\rho,E))=\Gamma(t_d,\rho). \tag{12}$$

[9]For X-endowed agents, we can see from (3) and (4) that holding ρ constant, only changes in x' and k that affect t_s affect $u(p)$. Hence, $u(p)$ can be reparameterized in terms of t_s and ρ. Similarly, for Y-endowed agents.

Let $\tilde{E} \equiv (\tilde{F}, \tilde{G})$ be the solution to the pair of equations above. That is,

$$\begin{aligned} &\tilde{F}(s(t_s, \rho, \tilde{E})) = \Phi(t_s, \rho), \\ &\tilde{G}(d(t_s, \rho, \tilde{E})) = \Gamma(t_s, \rho). \end{aligned} \tag{13}$$

$\tilde{E}$ as defined in (13) is the equilibrium of our model, in that agents' behavior in the environment $\tilde{E}$ serves to generate $\tilde{E}$ when agents' beliefs are correct. In the next section, we will show that such an $\tilde{E}$ does in fact exist and develop its properties.

6. Decentralized exchange and dispersed transactions prices

6.1. *The standard competitive solution*

It will be useful to examine the standard competitive model as it applies to our basic market setting, in order to establish a benchmark from which to analyze decentralized exchange. When there is implicitly an "auctioneer" coordinating all information and exchange, only the endowments and preferences of the agents (since they determine excess demand functions) are relevant to the analysis. As a consequence of assuming that only one unit of X is transferred in an exchange, the excess demand function of each agent for good X can be parameterized solely by his threshold price (t_s for an X-endowed agent, t_d for a Y-endowed agent). We characterize the set of X-endowed agents by the cumulative distribution $\Phi(t_s)$ of threshold supply prices among them and the set of Y-endowed agents by the cumulative distribution $\Gamma(t_d)$ of threshold demand price among them. Suppose now that the "auctioneer" displays a certain (relative) price p. What proportion of the X-endowed agents would be willing to trade at that price? Clearly, only those X-endowed agents whose threshold supply price is less than or equal to p (i.e., $\Phi(p)$). Thus, demand for X is $D(p) = \Phi(p)$. Similarly, $1 - \Gamma(p)$ defines the proportion of Y-endowed agents willing to trade at p, (i.e., $S(p) = 1 - \Gamma(p)$). Thus, the market clearing price $\hat{p}$ is simply the solution to $\Phi(p) = 1 - \Gamma(p)$.

6.2. *The exchange problem*

Assume for the moment that all X-endowed agents are identical and thus have identical threshold prices, $\bar{t}_s$. In the equilibrium of our model of decentralized exchange, each X-endowed agent would set the same offer supply price, since their (t_s, ρ) is the same. Denote that price by $\tilde{s} \geqslant \bar{t}_s$. We know that the standard competitive solution would have $\hat{p} = \bar{t}_s$. Assuming that $\tilde{s} = \hat{p}$, the corresponding equilibrium distribution of offer supply prices would be a point mass at $\hat{p}$, that is,

$$\tilde{F}(s) = \begin{cases} 0, & s < \hat{p}, \\ 1, & s \geqslant \hat{p}. \end{cases}$$

Facing $\tilde{F}$, Y-endowed agents with $t_d \geqslant \hat{p}$ maximize their gains from trade by setting $d = \hat{p}$, since the transactions price $p = \alpha d + (1-\alpha)s, 0 < \alpha < 1$. Those with $t_d < \hat{p}$ will simply set $d = t_d$. Thus, we have

$$\tilde{G}(s) = \begin{cases} \Gamma(d), & d < \hat{p}, \\ \quad 1, & k \geqslant \hat{p}. \end{cases}$$

Denoting the equilibrium distributions of transactions prices by $\tilde{\Theta}$, we have

$$\tilde{\Theta}(p) = \begin{cases} 0, & < \hat{p}, \\ 1, & p \geqslant \hat{p}. \end{cases}$$

That is, the single transactions price $\hat{p} = \bar{t}_s$ can characterize the equilibrium.[10] An analogous result would hold, of course, if all Y-endowed agents were identical.

Consider, though, what it means to have all threshold prices on at least one side of the market identical. Essentially, it implies that there is no "problem" in determining how exchange will take place. Suppose, for example, that in the context of our basic model X-endowed agents were arbitrarily paired with Y-endowed agents in a trade-or-no-trade setting and restricted from contacting any other agent. From simple Edgeworth Box analysis we know that the same proportion of the population would trade as would under an auctioneer setting. Furthermore, *any* arbitrary pairing would imply the same exchange behavior since one agent is a "perfect

[10]Furthermore, some single transactions price, $\tilde{p} \geqslant \bar{t}_s$, but not necessarily $\hat{p}$, *must* characterize the stationary state by the same argument. For an interesting extension of these arguments, consider a market slightly different from the one we have been dealing with. Suppose there is a continuum of consumers with preferences and endowments varying among them. Suppose also that this is a continuum of firms, all having access to the same, say constant returns to scale, technology. In this production context, as in pure exchange, our results would show that the competitive equilibrium (i.e., a single transactions price with $p = mc$), would be an equilibrium of a decentralized exchange process such as the one developed here.

substitute" for another as a trading partner if they have the same preferences and endowments.

Suppose now that agents differ in threshold prices across the population on both sides of the market and that an arbitrary pairing is conducted as above. In this case, the extent of trade depends critically upon the specific pairing, since agents are no longer "perfect substitutes in trade". It is really in this context that the whole notion of agents "searching" across the population on the other side of the market must be set. If there is no "exchange problem", there is no basis for a search-exchange process, the fundamental purpose of which is to solve such a problem.

6.3. The strategy for analyzing the equilibrium with heterogeneous agents

We now turn to analyzing the equilibrium when there *is* an "exchange problem", (i.e., when agents are heterogeneous on both sides of the market). We will continue to assume that agents have limited contacting ability. We will also assume, for convenience, that threshold prices and risk aversion are distributed independently across agents (i.e., $\Phi(t_s,\rho)=\Phi(t_s)\cdot\Phi(\rho)$ and $\Gamma(t_d,\rho)=\Gamma(t_d)\cdot\Gamma(\rho)$), and that $\Phi(t_s)$ and $\Gamma(t_d)$ are the cumulative distributions of uniform frequency distributions over the range $[0,1]$.[11] Thus, $\Phi(t_s)=t_s$ and $\Gamma(t_d)=t_d$.

It will be convenient to use the standard competitive solution as a benchmark from which to analyze the equilibrium of the decentralized market. We thus define a pair of offer price distributions with the property that transactions occur at the single market-clearing price $\hat{p}$. Denote these offer price distributions by $\hat{F}$ and $\hat{G}$:

$$\hat{F}(s)=\begin{cases} 0, & s<\hat{p}, \\ \Phi(s), & s\geqslant\hat{p}, \end{cases} \qquad \hat{G}(d)=\begin{cases} \Gamma(d), & d<\hat{p}, \\ 1, & d\geqslant\hat{p}. \end{cases} \tag{14}$$

Clearly, offer prices overlap only for those agents setting $d=\hat{p}$ and $s=\hat{p}$; thus, all transactions must occur at $\hat{p}$, regardless of the pattern of random contacts among the population of agents.

Our strategy in analyzing the equilibrium will be as follows. First we will assume the $(\hat{F},\hat{G})$ of (14) defines the environment and derive an exact

[11]Defining the range to be $[0,1]$ is not restrictive at all since with an appropriate change of units the range could be transformed to the general case, $[\underline{p},\bar{p}]$. The range of ρ we will take to be $[0,\bar{\rho}]$. Independence is not restrictive either. Uniformity, of course, is restrictive, but it serves the purpose of showing that heterogeneity can support dispersed prices. See Kormendi [15] for a more general treatment.

expression for the offer price decisions of agents facing that environment. Denote the relationships between s and (t_s,ρ) that generate $\hat{F}(s)$ and between d and (t_d,ρ) that generate $\hat{G}(d)$ by $\hat{s}(t_s,\rho)$ and $\hat{d}(t_d,\rho)$. Denote by $s(t_s,\rho,\hat{E})$ and $d(t_d,\rho,\hat{E})$ the *optimum* offer price of Y-endowed and X-endowed agents, respectively, who are in the assumed environment $\hat{E}=(\hat{F},\hat{G})$. Second, we will show that for a nonempty set of agents

$$s(t_s,\rho,\hat{E})<\hat{s}(t_s,\rho) \quad \text{and} \quad d(t_d,\rho,\hat{E})>\hat{d}(t_d,\rho),$$

implying that $(\hat{F},\hat{G})$ cannot in fact be an equilibrium. Third, we will show that no single transactions price can be an equilibrium. Fourth, we will show that an equilibrium $(\tilde{F},\tilde{G})$ exists and that it must be characterized by dispersed transactions prices.

6.4. *The offer price decision under* $(\hat{F},\hat{G})$[12]

In order to generate the offer price decision of agents facing $(\hat{F},\hat{G})$, we must derive the corresponding sequences, $\langle\hat{F}_r\rangle$ and $\langle\hat{G}_r\rangle$, using (A.6), (A.7) and (A.8) in Appendix 1; this is done in the following lemma.

Lemma 1. Given that $F_1=\hat{F}$ and $G_1=\hat{G}$, where $(\hat{F},\hat{G})$ are defined in (14),

$$\hat{F}_r(s)=\begin{cases}0, & s<\hat{p},\\ q_r+(1-q_r)\dfrac{[\Phi(s)-\Phi(\hat{p})]}{(1-\hat{q})}, & s>\hat{p},\end{cases}$$

$$G_r(d)=\begin{cases}(1-q_r)\dfrac{\Gamma(d)}{(1-\hat{q})}, & d<\hat{p},\\ 1, & d\geqslant\hat{p},\end{cases} \tag{15}$$

where $\hat{q}=\hat{F}(\hat{p})=1-\hat{G}(\hat{p})$ and $q_r=\hat{q}/(1+(r-1)\hat{q})$.

Proof. See Appendix 2.

As rounds of contacting advance, $q_r=\hat{q}/(1+(r-1)\hat{q})$, the proportion of potential trading partners in round r, decreases in value, and correspondingly the weight $(1-q_r)/(1-\hat{q})$ increases. This simply reflects the fact that

[12]The material in this subsection is of a somewhat detailed nature. The reader wishing to skip it can proceed to section 6.5 with little loss of continuity.

only the Y-endowed agents with $s=\hat{p}$ and the X-endowed agents with $d=\hat{p}$ are finding trading partners, and hence as rounds proceed the rest of the population becomes an increasing proportion of the remaining total population.

Given the sequences $\langle \hat{F}_r \rangle$ and $\langle \hat{G}_r \rangle$ from Lemma 1 we can now see whether $(\hat{F}, \hat{G})$ is a solution to (12). Denote the total gain associated with offer price s for an X-endowed agent by $V(s|t_s, \rho, \hat{E})$. Similarly, let $W(d|t_d, \rho, \hat{E})$ represent the total gain of a Y-endowed agent. We focus on the population of X-endowed agents; since the environment is qualitatively symmetric, our results will carry over directly to Y-endowed agents.

Every X-endowed agent is facing the sequence of distributions $\langle G_r \rangle$ in the equilibrium. It is clear that an X-endowed agent will not set $s>\hat{p}$ (unless $t_s>\hat{p}$) since $g(d)=0$ for $d>\hat{p}$. Clearly then, whether $(\hat{F}, \hat{G})$ is an equilibrium depends upon whether $s(t_s, \rho, \hat{E})=s(t_s, \rho)$ for *all* $(t_s, \rho) \in [0, \hat{p}] \times [0, \bar{\rho}]$. This cannot hold true, however, if at $s=\hat{p}$

$$\frac{\mathrm{d}V(s|t_s, \rho, \hat{E})}{\mathrm{d}s} < 0, \quad \text{for some } (t_s, \rho) \in [0, \hat{p}] \times [0, \bar{\rho}]. \tag{16}$$

Given $\langle \hat{G}_r \rangle$, we can substitute into (10) as follows (where $q_0 \equiv 0$ and $\beta = 1-\alpha$):

$$V(s|t_s, \rho, \hat{E}) = \sum_{r=1}^{R} \left[\frac{\hat{G}(s)}{(1-\hat{q})} \right]^{r-1} \left[\prod_{i=0}^{r-1} (1-q_i) \right] \left\{ (1-q_r) \int_s^1 \frac{u(p)}{1-\hat{q}} \mathrm{d}\hat{G}(d) + q_r u(\alpha\hat{p} + \beta s) \right\}. \tag{17}$$

To find out whether (16) holds true, we differentiate (17) with respect to s at $s=\hat{p}$ to get[13]

$$V_s(\hat{p}|t_s, \rho, \hat{E}) = \sum_{r=1}^{R} \frac{(1-\hat{q})}{[1+(r-2)\hat{q}][1+(r-1)\hat{q}]} [\beta\hat{q}u'(\hat{p}) - u(\hat{p})\hat{g}(\hat{p})]. \tag{18}$$

[13]Differentiating (17) with respect to s at $s=\hat{p}$ yields

$$V_s(\hat{p}|t_s, \rho, \hat{E}) = \sum_{r=1}^{R} \left[\prod_{i=1}^{r-1} (1-q_i) \right] \left\{ q_r \beta u'(p) + \frac{u(\hat{p})g(\hat{p})}{1-\hat{q}} (rq_r - 1) \right\}.$$

Given the definition of $q_i = \hat{q}/(1+(i-1)\hat{q})$, we can write $\prod_{i=1}^{r-1}(1-q_i) = (1-\hat{q})/(1+(r-1)\hat{q})$. Substituting the definition of q_r into $V_s(p|\ldots)$ yields (18).

Clearly, the sign of the above expression depends upon the sign of the last term in brackets. Recall now equation (7). Given the nature of $\hat{G}(S)$, we can see that the expression in brackets is simply

$$\int_{\hat{p}}^{1} \beta u'(p)\mathrm{d}\hat{G}(d) - u(\hat{p})\hat{g}(\hat{p}), \tag{19}$$

which is the derivative of (7) evaluated at $\hat{p}$ when $G_1 = \hat{G}$. Thus, we are back to asking a variant of the essential question isolated earlier: for all agents with $(t_s, \rho) \in [0,\hat{p}] \times [0,\bar{\rho}]$, is the loss from trading with agents within the margin of lowering s below $\hat{p}$ offset by the gain from picking up potential partners at the margin?

Lemma 2. For $\Phi(t_s)$ and $\Gamma(t_d)$ uniform over (0, 1) and $(\hat{F}, \hat{G})$ as defined in (14), there is a set of X-endowed agents for whom $s(t_s, \rho, \hat{E}) < \hat{s}(t_s, \rho)$.

Proof. From Proposition 2, we know that $V_s(s \mid t_s, \rho, \hat{E}) < V_s(s \mid t_s, 0, \hat{E})$ for all $\rho > 0$. Thus, if we find that for some set of agents $A \subseteq [0, \hat{p}]$, $V_s(\hat{p} \mid t_s, 0, \hat{E}) < 0$ all $t_s \in A$, we have proved the proposition. Looking at (19), using the fact that $\rho = 0$ and the fact that $\hat{g}(\hat{p}) = \gamma(\hat{p}) = 1$, since $\gamma(\hat{p})$ is uniform on [0, 1], we get $[\beta\hat{q}u'(\hat{p}) - u(\hat{p})\hat{g}(\hat{p})] = \beta\hat{q} - (\hat{p} - t_s)$. Since $\beta \in (0, 1)$ and $\hat{p} = \hat{q} = \frac{1}{2}$, we find that $V_s(\hat{p} \mid t_s, 0, \hat{E}) < 0$, for all agents with $t_s < (1 - \beta)/2$. QED

The corresponding lemma for Y-endowed agents is derived in an analogous manner. We exhibit it as:

Lemma 3. For $\Phi(t_s)$ and $\Gamma(t_d)$ uniform over [0, 1] and $(\hat{F}, \hat{G})$ as defined in (14), there is a set of Y-endowed agents for whom $d(t_d, \rho, \hat{E}) > \hat{d}(t_d, \rho)$.

Proof. Follows the proof of Lemma 2.

6.5. *A dispersed price equilibrium*

Essentially, Lemma 2 shows that there is a set of X-endowed agents who would want to set their offer supply price *lower* than $\hat{p}$ if the environment were in fact $(\hat{F}, \hat{G})$ as defined in (14). Similarly, from Lemma 3, there is a set of Y-endowed agents who would want to set their offer demand price *higher* than $\hat{p}$ if the environment were $(\hat{F}, \hat{G})$. Thus, $(\hat{F}, \hat{G})$ cannot be an equilibrium. We now wish to show that no environment $(\bar{F}, \bar{G})$ that would yield transactions *at only one price*, $\bar{p} \in [0, 1]$, can be an equilibrium of our model of decentralized exchange. Define $(\bar{F}, \bar{G})$ generally as:

$$\bar{F}(s) = \begin{cases} 0, & s < \bar{p}, \\ \Phi(s), & s \geqslant \bar{p}, \end{cases} \qquad \bar{G}(d) = \begin{cases} \Gamma(d), & d < \bar{p}, \\ 1, & d \geqslant \bar{p}, \end{cases} \tag{20}$$

which is necessary and sufficient for a single transactions price to rule.

Proposition 3. The environment $(\bar{F}, \bar{G})$ as defined in (20) cannot be an equilibrium as defined in (13).

Proof. Lemmas 2 and 3 directly prove the proposition for $\bar{p} = \hat{p}$. We consider, therefore, any arbitrary $\bar{p} > \hat{p}$, and show that $s(t_s, \rho, \bar{E}) < \bar{s}(t_s, \rho)$ for some set of X-endowed agents, where $\bar{s}(t_s, \rho)$ is defined analogously to $\hat{s}(t_s, \rho)$. Again, we focus on those agents with $\rho = 0$, since $s(t_s, \rho, E) < s(t_s, 0, E)$ all $\rho > 0$. Consider substituting into (18) $\bar{q} = 1 - \Gamma(\bar{p})$ for $\hat{q}$ and $\bar{p}$ for $\hat{p}$. From Lemma 2, the sign depends upon $[\beta q u'(\bar{p}) - u(\bar{p}) q(\bar{p})] = \beta \bar{q} - (\bar{p} - t_s)$. Since $\bar{p} > \hat{p} = \hat{q} > \bar{q}$, $\bar{p} - \beta \bar{q} > 0$ for all $\beta \in (0, 1)$. Hence, the set of agents for whom $t_s < \bar{p} - \beta \bar{q}$ would want to set $s < \bar{p}$. Simply substituting in $\bar{q}$ and $\bar{p}$ into (18) would be correct, however, only if $\Phi(\bar{p}) = 1 - \Gamma(\bar{p})$. In fact, $\Phi(p) > 1 - \Gamma(\bar{p})$ when $\bar{p} > \hat{p}$. Denote by $\langle \bar{G}_r \rangle$ the sequence deriving from $(\bar{F}, \bar{G})$. Denote by $\langle \bar{\bar{G}}_r \rangle$ the sequence derived from (15) replacing $\hat{q}$ with $\bar{q}$ and $\hat{p}$ with $\bar{q}$. For $r = 1$, $\bar{\bar{G}}_1 = \bar{G}_1 = \bar{G}$. For $r > 1$, $\bar{\bar{g}}_r(d) < \bar{g}_r(d)$ all $d < \bar{p}$ and $\bar{\bar{q}}_r = \int_{\bar{p}}^{1} g_r(d)\,\mathrm{d}d > \int_{\bar{p}}^{1} \bar{g}(d)\,\mathrm{d}d = \bar{q}_r$. Letting $V_s(\bar{p} \mid t_s, \rho, \bar{\bar{E}})$ represent the derivative of (10) under $\langle \bar{\bar{G}}_r \rangle$, and $V_s(\bar{p} \mid t_s, \rho, \bar{E})$ represent the derivative of (10) under $\langle \bar{G}_r \rangle$, $V_s(\bar{p} \mid t, \rho, \bar{E}) < V_s(\bar{p} \mid t_s, \rho, \bar{\bar{E}})$. Hence, since under $\langle \bar{\bar{G}}_r \rangle$ all agents with $t_s < \bar{p} - \beta \bar{q}$ would set $s < \bar{p}$, they also would under $\langle \bar{G}_r \rangle$. The proof for $\bar{p} < \hat{p}$ is analogous. QED

Proposition 3 says that when agents are heterogeneous the equilibrium of our market model *cannot* involve transactions at a single price whether it be the competitive price $\hat{p}$ or any other. This is basically because under $(\hat{F}, \hat{G})$ there are X-endowed agents wishing to set their offer supply price lower than $\hat{p}$ and Y-endowed agents wishing to set their offer demand prices higher than $\hat{p}$. Furthermore, under any other single price environment $(\bar{F}, \bar{G})$, agents on the "long side of the market" (i.e., X-endowed agent if $\bar{p} > \hat{p}$ and Y-endowed agents if $\bar{p} < \hat{p}$) have even a greater incentive to alter their offer prices than under $(\hat{F}, \hat{G})$. As a result, even if a decentralized market ever got to a state such that transactions were at a single price across all agents, it would be in the interest of some (not all) agents, specifically those with the most intense tastes for a good and those most risk averse, to alter their offer prices in an attempt to increase their probability of trading. Such individual action obviously implies that, if an equilibrium exists, it must involve dispersed transactions prices. We now proceed to establish that some $(\tilde{F}, \tilde{G})$ does in fact satisfy (13).

Proposition 4. Let $\mathcal{D}$ be the space of all distribution functions defined on [0, 1]. An equilibrium as defined in (13) exists in $\mathcal{D} \times \mathcal{D}$.

Proof. The pair of equations in (12) forms a compound mapping T: $\mathcal{D} \times \mathcal{D} \rightarrow \mathcal{D} \times \mathcal{D}$. T can be considered to be made up of three mappings. The first is the continuous mapping that takes (F, G) into the pair of sequences $(\langle F_r \rangle, \langle G_r \rangle)$ as characterized in equations (A.6), (A.7) and (A.8) of Appendix 1. The second is simply the continuous mapping that takes the pair $(\langle F_r \rangle, \langle G_r \rangle)$ into a pair of offer price functions $[d(t_d, \rho), s(t_d, \rho]$. The third is the continuous mapping that takes $(d(t_d, \rho, E), s(t_s, \rho, E))$ back into (F, G) given the underlying $(\Phi(t_d, \rho), \Gamma(t_d, \rho))$ as shown in (12). The space $B[0, 1]$ of all bounded functions defined on [0, 1] is a Banach Space, using the supnorm as the metric (see Dunford and Schwarz [7, p. 240]. The space, $\mathcal{D}$, of all cumulative distribution functions on [0, 1] is clearly a convex subset of $B[0, 1]$, which is a linear metric space. $\mathcal{D}$ is also compact in the following sense. $\bar{\mathcal{D}}$, the closure of $\mathcal{D}$ is compact. The set that closes $\mathcal{D}$ is the set of functions on [0, 1] that have all the usual properties of distribution functions except that they have right limits at their points of discontinuity (distribution functions are defined here to have *left* limits). However, in the mapping T, functions that differ only with respect to the limits at their points of discontinuity are identical. Hence, with respect to the mapping T, $\mathcal{D}$ is equivalent to $\bar{\mathcal{D}}$. Thus, $T: \bar{\mathcal{D}} \times \bar{\mathcal{D}} \rightarrow \bar{\mathcal{D}} \times \bar{\mathcal{D}}$ has a fixed point in $\mathcal{D} \times \mathcal{D}$ by the Schauder theorem [7, p. 456]. QED

The development of the argument in this section has led to two important propositions. Proposition 4 shows that an equilibrium in our model of decentralized exchange as defined in (13) does in fact exist. Proposition 3 tells us that the equilibrium cannot be characterized by transactions occurring all at a single transactions price. Taken together, these propositions imply that the equilibrium of our model must be characterized by dispersed transactions prices. We capture this conclusion in the following proposition.

Proposition 5. The equilibrium distribution of transactions prices, $\tilde{\Theta}$, which derives from the equilibrium $(\tilde{F}, \tilde{G})$ as defined in (13) has the following properties. Defining $p_* = \sup\{s: \tilde{F}(s) = 0\}$, $p^* = \inf\{d: \tilde{G}(d) = 1\}$: $0 < p_* < p^* < 1$ and $0 = \tilde{\Theta}(p_*) < \tilde{\Theta}(p) < \tilde{\Theta}(p^*) = 1$ for $p \in [p_*, p^*]$.

Proof. In Appendix 2.

7. The nature of dispersed transactions prices and resource allocation

7.1. Unlimited contacting

The results of the last sections show that when agents are heterogeneous and are limited in the ability to contact potential trading partners, dispersed transactions prices characterize the equilibrium. We also saw that if agents are homogeneous a single transactions price must characterize the equilibrium. Let us now look at the case in which agents are not limited in the number of potential trading partners they may contact but in which agents are heterogeneous. In doing so, we will show the role played by the assumption of limited contacting in generating our results.

Consider the sequence of distributions facing an X-endowed agent when $(\hat{F}, \hat{G})$ as defined in (14) is the environment and $R = \infty$, $\langle \hat{G}_r \rangle_{r=1}^{\infty}$. Under this specific environment, an X-endowed agent with $s = \hat{p}$ is concerned only with the probability of finding a trading partner in any given round. This is simply the proportion of Y-endowed agents with $d = \hat{p}$ in round r (i.e., $q_r = \hat{q}/[1 + (r-1)\hat{q}]$) as derived in Lemma 1. From the point of view of setting his initial offer supply price, the probability of trading in round r (i.e., not having traded prior to round r, but finding a partner in round r) is $\prod_{i=0}^{r-1} (1 - q_i) \cdot q_r$, where $q_0 \equiv 0$. Thus, for an agent with $s = \hat{p}$, the probability of consummating trade under $(\hat{F}, \hat{G})$ when $R = \infty$ is

$$\sum_{r=1}^{\infty} \left[\prod_{i=0}^{r-1} (1 - q_i) \right] \cdot q_r .$$

It can be shown that this infinite sum equals 1.[14]

Since the environment is symmetric, a similar statement holds for any Y-endowed agent who sets $d = \hat{p}$ under $(\hat{F}, \hat{G})$—he will trade at $\hat{p}$ with

[14] Let $\Sigma_R = \Sigma_{r=1}^{R} q_r \Pi_{i=0}^{r-1} (1 - q_i)$ and $\Pi_R = \Pi_{i=0}^{R} (1 - q_i)$. It is easy to show that $\Sigma_R + \Pi_R = \Sigma_{R-1} + \Pi_{R-1}$. Furthermore, $\Sigma_1 + \Pi_1 = q_1 + (1 - q_1) = 1$. Therefore, $\Sigma_R + \Pi_R = 1$ all $R < \infty$. But $\lim_{R \to \infty} \Pi_R = 0$, since $\Sigma q_r = \infty$, and hence $\lim_{R \to \infty} \Sigma_R = 1$.

probability 1. Thus, we have all X-endowed agents with $t_s \leqslant \hat{p}$ and all Y-endowed agents with $t_d \geqslant \hat{p}$ trading at $\hat{p}$ with probability 1 if they set their offer prices at $\hat{p}$. Furthermore, an agent would not trade at all if he set $s > \hat{p}$ or $d < \hat{p}$, and would trade only at a less attractive transactions price if he sets $s < \hat{p}$ or $d > \hat{p}$. We have thus proved Proposition 6.

Proposition 6. $(\hat{F}, \hat{G})$ as defined in (14) is an equilibrium of the model when $R = \infty$.

From Proposition 6, we can see that heterogeneity of agents alone does not guarantee that dispersed transactions prices characterize the equilibrium. If agents can contact other agents without limit, then the result of a decentralized exchange process can be transactions at a single market clearing price. Thus, both heterogeneity of agents and limited contacting are crucial for dispersed transactions prices to characterize the equilibrium.

7.2. The allocation of resources in decentralized exchange

The final question to which we wish to address ourselves concerns the properties of the allocation of resources when dispersed transactions prices characterize the equilibrium. As we shall see, the allocation of resources underscores the essential tradeoff facing agents in an environment of dispersed prices: that between the probability of consummating trade and the price at which trade is consummated.

The probability of the single X-endowed agent actually consummating trade given that he sets offer price s is:

$$\pounds(s) = \sum_{r=1}^{R} \left[\prod_{i=0}^{r-1} \tilde{G}_i(s) \right] \left[\int_s^1 \mathrm{d}\tilde{G}_r(d) \right]. \tag{21}$$

$\pounds(s)$ is a decreasing function of s.[15] The probability of an agent with offer price s consummating trade at transactions price p or higher conditional

[15]In general, the sign of $\pounds'(s)$ would depend upon the particular nature of $\langle \tilde{G}_r \rangle$. Given that $\langle \tilde{G}_r \rangle$ is the equilibrium environment, however, we can show that $\pounds'(s) \leqslant 0$ must be the case for all $s \in [0, 1]$. Suppose that $\pounds'(s_1) > 0$, where s_1 is the offer price of some set of agents. Clearly, they could increase their probability of transacting by raising s, but also, a higher s implies greater gains from trade when trade occurs. Thus, s_1 could not have been the optimum offer supply price, violating $\langle \tilde{G}_r \rangle$ being an equilibrium. Since an equilibrium exists, $\pounds'(s) \leqslant 0$ must be the case for all $s \in [0, 1]$. Furthermore, since $\pounds(0) = 1$ and $\pounds(1) = 0$, $\pounds'(s) < 0$ must be the case for some set of $s \in [0, 1]$.

upon consummating trade is:

$$\bar{\mathfrak{L}}(p, s) = \frac{\sum_{r=1}^{R}\left[\prod_{i=0}^{r-1}\tilde{G}_i(s)\right]\left[\int_{(p-\beta s)/\alpha}^{1} \mathrm{d}\tilde{G}_r(d)\right]}{\mathfrak{L}(s)} \tag{22}$$

where $p \in [s, 1]$. Clearly, $\bar{\mathfrak{L}}$ is a decreasing function of p; it is also an increasing function of s.

Since $\tilde{\mathfrak{L}}$ is an increasing function of s, agents with higher offer supply prices can expect to trade at higher prices when they do trade. Since $\mathfrak{L}$ is a decreasing function of s, however, agents with higher offer supply prices can expect to consummate trade less frequently. Recalling the relationships between s and the parameters (x', k, ρ), we can see that those X-endowed agents with larger endowments of X (higher x'), less intense tastes for X (lower k), and greater risk aversion (higher ρ), will consummate trade (supply X) more frequently, but on average at lower transactions prices. Similarly, those Y-endowed agents with larger endowments of Y (higher y'), more intense tastes for X (higher k), and greater risk aversion (higher ρ) will succeed in trading (purchasing X) more frequently, but will pay higher transactions prices.

These results have interesting implications for the allocation of resources. In equilibrium, holding risk aversion constant, those Y-endowed agents who place a higher value on X *relative to* Y have a higher probability of getting X allocated towards them through trade. Similarly, those X-endowed agents who value Y relatively more highly have a higher probability of getting Y allocated towards them. Therefore, though pure Pareto optimality does not characterize the allocation of resources, we have a "quasi-optimality" result which tells us that resources flow with higher probability to higher value uses, holding risk aversion constant.

In the standard competitive setting, risk aversion plays no role in reallocating resources across agents. In decentralized exchange, however, when there is limited contacting, risk aversion does in fact affect the allocation of resources. Since $\partial s/\partial\rho < 0$ and $\partial d/\partial\rho > 0$, we know that the more risk averse an agent is, the greater will be the probability that he will trade. Thus, to incorporate the effects of risk aversion into the quasi-optimality result requires a proper reinterpretation.

In the equilibrium of decentralized exchange, achieving gains by trading for higher-valued goods is a probabilistic proposition. The relative value an agent places on a good is a certainty measure (i.e., conditional upon consummating the exchange). The degree of risk aversion an agent has should be thought of as weighting that agent's relative value by the probability of achieving the particular exchange that is being evaluated. Thus, an X-endowed agent with a low value of X relative to Y might, in a setting in which exchange is a probabilistic occurrence, place higher value on actually consummating the exchange if he has a high degree of risk aversion than an agent with a high value of X relative to Y and low risk aversion. This higher value on consummating the exchange is reflected as we have seen in a lower offer price. Thus, we find that with risk averse agents, resources flow with higher probability to those agents with higher relative value of consummating trade for the good.

To summarize, in a dispersed price equilibrium there exists a trade-off between the gains from trade and the probability of trading, with agents choosing their optimum "price–probability" pair from this opportunity set. Where they choose to locate depends upon their relative tastes for the goods, their endowment and their risk aversion. Looked at in this way, one can see a direct analogy to the full information "hedonic price function" models (e.g., Rosen [22]). In those models there is an intrinsic price-quality trade-off in equilibrium supported by the heterogeneity of agents. In our model, the limited information generates a stochastic trade-off between price and probability of trading, again supported by the heterogeneity of agents.

Appendix 1

In this appendix we derive from any initial pair of offer price distributions (F_1, G_1), the pair of corresponding sequences, $(\langle F_r\rangle, \langle G_r\rangle)$.

Start with round 1, and consider first those X-endowed agents who have set their offer supply prices within the range $s \pm \epsilon$, where $\epsilon > 0$. The condition for consummating trade, of course, is overlapping offer prices (i.e., $d \geqslant s$). Thus, the proportion of Y-endowed agents with overlapping offers is approximately $\int_s^{\bar{p}} \mathrm{d}G_1(d) = 1 - G_1(s)$, where the approximation is better the smaller is ϵ. By the definition of random contacting, this is true for every s. Since the proportion of X-endowed agents within the range $s \pm \epsilon$ (letting ϵ be arbitrarily small) is $f_1(s)ds$, we can express the number of X-endowed agents entering round 1 with their offer prices set less than s who succeed in consummating trade, as a proportion of all X-endowed agents, as:

$$C_1^X(s) = \int_{\underline{p}}^{s} f_1(u)[1 - G_1(u)]\mathrm{d}u. \tag{A1}$$

The number of X-endowed agents entering round 1 with offer prices set less than s who do *not* consummate trade, as a proportion of all X-endowed agents, is simply:

$$F_1(s) - C_1^X(s) = \int_{\underline{p}}^{s} f(u)[G_1(u)]\mathrm{d}u. \tag{A.2}$$

From (A.2) we can move directly to the cumulative distribution of offer supply prices remaining active after round 1:

$$F_2(s) = \frac{F_1(s) - C_1^X(s)}{1 - C_1^X} = \frac{\int_{\underline{p}}^{s} f_1(u)[G_1(u)]\,\mathrm{d}u}{\int_{\underline{p}}^{\bar{p}} f_1(u)[G_1(u)]\mathrm{d}u}, \qquad \text{where } C_1^X = C_1^X(\bar{p}). \tag{A.3}$$

Equation (A.3) follows directly from the fact that those agents who do not succeed in trading in round 1 go into round 2, while all those who traded in round 1 drop out of the picture.

The derivation of $G_2(d)$ from the round 1 distributions F_1 and G_1 is nearly identical. The number of Y-endowed agents entering round 1 with offer demand prices less than d who consummate trade, as a proportion of all Y-endowed agents, is simply:

$$C_1^Y(d) = \int_{\underline{p}}^{d} g_1(v)[F_1(v)]\mathrm{d}v. \tag{A.4}$$

Thus, the cumulative distribution of offer demand prices remaining active after round 1 (i.e., the distribution of offer demand prices in round 2), is:

$$G_2(d) = \frac{G_1(d) - C_1^Y(d)}{1 - C_1^Y} = \frac{\int_{\underline{p}}^{d} g_1(v)[1 - F_1(v)]\mathrm{d}v}{\int_{\underline{p}}^{\bar{p}} g_1(v)[1 - F_1(v)]\mathrm{d}v},$$

$$\text{where } C_1^Y = C_1^Y(\bar{p}). \tag{A.5}$$

Once F_2 and G_2 are derived from F_1 and G_1, the process can be repeated to derive F_3 and G_3 from F_2 and G_2 and so on. In general, the relationships between the distributions going from rounds r to $r+1$ can be given as follows:

$$F_{r+1}(s)=\frac{F_r(s)-C_r^X(s)}{1-C_r^X}, \tag{A.6}$$

$$G_{r+1}(d)=\frac{G_r(d)-C_r^Y(d)}{1-C_r^Y}, \tag{A.7}$$

$$C_r^X=C_r^Y. \tag{A.8}$$

Thus, to describe the market environment, it is sufficient to refer to the pair of offer price distributions $(F_1,\ G_1)$ – or simply $(F,\ G)$, dropping the subscripts.

Appendix 2

Proof of Proposition 1

We will prove the proposition for X-endowed agents. The proof for Y-endowed agents is similar. Define a transformation $w(p)=u(p-\Delta)$, where $\Delta=t_s^2-t_s^1>0$. This is illustrated in figure 4.1. Let $s(\cdot)$ be the unique solution to $\mathrm{d}V/\mathrm{d}s=0$ where $V(s)$ is defined in (10) when t_s takes on a given value. If $s(t_s^1)<t_s^2$, then $s(t_s^2)\geqslant t_s^2>s(t_s^1)$. So consider $t_s^1<t_s^2<s(t_s^1)$, and construct the transformation $z(p)=K(s_1)w(p)$, where $K(s)=u(s_1)/w(s_1)$ and $s_1\equiv s(t_s^1)$. This is also illustrated in figure A.1.

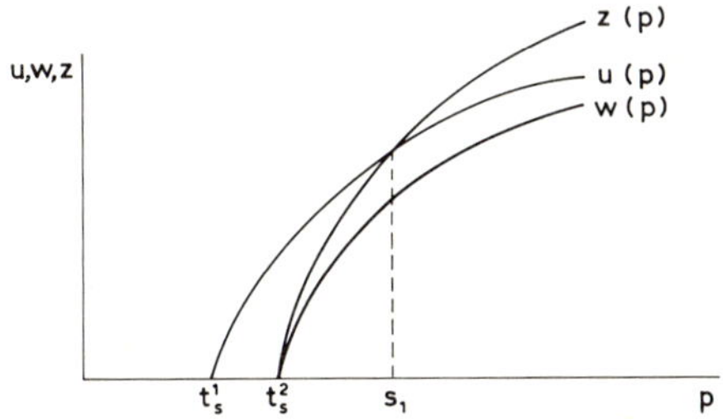

Figure A.1

In order to prove the proposition, it is sufficient to show that: (a) $z(p)>u(p)$ all $p>s_1$; and (b) $z'(p)>u'(p)$ all $p\geqslant s_1$. We will first show that conditions (a) and (b) will prove the proposition.

Rewriting (10) as $V(s)=\Sigma_{r=1}^{R}A_rB_r$, where A_r and B_r are the two bracketed terms in (10), we can write the first-order condition as:

$$\mathrm{d}V/\mathrm{d}s=\sum_{r=2}^{R}\left[\sum_{j=1}^{r-1}g_j(s)\cdot A_r/G_j(s)\right]B_r$$

$$+\sum_{r=1}^{R}A_r\left[\int_s^{\infty}(1-\alpha)u'(p)dG_r(d)\right]-\sum_{r=1}^{R}A_r[u(s)g_r(s)]=0.$$

If condition (a) holds, $B_r^z>B_r^u>0$, where the superscripts refer to $z(p)$ and $u(p)$, respectively. If condition (b) holds, $\int_s^{\infty}(1-\alpha)z'\mathrm{d}G_r>\int_s^{\infty}(1-\alpha)u'\mathrm{d}G_r>0$. By construction, $z(s_1)=u(s_1)$. Hence $\mathrm{d}v^z/\mathrm{d}s>0$ at s_1, implying that $s_2=s(t_s^2)$ is greater than s_1. Since $z(p)$ is a linear transformation of $w(p)$, the solution to $\mathrm{d}v^z/\mathrm{d}s=0$ is the same as to $\mathrm{d}v^w/\mathrm{d}s=0$. It remains to prove that conditions (a) and (b) hold true.

First (b): $w'(p)=u'(p-\Delta)$ and hence $w'(p)\geqslant u'(p)$ (=only if $u''=0$, i.e., $\rho=0$). Since $w(p)<u(p)$, $k(s_1)>1$, implying that $z'(p)=k(s_1)$. $w'(p)>w'(p)$.

Now (a): $z(p)=z(s_1)+\int_{s_1}^{\infty}z'(m)\mathrm{d}m$ all $p>s_1$. And, $u(p)=u(s_1)+\int_{s_1}^{p}u'(m)\mathrm{d}m$ all $p>s_1$. Since $z(s_1)=u(s_1)$ by construction and $z'(m)>u'(m)$ (all m, $s_1\leqslant m\leqslant p$), $z(p)>u(p)$ for all $p>s_1$.

Proof of Proposition 2

We prove the proposition for X-endowed agents. The proof for Y-endowed agents is similar. Rewrite (3) as $u(p)=-kA(x)(1-\mathrm{e}^{-\rho_1})+1-\mathrm{e}^{-\rho_1 p}$. Using (4) yields $u(p)=\mathrm{e}^{-\rho_1 t_s}-\mathrm{e}^{-\rho_1 p}$. Letting $z=p-t_s$, $u(z)=1-\mathrm{e}^{-\rho_1 z}$. Consider now an indirect utility function $w(p)$ such that $-w''/w'=\rho_2>\rho_1$. As above, $w(z)=1-\mathrm{e}^{-\rho_2 z}$. $u(z)$ and $w(z)$ are illustrated in figure 4.2. Let s_1 be the unique solution to max $V(s)$ under $u(p)$ and define $K(z_1)=u(z_1)/w(z_1)$, where $z_1=s_1-t_s$. Now construct the transformation $v(z)=K(z_1)w(z)$. Clearly, $v(z_1)=u(z_1)$. This is illustrated in figure 4.2.

As with Proposition 1, in order to prove Propositon 2 it is sufficient to show that: (a) $u(z)>v(z)$ all $z>z_1$; and (b) $u'(z)>v'(z)$ all $z\geqslant z_1$.

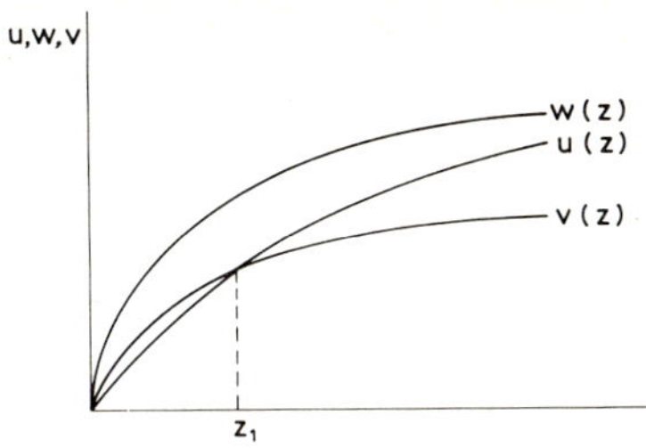

Figure A.2

First (b): let $R(z) \equiv v'(z)/u'(z)$. $R(z) = K(z_1)(\rho_2/\rho_1)e^{(\rho_1 - \rho_2)z}$ from definition of $v(z)$ and $u(z)$. Thus, $dR/dz = R(z) \cdot (\rho_1 - \rho_2) < 0$, since $\rho_2 > \rho_1$. If $R(0) \leqslant 1$, then since $dR/dz < 0$, $u(z_1) = \int_0^{z_1} u'(z)dz > \int_0^{z_1} v'(z)dz = v(z_1)$. This violates the fact that $v(z_1) = u(z_1)$ by construction. Hence $R(0) > 1$. $R(0) > 0$ and $dR/dz < 0$ imply a unique intersection between $u(z)$ and $v(z)$ at z_1, with $u'(z_1) > v'(z_1)$. Then, since $dR/dz < 0$, $u'(z) > v'(z)$ all $z > z_1$ must hold, which proves (b).

Now (a). For $z > z_1$, $u(z) = u(z_1) + \int_{z_1}^{z} u'(r)dr$ and $v(z) = v(z_1) + \int_{z_1}^{z} v'(r)dr$. But since $u(z_1) = v(z_1)$ by construction and condition (b) holds true, $u(z) > v(z)$ for $z > z_1$.

Proof of Lemma 1

Given the definition of $(\hat{F}, \hat{G})$, we can define $q_r \equiv \hat{F}_r(\hat{p}) = 1 - \hat{G}_r(\hat{p})$ and see that $C_r^X = C_r^Y = q_r^2$. Then (A.6) yields $q_r = q_{r-1}/(1 + q_{r-1})$. Repeated backward substitution yields $q_r = \hat{q}/[1 + (r-1)\hat{q}]$.

We now derive $\hat{F}_r(s)$. For $s < \hat{p}$, $\hat{F}(s) = 0$, and thus $\hat{F}_r(s) = 0$. For $s = \hat{p}$, $\hat{F}_r(\hat{p}) = q_r$. For $s > \hat{p}$ we must prove that $(\hat{F}_r(s) - q_r/1 - q_r) = (\hat{F}_{r+1}(s) - q_{r+1})/(1 - q_{r+1})$. From (A.6), $\hat{F}_r(s) = (\hat{F}_r(s) - q_r^2)/(1 - q_r^2)$. Thus,

$$\frac{\hat{F}_{r+1}(s) - q_{r+1}}{1 - q_{r+1}} = \frac{(\hat{F}_r(s) - q_r^2)/(1 - q_r^2) - (q_r/(1 + q_r))}{(1/1 + q_r)} = \frac{\hat{F}_r(s) - q_r}{1 - q_r}.$$

Using this relationship yields $(\hat{F}(s) - \hat{q})/(1 - \hat{q}) = (\hat{F}_r(s) - q_r)/(1 - q_r)$. But $\hat{F}(s) - \hat{q} = \Phi(s) - \Phi(\hat{p})$. Thus, for $s > \hat{p}$, $\hat{F}_r(s) = q_r + [(1 - \hat{q}_r)/(1 - \hat{q})][\Phi(s) - \Phi(\hat{p})]$. $\hat{G}_r$ can be derived analoguously.

Proof of Proposition 5

Construct from $(\tilde{F}_r, \tilde{G}_r)$ an $\tilde{H}_r$, the joint distribution of X-endowed and Y-endowed agents over $[0,1]\times[0,1]$. Also construct the subset of $[0, 1]\times[0, 1]$ for which transactions would be at a price less than p. Denote the subset $\Delta(p)$, whence $\Delta(p)=\{(s,d)\,|\,d\geqslant s \text{ and } \alpha d+\beta s>p\}$. This is illustrated in figure A.3.

The proportion of transactions consummated in round r at prices less than p is simply the joint probability that (s,d) will fall in $\Delta(p)$ in round r, or

$$\tilde{\Theta}_r(p)\equiv \int_{\Delta(p)} \mathrm{d}\tilde{H}_r(s,d)=\int_0^p \mathrm{d}s \int_s^{\min[(p-\beta s)/\alpha,1]} \tilde{H}_r(s,d)\mathrm{d}d.$$

Letting $\tilde{W}^r=\prod_{i=1}^{r-1}(1-\tilde{C}_i)$,

$$\tilde{\Theta}(p)=\frac{\sum_{r=1}^{R}\tilde{\Theta}_r(p)\cdot\tilde{W}^r}{\sum_{r=1}^{R}\tilde{\Theta}_r(1)\cdot\tilde{W}^r}.$$

By the definition of p_* and p^*, $\tilde{\Theta}_r(p)=\int_{p*}^{p}\mathrm{d}s\int_s^{\min[p/\alpha-\beta/\alpha s,p^*)}\tilde{H}_r(s,d)\mathrm{d}d$, implying $\tilde{\Theta}_r(p^*)=\tilde{\Theta}_r(1)$ and $\tilde{\Theta}_r(p_*)=\tilde{\Theta}_r(0)$. Thus, $\tilde{\Theta}(p^*)=1$ and $\tilde{\Theta}(p_*)=0$.

Construct now $\Delta^*(p)$, which denotes the pairs (s,d) such that $d>s$, $s>p_*$, $d\leqslant p^*$, and $\alpha d+\beta s<p$:

$$\Delta^*(p)=\Delta(p)\cap(p_*,p^*)\times(p_*,p^*).$$

For any $(s\,d)\in\Delta^*(p)$, $0<\tilde{F}_r(s)<1$ and $0<\tilde{G}_r(d)<1$. Thus, $0<\tilde{H}_r(s,d)<1$ all $(s,d)\in\Delta^*(p)$, implying that $0<\tilde{\Theta}(p)<1$ all $p\in(p_*,p^*)$.

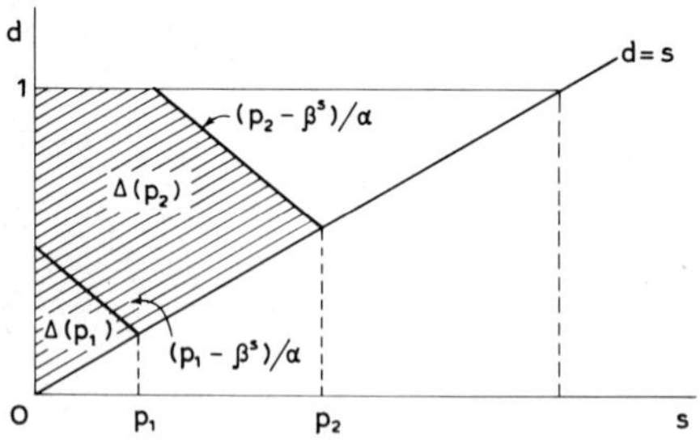

Figure A.3

References

[1] Alchian, A. A., "Information costs, pricing and resource unemployment", *Western Economics Journal*, 7 (1969).

[2] Arrow, K. J., "Toward a theory of price adjustment", in Baran, P. A., Scitovsky, T., and Shaw, E. S., (eds.), *The Allocation of Economic Resources*, Stanford University Press, Stanford, California, 1958.

[3] Arrow, K. J., *Essays in the Theory of Risk Bearing*, Markham Publishing Company, Chicago, 1971.

[4] Arrow, K. J., "Limited knowledge and economic analysis", *American Economic Review*, 64 (1974), 1–10.

[5] Arrow, K. J., and Hahn, F. H., *General Competitive Analysis*, Holden-Day, San Francisco, 1971.

[6] Butters, G., "Equilibrium distribution of prices and advertising", *Review of Economic Studies* 44 (1977).

[7] Dunford, N. and Schwartz, J. T., *Linear Operators Part I: General Theory*, John Wiley, New York, 1957.

[8] Edgeworth, F. Y., *Mathematical Psychics*, Routledge Kegan Paul, London, 1881.

[9] Fisher, F. M., "Quasi-competitive price adjustments by individual firms: a preliminary paper", *Journal of Economic Theory* 2 (1970).

[10] Fisher, F. M., "On price adjustment without an auctioneer", *Review of Economics Studies*, 39 (1972).

[11] Green, J. R., and Majundar, M., "The nature of stochastic equilibria", *Econometrica*, 43 (1975).

[12] Hildenbrand, W., *Core and Equilibria in a Large Economy*, Princeton University Press, Princeton, New Jersey, 1974.

[13] Ionnides, Y. M., "Market allocation through search: equilibrium adjustment and price dispersion", *Journal of Economic Theory* (1975).

[14] Jevons, W. S., *The Theory of Political Economy*, Macmillan, London, 1871.

[15] Kormendi, R. C., "On the nature of decentralized pure exchange", unpublished PhD dissertation, University of California, Los Angeles, 1976.

[16] Lippman, S. A., and McCall, J. J., "The economics of job search: a survey", *Economic Inquiry*, 14 (1976), 155–189.

[17] Lucas, R. E., and Prescott, E. C., "Equilibrium search and unemployment", *Journal of Economic Theory*, 7 (1974).

[18] Marshall, A., *Principles of Economics*, Macmillan, New York, 1920.

[19] Mortensen, D. T., "Rational price dispersion, search and adjustment", unpublished paper, Northwestern University, 1974.

[20] Ostroy, J., "The informational efficiency of monetary exchange, *American Economic Review*, 63 (1973), 579–610.

[21] Reiter, S., "A market adjustment mechanism", unpublished paper, Purdue University, 1959.

[22] Rosen, S., "Hedonic prices and implicit markets", *Journal of Political Economy*, 82 (1974).

[23] Rothschild, M., "Models of market organization with imperfect information: a survey", *Journal of Political Economy*, 8 (1973), 1283–1308.

[24] Rothschild, M., "A two-armed bandit theory of market pricing", *Journal of Economic Theory*, 9 (1974).

[25] Stigler, G. J., "The economics of information", *Journal of Political Economy*, 69 (1961).

[26] Stuart, C., "A model of price formation in a market with search", unpublished paper, Lund University, 1975.

[27] Telser, L. G., "Equilibrium price distribution", unpublished paper, University of Chicago, 1975.

[28] Walras, L., *Elements of Pure Economics*, (trans Jaffe, W.) Irwin, Homewood, Ill., 1954.

CHAPTER 5

The theory of search and equilibrium in a nonauctioneered market

JOSEPH BROOKE WHARTON*

Southern California Edison Company

1. Introduction

The theory of search was delivered into this world in 1961 by the gentle hands of Dr. Stigler [22, 23]. He gave us the *gedanken*–thought experiment —which continues to unify the subject matter today. An individual economic agent *knowingly* faces a range of prices within which he can transact for a given commodity. (The ambiguous word "transact" is used purposefully to leave open whether the agent is potentially a buyer or a seller, because search theory can be and has been applied to both product and factor markets.) The location or source of any specific offer is, however, originally unknown and can be determined only by a random draw from among the group of potential exchange partners (i.e., by *search*). These random draws or observations are made sequentially and are costly. The searching agent exercises the option to stop when he feels that a satisfactory offer has been found.

The present collection of papers, as well as the recent survey by Lippman and McCall [14], evidence the intellectually satisfying diversity of models which now exist. Having reached the age of sixteen, search theory exhibits the common characteristics of adolescence: novelty, variety, independence and promise. This paper presents an insight into some core concepts of economic science which I have gleaned from work in this field. To put it simply, the theory of what a *market* is can be clarified and expanded.

*The views herein expressed are solely those of the author and are not a reflection of the attitudes of either the management or the stockholders of the Southern California Edison Company.

I consider a market for labor services (i.e., a market where households are sellers and firms are buyers). This concreteness merely simplifies exposition; no institutional or empirical features of labor markets are consciously introduced. The market consists of a finite group of firms who hire households each week. A firm attracts its work force simply by making its wage offer available to searching households. This offer is arrived at in a "satisficing" manner independently of other firms; the firm simply moves its offer some part of the way towards its known value of the marginal product (VMP) for whatever size work force turned up last week.

A household is notified each week how much it will receive if it stays with its present firm, and also what is the distribution of offers at other firms. If it is willing to bear the cost, it can get a concrete offer by sampling randomly from those other firms. After a finite number of such searches, it decides to go to work at the observed firm with the highest offer. The household is myopic, only worrying about what its earnings are to be next week.

Mathematically this market is a finite state Markov chain. The state of the market is describable each week by the vector of work force allocations and wage offers at all the firms. The questions this study focuses on are what do the equilibrium states look like? How many are there? Do they have a dispersion of wage offers?

One subset of states is important to distinguish: the stationary wage states (SW) are those for which all firms have wage offers *on their VMP curves*. Unless the size of the work forces change, such firms will not change their offers. There is assumed to exist within SW a unique competitive equilibrium state (CE); the allocation of households across firms is such that the VMPs, and thus wage offers, are all *equal*. When all households know that they are receiving the same wage, there is no incentive to search; and so, CE is an equilibrium state. When there is price dispersion and households from low paying firms search, some will with positive probability find better offers and relocate. The state of the system will change, indicating a previous disequilibrium. Within SW, the key to whether a state is an equilibrium is whether households are searching. This depends on household search behavior.

The line of proof used here requires that there be a bound on the number of observations taken. Within the class of household search models satisfying that constraint, I use two basic variants. Version A exhibits bounded search because the costs of successive observations rise until search is uneconomic. Version B simply postulates a bound N, explicable perhaps as a time constraint, and constant search costs.

The first theorem considers version A and exhibits a bound on the cost of the *first* observation. If across all households this bound is not exceeded, then with probability one the market will reach the competitive equilibrium state with certainty in some finite (but perhaps unbounded) number of periods and remain there. For version B, a similar constraint is placed on the observation cost and the size of N, and convergence to competitive equilibrium is similarly demonstrated.

I then restrict my discussion to the class of models for which the demand or VMP curves are linear and of equal slope, and households have identical search costs. In the third theorem, I consider only version A and exhibit a *sequence of intervals* on the range of possible values of the cost of the first observation. Corresponding to each interval, there is a group of SW states which are equilibria if the first search cost lies in that interval. For example, the group corresponding to the interval with the smallest values contains only the competitive equilibrium state; this is simply a restatement of the first theorem. The group corresponding to the next interval also contains SW states in which the lowest paying firms have exactly *one* more household than they would in competitive equilibrium. The group corresponding to the third interval adds those SW states in which the lowest paying firms have exactly *two* more households than they would in competitive equilibrium, and so forth. A similar, but much less simple partitioning of the set of SW states takes place in the nonlinear, nonhomogeneous market, and I discuss briefly why the complexity arises.

In the case where there are multiple equilibria, one of them will be reached in a finite number of weeks. The final state reached depends upon the initial state of the market system and may be inherently uncertain because of the probabilistic nature of search. The calculation of these "first passage" probabilities, which has not been done, appears conceptually simple, but prohibitively expensive for all but the smallest systems.

To summarize, the model shows the equilibrium properties of a dynamic market where search is the driving force for bringing about an orderly pattern of exchange. The propostitions demonstrate the competitive equilibrium is reached with certainty only when search costs are low enough. This result has some affinity with the perfect information assumption in neoclassical price theory, although an explicit market model is necessary to give this phrase precise meaning. To me the most straightforward interpretation of the neoclassical market model is that of an auction run at a single place and time by an auctioneer *ã la* Walras [25]. The high degree of organization required for an auction and, correspondingly, its relative infrequency in economic life are in contrast to its central theoretical position. Although the nonauctioneered market is highly simplified, I believe that it makes explicit a process which is fundamental to the operation of many real world markets.

2. A philological digression[1]

Since the simple idea of searching for a bargain in some product market or for a better paying job in some labor market is part of the immediate experience of most people, it is striking to realize that search has no *explicit* role in the neoclassical theory of price. For there to be search, there must be a range of prices. For there to be a range of prices, the decision as to what prices to charge must be left in the hands of individual economic agents. Rothschild [18] points out that price setting firms are a natural and necessary complement to the household search model. In the neoclassical world of Walras [25], Jevons [10], Debreu [5], and Arrow and Hahn [3], the price setting function is centralized in the person, or better, *deus ex machina*, of the auctioneer. The potential transactors, firms and households, receive word in some unspecified way of the auctioneer's price and then respond in terms of the quantities of the commodity they wish to buy or sell.

Both Walras [25, p. 83–84] and Jevons [10, p. 132] were careful to indicate that special assumptions concerning their respective processes of price formation were being made in order to yield a single price. Walras introduced the auctioneer, but stated in passing that something closely akin to it determines prices in nonauctioneered markets. Jevons assumed that transactors have complete or perfect information about all bid and ask prices, and enunciated his famous Law of Indifference—that only one price can reign. The modern discussions I have seen are usually less explicit about what assumptions lie behind the single price. It seems to me that the act of summing the quantities of a commodity supplied and demanded by individual agents at each of several prices and then the use of this *market excess* demand function as a description of the behavior of the group are tantamount to assuming there is an auction for the commodity.

[1]This section contains my thoughts about the relation of this work to the neoclassical main stream and can be skipped by readers interested in the model *per se*. My dictionary tells me "philology" is a synonym for linguistics and I eventually came to see a central purpose of the model as pinning down a meaning of the word "market".

Is the question of whether there is a single price for each commodity moot? In Stockholm, Arrow synopsized the neoclassical tradition as the study of the coordination which *free markets* in capitalistic economies achieve among vast numbers of agents, each of whom is guided by his own individual desires. Arrow [1, p. 254] points to the marginalists, Walras and Jevons, as having first provided clear answers to how this takes place:

> It was the fact that all agents in the economy faced the same set of prices that provided the common flow of information needed to coordinate the system. There was, so it was argued, a set of prices one for each commodity, which would equate supply and demand for all commodities,...

In fact, most commodities are not sold at auctions and, possibly as a result, there is a price dispersion for some commodities. What is the implication of price dispersion for general equilibrium analysis? If price dispersion is generated by a process similar to that shown in my model, it may well be a second order effect in the overall question of resource allocation. On the other hand, there may be substantive questions raised by a general investigation into which processes are used for setting prices and exchanging commodities in atomistic but nonauctioneered markets and how closely these are approximated by the auction market model.

Dissatisfaction with the auctioneer and, more generally, with the neoclassical handling of the process of market adjustment has been sounded from many quarters. My own introduction to this missing dimension was through the monetary theory of Clower [4], Leijonhufvund [12], [13] and Ostroy [17]. It is pointed out particularly clearly in the latter that after the market clearing prices are found, neoclassical theory offers few clues as to how individual buyers and sellers proceed to effect the exchanges which in aggregate are possible.

A corollary to the lack of attention to the process of exchange in modern price theory is that the question of what a market is, once pondered by Walras and Jevons, is no longer asked. The common connotation of "market" in economic discussions is that of the place where exchange occurs. Despite the omnipresence of the word, one searches in vain for a denotation of "market" in the neoclassics: Hicks [9], Samuelson [20], Debreu [5], Arrow and Hahn [3]. Arrow [2] recognizes this lacuna in describing the two cornerstones of general competitive analysis as the *concrete* optimization of the individual and the *ethereal* coordination of the market. Perhaps without Arrow's intention, this draws an interesting parallel between the market of twentieth century economics and the ether of nineteenth century physics. Without identifiable properties, each manages to serve as a medium by which signals are transmitted.

There is an older tradition of defining the market as the area within which the price of a commodity *tends* to uniformity. Stigler [24] is the only place I have seen this still being used. It can be traced back to Adam Smith's celebrated chapter of "Of wages and profits in the different employments of labour and stock", in the *Wealth of Nations* [21, Book I, Ch. X, pp. 201–247]:

> The whole of the advantages and disadvantages of the different employments of labor and stock must, in the same neighborhood, be either perfectly equal or continually tending to equality. If in the same neighborhood, there was any employment evidently either more or less advantageous than the rest, so many would crowd into it in the one case and so many would desert it in the other that its advantages would soon return to the level of other employments.

My model can well be seen as an attempt to capture one aspect of this. I see three problem areas in modeling Smith's total gestalt and thus rigorously defining the ways in which the market functions as a stage for the process of exchange:

(1) Does a market pertain to trade in a single commodity (other than money) or to a group of commodities? Behind this is the elusive question: What is a distinct commodity?
(2) Is the market primarily one or a number of locations and, more generally, what is the spatial and temporal extent of the market?
(3) What is the nature and importance of the major structural features: numbers of buyers and sellers, modes of communication, procedures for setting prices and effecting exchanges?

Search theory has a natural role in the third area, as I hope my model demonstrates.

3. The model

The general form of the model's state space description is from Mirman and Porter [16]. There are two groups of immortal economic agents: households and firms. The sets $\mathcal{H}$ of households and $\mathcal{F}$ of firms are both finite, containing H and F elements, respectively.

Time is discrete; the unit period or *week* is that time between simultaneous revisions by all firms of their wage offers. The labor services commodity is homogeneous across households and sold in discrete units. Every week each household supplies one unit to that firm at which the highest offer was observed during the previous week's search. This corresponds to what Lippman and McCall [14] label "on-the-job" search. An *allocation*, $\langle a_1, \ldots a_f, \ldots a_F \rangle$, of the total market supply of labor to the firms is an F-tuple of nonnegative integers with the property that $\Sigma \mathcal{F} a_f = H$, where a_f is the number of households employed at firm f. It may be useful to think of this allocation process as the periodic distribution of H marbles to F urns.

Assumption 1. With each firm f, there is associated a nonnegative, integer-valued function V_f such that the value to the firm f of employing n units of labor is

$$\sum_{k=0}^{n} V_f(k), \qquad n = 0, 1, 2, \ldots, H,$$

(i.e., $V_f(n)$ is the value of the marginal product). Moreover, there is an integer, $M_f \leqslant H$, such that the law of diminishing returns holds up to M_f and then additional households produce nothing:

$$V_f(n) > V_f(n+1), \qquad n = 0, 1, \ldots, M_f - 1, \tag{1}$$

and

$$V_f(n) = 0, \qquad n \geqslant M_f. \tag{2}$$

Assumption 2. The wage offer firm f sets in week t, w_f^t, will be in effect for all households who observe this offer during week t and choose to be employed by firm f in week $t+1$.[2] The set of possible wage offers is simply the integers between 0 and

$$W = \max_{f \in \mathcal{F}} V_f(0).$$

[2]This somewhat awkward use of the symbol w_f^t to refer to the wage earned in period $t+1$ is necessary since these "future prices" govern search in period t.

If not on its VMP, every firm moves its wage offer *one* unit toward its VMP,

$$w_f^t = \begin{Bmatrix} w_f^{t-1}+1 \\ w_f^{t-1} \\ w_f^{t-1}-1 \end{Bmatrix}, \quad \text{if} \quad V_f(a_f^t)\begin{Bmatrix} > \\ = \\ < \end{Bmatrix} w_f^{t-1}. \tag{3}$$

This mode of wage adjustment may seem arbitrary, but it is a clear representation of a firm passively moving its offer to its demand curve. All the theorems can be derived from a Koyck-type adjustment function of the type:

$$w_f^t = \alpha\cdot\left(w_f^{t-1}\right) + (1-\alpha)\cdot V_f\left(a_f^t\right).$$

I think this complicates but does not strengthen the theory. The theory would be strengthened measurably if, as Rothschild [18] points out, the firms were to exploit their monopsony power. I have achieved no definitive results in this direction.

Assumption 3. A firm f notifies, at no cost, its own employees of its wage offer, w_f^t. These households then do not have to search to remain employed, but do have to search to learn of other firms' offers. Let n_i be the number of firms who are willing to pay the wage $i, i=0,1,\ldots,W$. Then the probability mass function ${}_fp = \langle {}_fp_0, {}_fp_1, \ldots, {}_fp_W\rangle$ of the wage offer distribution for a household employed by firm f in week t is given by:

$${}_fp_i = \begin{cases} n_i/(F-1) & \text{if} \quad i \neq w_f^t, \\ (n_i-1)/(F-1) & \text{if} \quad i = w_f^t. \end{cases} \tag{4}$$

It is assumed that job search is done *with replacement* (i.e., the same firm can be sampled repeatedly). Search for a household currently employed at firm f then consists of a sequence $X_0, X_1, X_2 \ldots$, where $X_0 = w_f^t$ and $X_1, X_2, \ldots$ is a sequence of independent, identically distributed random variables, whose distribution is ${}_fp$. Replacement is a standard simplifying assumption made in search theory. If firms once sampled were deleted from the group to be sampled, the distribution would be hypergeometric. Such a distribution would not depart too far from the multinomial distribution ${}_fp$ if the number of observations were small in relation to the number of firms, but the implications of this have not been investigated.

Assumption 4. Household h incurs a (small) positive cost γ_h in changing jobs; γ_h is small in the sense that it keeps households from moving between firms with the same wage offer, but can otherwise be ignored.

Households seek to maximize their expected earnings from job *found* this week and *taken* next week, net of the costs of search and changing jobs. With respect to planning, the households are myopic; the planning horizon involves only the following week and ignores the infinite span of time after that.

Assumption 5A. Each household h can take an unlimited number of observations with recall[3] (i.e., previous opportunities are not lost by continuing search). The household must pay according to the sequence $\langle c_{h,1}, c_{h,2}, c_{h,3}, \ldots \rangle$. These successive observation costs increase and eventually exceed even the highest wage offer.

$$c_{h,n} < c_{h,n+1} \qquad \text{all } h, \quad \text{all } n. \tag{5a}$$

For every h there exists some n such that

$$c_{h,n} \geqslant W. \tag{5b}$$

Under this assumption, the optimal stopping rule for household h is to solve for the sequence of reservation wages, $w_1^*, w_2^*, \ldots$, where w_n^* is the smallest *integer* such that:

$$c_{h,n} > \sum_{j=w_n^*}^{W} (j - w_n^*) \cdot {}_f p_j, \qquad n = 1, 2, \ldots. \tag{6}$$

The right hand side of this inequality is an expression for the expected gain from search for a household whose current best offer is w_n^*. By stopping rule is meant that the nth observation should not be taken—search should stop—if the best offer received is greater than or equal to w_n^*, the reservation wage:[4]

$$\max\{X_j : j = 0, 1, \ldots, n-1\} \geqslant w_n^*, \qquad n = 1, 2, \ldots. \tag{7}$$

[3]Recall is necessary for a simple solution to this problem.

[4]This ensures the finitude of search in the following manner. If search has not already ceased when $c_{h,n}$ reaches the mean of the distribution ${}_f p$, it is well known from search theory that the reservation wage becomes zero.

Assumption 5B. Every household h can take at most $N(h)$ observations at constant cost c_h, but if another observation is taken the previous opportunity is lost.[5] Under this assumption the optimal sequence of reservation wages is calculable by backward induction using the $N(h)$ equations:

$$w^*_{N(h)} = \mu_f - c_h. \tag{8a}$$

$$w^*_n = w^*_{n+1} + T_f(w^*_{n+1}) - c_h \qquad n = N(h)-1, N(h)-2, \dots, 1. \tag{8b}$$

where μ_f is the mean of ${}_fp$, $]x[$ is the smallest integer $\geqslant x$, and

$$T_f(x) = \sum_{j=]x[}^{W} (j-x)\cdot {}_fp_j \qquad n = 1, 2, \dots, N(h)-1. \tag{9}$$

For any $N(h)$, w^*_n is increasing with n as shown by Lippman and McCall [14, p. 167]. As c_h approaches μ_f, w^*_n approaches 0 for all n. The optimal stopping rule is *not* to take the nth observation if:

$$X_{n-1} \geqslant w^*_n. \tag{10}$$

It is noteworthy that for both household search models, (Assumptions 5A and 5B), the reservation wage for the *first* observation is the highest. From (7) and (10), it is clear that no search will occur unless this initial reservation wage exceeds the offer from the household's own firm. This fact figures predominantly in the proofs.

A *state* of the system is a $2F$-tuple:

$$s = \langle a_1, \dots, a_F;\ w_1, \dots, w_F \rangle.$$

The *nonauctioneered market system* (NMS) is the Markov chain satisfying Assumptions 1, 2, 3, 4, and either 5A or 5B.

The set SW of *stationary wage* states consists of those states for which $w_f = V_f(a_f)$ for all $f \in \mathfrak{F}$. If the allocation, $\langle a_1, \dots, a_F \rangle$, remains the same for all firms, then the wage vector remains the same, because firms are on their VMP curves.

[5]Nonrecall is assumed in order to yield a solution of strictly increasing reservation wages, parallel to that for Assumption 5A; recall would imply a constant reservation wage and could equally well have been developed.

Assumption 6. There is assumed to exist a unique *competitive equilibrium* (CE) state $\langle a_1^e,\ldots,a_F^e;\ w^e,\ldots,w^e\rangle$ in SW, where:

$$a_f^e < M_f, \qquad \text{all } f \in \mathfrak{F},$$
$$w^e = V_f(a_f^e), \quad \text{all } f \in \mathfrak{F}.$$

This assumption places certain restrictions on the set $\{V_f\}, f \in \mathfrak{F}$. For example, if all V_f are identical, then it must be that $k \cdot F = H$, for some positive integer k. The competitive allocation would then be $a_f^e = k$. I do not see assuming away the existence problems as a fault of the theory. Consideration of existence would only blur the focus on the dynamic adjustment process.

A state s_1 *leads to* a state s_n (or s_n is *accessible from* s_1) if there exists a finite sequence of states $\langle s_1, s_2, \ldots, s_n\rangle$ such that there is positive probability of the NMS making the transition from s_i to s_{i+1} for all i. An *absorbing state* is one that leads only to itself; a prime example is CE. The uniformity of offers in CE makes search uneconomic for the households and without search the allocation remains unchanged. Under the adjustment rule of equation (3), this implies that the wage offers remain the same. By the same logic, any SW state is absorbing if the households do not search.

Fact 1. If for each nonabsorbing state s there is an absorbing state s' which is accessible from s, then with probability one the NMS remains among the nonabsorbing states for only a finite number of weeks (see Doob [7, p. 180]).

4. Propositions

The reader should now fix in his or her mind a couple of crucial structural features of the NMS. First, there is a distinguished state CE, for which the VMPs and wage offers of all firms are equal. The best way to visualize other states is not through their formal description, $\langle a_1,\ldots,a_F;\ w_1,\ldots,w_F\rangle$, since the firms may be of widely divergent sizes. It is better to consider the allocation a_f of each firm in terms of its *excess* or *deficit vis-à-vis* the competitive equilibrium allocation, a_f^e:

$$x_f = a_f - a_f^e, \qquad f \in \mathfrak{F}. \tag{11}$$

From the fact that the VMP curves are monotonically decreasing by (1) and (2), a surplus (deficit) firm will be adjusting its wage offer toward a value below (above) w^e.

To describe all possible states of the system would require determining all possible ways of allocating the households across firms and then taking the Cartesian product of this set with the set of possible wage offers at all firms. The number of states gets large and unwieldy very quickly as F and H increase. Many of these states would be illogical from an economic viewpoint. In some, firms would have widely disparate VMPs because their surpluses or deficits would be large. In some states, firms' wage offers would be far above or below their VMPs. Both of these situations, which are by no means mutually exclusive, can be expected to be corrected by the rational behavior of households and firms over time. However, the proofs must be arranged to give all possible states their due. To aid in understanding the dynamics of the NMS, consider the following example.

Example 1. There are three households and three firms with the identical VMP:

$$V_f(a_f)=\begin{cases} 2-a_f, & (0\leqslant a_f\leqslant 2),\\ 0, & (a_f=3). \end{cases}$$

The households behave according to Assumption 5A and pay for observations according to the schedule $\langle 1,100,101,\ldots,\rangle$ (i.e., they will take just one observation). If the NMS were at state $\langle 3, 0, 0; 2, 0, 0\rangle$, then no search would take place because the three households at firm 1 have nothing to gain. The firms will adjust their offers by unity toward their VMPs, which are $\langle 0, 2, 2\rangle$, according to (3). The initial transition is

$$\langle 3,0,0;2,0,0\rangle\rightarrow\langle 3,0,0;1,1,1\rangle.$$

Again no search is warranted and the next transition is

$$\langle 3,0,0;1,1,1\rangle\rightarrow\langle 3,0,0;0,2,2\rangle.$$

The expected gain for all three households if they search is now 2 with a cost of 1. Search must succeed and four new allocations are possible, $\langle 0,3,0\rangle$, $\langle 0,2,1\rangle$, $\langle 0,1,2\rangle$, and $\langle 0,0,3\rangle$ with probabilities 1/8, 3/8, 3/8, 1/8 respectively. Thus the following transitions are possible:

$$\begin{aligned}\langle 3,0,0;0,2,2\rangle&\rightarrow\langle 0,3,0;1,1,2\rangle\\ &\rightarrow\langle 0,2,1;1,1,1\rangle\\ &\rightarrow\langle 0,1,2;1,1,1\rangle\\ &\rightarrow\langle 0,0,3;1,2,1\rangle.\end{aligned}$$

Thus, the dyamics of the NMS are straight forward. However, as the number of agents increases, the number of possible transitions multiplies quickly.

To cut through the maze of possible transitions, it is convenient to distinguish two mutually exclusive classes of states: those inside and those outside SW. Recall that the Stationary Wage states, SW, are those for which each firm has reached the target wage on its VMP curve. These states have two cardinal virtues. First, they are the only potential absorbing states in the NMS and thus the only candidates to be equilibrium states. Second, all the firms with a *surplus* of workers, $x_f > 0$, have wage offers below w^e and thus below the wage offers of all firms with a *deficit* of workers, $x_f < 0$, whose wage offers are above w^e. (The only state in SW without any surplus or deficit firms is CE itself.) This follows from (1), the assumption that the VMPs are strictly decreasing in the neighborhood of a_f^e.

If households from all the *surplus firms* (those with a surplus labor force) engage in search, which is not unnatural since they are the worst paid, there is the possibility that each *surplus household* (those employed at surplus firms) observes the wage offer at any particular deficit firm. If there is also the case that search *may fail* for any household, as elaborated below, it can be shown that there is a possible transition in which *exactly* x_f households leave each surplus firm f and *exactly* $x_{f'}$ households enter each deficit firm f'. This follows because the sum of all surpluses must equal the sum of all deficits. Such a transition will bring about the competitive allocation, $\langle a_1^e, \ldots, a_F^e \rangle$, although not necessarily CE itself. To reach CE then requires that all households remain at their new employers long enough for the wage offers of those employers to reach the common value of their respective VMPs — w^e. Such stability of work forces can result from either the households not engaging in search or search failing to turn up better offers.

The sequence of transitions outlined above has taken the NMS from an arbitrary state in SW to CE. A complete convergence proof requires an additional demonstration that an arbitrary initial state leads to a state in SW. The complete proof consists of three parts, or interim assumptions, which will be explored below.

Interim Assumption 1. For an arbitrary initial state s, s leads to some s' in SW.

Interim Assumption 2. At any surplus firm f in any SW state except CE itself, at least x_f (the surplus) households with positive probability engage in search and $a_f - x_f = a_f^e$ households with positive probability either do not engage in search or are unsuccessful in their search, and so remain with firm f.

Interim Assumption 3. After the transition to a state with a competitive allocation and in subsequent transitions until CE is reached, there is positive probability that all households at the firm(s) with the lowest wage either do not search or are unsuccessful in their search, and so remain with their present firm(s).

In these interim assumptions, the phrase "with positive probability" is prominent. It is the nature of a Markov chain that the *possibility* of the system moving from an arbitrary initial state to a unique absorbing state is sufficient to insure that the system will *with certainty* reach that absorbing state, as indicated in Fact 1. None of the interim assumptions follows from Assumptions 1, 2, 3, 4, 5A or 5B and 6 used in defining the NMS. Part of Interim Assumption 2 can and will be derived from Assumption 5A or 5B by placing suitable *restrictions* on ${}_hc_1$ and $\langle N(h), c_h\rangle$, respectively. Laying out these restrictions is the principle substantive condition for convergence of the NMS.

Interim Assumptions 1, 3, and the remaining part of 2 all require that the NMS possess a certain amount of inertia or stability. I consider this to be a technical problem caused by the line of proof developed. As indicated above, the problem can be approached in two ways: at the appropriate times, households can not engage in search *or* search can fail to locate higher offers and bring about relocation. Before specifying these options in detail, which will be Assumptions 7 and 8, the nature of the problem will be more fully explicated with two examples.

Example 2. Two firms have the identical linear VMP, $V_f(a_f) = 2 - a_f$. Without specifying Assumption 5A or 5B and appropriate parameter values, assume that each of two households searches once when its firm has a lower wage offer than the other firm. Table 1 below presents a succinct description of the dynamics of Example 2. It uses arrows (→) to denote transitions.

This system is so simple that all transitions are deterministic rather than probabilistic. The possible states total 27: three possible allocations ⊗ three wage offers at firm 1⊗ three wage offers at firm 2. The last nine states are not represented as the system's perfect symmetry implies that they are mirror images of the first nine. The dynamics are simple: the firm

Table 5.1. Dynamics of example 2.

States with correct signals
$1\langle 2,0;1,2\rangle \underset{1}{\rightarrow} \langle 0,2;2,1\rangle \underset{2}{\rightarrow} \langle 2,0;1,2\rangle$ cycle
$2\langle 2,0;0,2\rangle \underset{1}{\rightarrow} \langle 0,2;1,1\rangle \underset{2}{\rightarrow} \langle 0,2;2,0\rangle \underset{3}{\rightarrow} \langle 2,0;1,1\rangle \underset{4}{\rightarrow} \langle 2,0;0,2\rangle$ cycle
$3\langle 2,0;0,1\rangle \underset{1}{\rightarrow} \langle 0,2;1,0\rangle \underset{2}{\rightarrow} \langle 2,0;0,1\rangle$ cycle
States with no search
$4\langle 2,0;2,2\rangle \rightarrow \langle 2,0;1,2\rangle$
$5\langle 2,0;1,1\rangle \rightarrow \langle 2,0;0,2\rangle$
$6\langle 2,0;0,0\rangle \rightarrow \langle 2,0;0,1\rangle$
States with reverse signals
$7\langle 2,0;2,1\rangle \rightarrow \langle 2,0;1,2\rangle$
$8\langle 2,0;2,0\rangle \rightarrow \langle 2,0;1,1\rangle$
$9\langle 2,0;1,0\rangle \rightarrow \langle 2,0;0,1\rangle$
States with no search
$10\langle 1,1;2,2\rangle \underset{1}{\rightarrow} \langle 1,1;1,1\rangle$ CE, absorbing
$11\langle 1,1;1,1\rangle$ CE
$12\langle 1,1;0,0\rangle \underset{1}{\rightarrow} \langle 1,1;1,1\rangle$ CE
Other states
$13\langle 1,1;2,1\rangle \rightarrow \langle 2,0;1,2\rangle$
$14\langle 1,1;2,0\rangle \rightarrow \langle 2,0;1,1\rangle$
$15\langle 1,1;1,0\rangle \rightarrow \langle 2,0;0,1\rangle$
$16\langle 1,1;1,2\rangle \rightarrow \langle 0,2;2,1\rangle$
$17\langle 1,1;0,2\rangle \rightarrow \langle 0,2;1,1\rangle$
$18\langle 1,1;0,1\rangle \rightarrow \langle 0,2;1,0\rangle$

with the higher wage collects both households because households are assumed to search and, with only two firms, search must succeed. States 1, 2 and 3 exhibit correct wage signals in the sense that the firm with the smallest work force and thus the largest VMP has the largest wage offer. These three states are seen to lead into cycles with periods of 2, 4 and 2 weeks respectively. States 4, 5, 6, 7, 8, 9, 13, 14, 15, 16, 17 and 18 are shown to lead directly to a state in one of these cycles. Only states 10 and 12 lead to CE, state 11. The cyclicity, or nonconvergence, is a result of the instability or lack of inertia in the system. If the households move, they move together; and they always move when wage signals are right. Under certain conditions, this phenomena may be eliminated by simply enlarging the NMS as shown in Example 3.

Example 3. Consider the case of eight households and four firms with the common $V_f(a_f)=4-a_f$. Again assume that a household searches once if his own firm's offer is not maximal. The following sequence is typical:

$$\langle 8,0,0,0;0,4,4,4\rangle \underset{1}{\rightarrow} \langle 0,3,3,2;1,3,3,3\rangle \underset{2}{\rightarrow}$$

$$\langle 0,3,3,2;2,2,2,2\rangle \underset{3}{\rightarrow} \langle 0,3,3,2;3,1,1,2\rangle \underset{4}{\rightarrow}$$

$$\langle 0,3,3,2;4,1,1,2\rangle,\ SW \text{ state } \underset{5}{\rightarrow}$$

$$\langle 2,2,2,2;3,2,2,2\rangle \underset{6}{\rightarrow} \langle 2,2,2,2;2,2,2,2\rangle\ CE.$$

These transitions are all possible, but not necessary. The crucial difference between Example 3 and Example 2 is evident in transitions 4, 5 and 6. Firms with lower wage offers are nonetheless able to retain all or part of their work forces, because of the multiplicity of these low wage offers. This multiplicity in conjunction with the replacement assumption and the finitude of search imply that *search may fail*—all of an individual's observations may be offers of equivalent or lower magnitude than his own firm's offer.

Fact 2. The sufficient conditions for the set SW to be accessible from all initial states are (1) there are at least four firms; and (2) two of these firms have VMPs with the same slope. The proof of Fact 2 is in Appendix 1.

Assumption 7. The NMS satisfies the hypothesis of Fact 2.

The second and simpler option is to assume that during each week there is some probability *less* than unity that each household *considers* searching for a better job, in the sense of calculating his sequence of reservation wages and comparing the initial value, w_1^*, with the initial value, w_f, with his present firm's offer.[6] There is then some residual positive probability that no search takes place regardless of the present firm's wage offer.

Assumption 8. For every household h there is probability p_h that search will be considered during any week, where $0<p_h<1$.

Either Assumption 7 or 8 simultaneously satisfies the Interim Assumptions 1, 3 and the stability aspect of 2. Are these legitimate simplifying

[6]This is simpler than the distinction between observations and job offers which is developed by Lippman and McCall [14, p. 164], which might be put to the same purpose.

assumptions or do they violate the spirit of the analysis? Assumption 7 and its usage in the proof put considerable weight on the replacement assumption. As in Example 3, another firm with the identical, lowest wage offer is observed every time an observation is taken by a household at one of the lowest paying firms. This gets increasingly improbable as F grows. Assumption 8 gets rid of the problem directly. In both cases the stability must be maintained over the number of weeks necessary for firms to reach their VMP curves, so the paths may well represent sequences of improbable transitions.

The improbability of the exhibited path to CE is of little consequence. The general NMS is a complex system which is not easy to describe. The virtue of the proof developed is that it is simple. The basic dynamics of the NMS are what is important and CE has a unique relationship to these dynamics. First, the firms' wage adjustment processes continually set the wage signals high for deficit firms and low for surplus firms. This has the effect of drawing households out of surplus firms and into deficit firms. CE is that middle ground where the surpluses and deficits have been eliminated and wage offers signal households to stay put. Second, the NMS will miss CE only if the movement toward it always overshoots, and surplus firms become deficit firms and vice versa in a single transition, as is seen in the cycles of Example 2. This overshooting does not seem to be the principle concern in an investigation of a market with no organizing force except the actions of individual agents. Rather, the problem one starts out with is just the opposite—showing that individual search is enough of a force to equalize wage offers.

All that remains for the convergence proof is then to delineate the bounds on the values of parameters of alternative household search models in Assumptions 5A and 5B. This task is best approached backwards by asking the question: how small a value does the expected gain from search reach across all SW (and thus potential equilibrium) states except CE and all surplus households? Designate this minimum as $EG_{\min}$. It will be found among the *unitary surplus* states, US; US consists of those states in SW for which there is a subset $\mathfrak{F}_1$ of firms with a surplus of one, $x_f = 1$, and in which the remaining firms $\mathfrak{F}/\mathfrak{F}_1$ exhibit a deficit, $x_f \leqslant 0$. Equations (6), (8) and (9) show that wage differentials make search valuable. Since states in the set US by definition exhibit minimal deviations from the CE allocation, they also exhibit minimum wage differentials in SW. For every state in SW, there is a state in US in which exactly the same firms exhibit surpluses or deficits, and for which the surpluses and deficits are (weakly) smaller in absolute value. By (1), this implies that the wage differentials are smaller.

Within US, it cannot be determined *a priori* which states exhibit $EG_{\min}$. As the number of surplus firms ranges from 1 to F-1, the size of the wage differential(s) grows because the total deficit grows, but the number of deficit firms with the better offers decreases. Which consideration is more important depends upon the slopes of the VMPs. For the special case in which the slopes are all linear and equal, all US states exhibit $EG_{\min}$.

Consider the household model in Assumption 5A. For households at any surplus firm f in a US state s, (6) indicates that the first observation will be worthwhile to take only if:

$$_hc_1 < \sum_{i=w_f}^{W} (i-w_f)\cdot {}_fp_i. \tag{12}$$

For any state s, let the right hand side of this equation be the expected gain from the first observation, EG(s). Then it follows:

$$EG_{\min} = \min_{\substack{s\in \text{US} \\ f \text{ with } x_f=1}} EG(s). \tag{13}$$

This completes explication of the interim assumptions.

Theorem 1. An NMS satisfying Assumptions 5A, 6, and either 7 or 8 will converge to CE in a finite number of weeks probability one if:

$$\max_{\mathcal{H}} ({}_hc_1) < EG_{\min}. \tag{14}$$

Proof. All the pieces of the proof have been laid out and need only to be brought together. Starting from an arbitrary initial state, the NMS has positive probability of going to an SW state by either Assumption 7 or 8. If this is not CE, then under the conditions of Assumption 5A and (14), households at every surplus firm will have the incentive to search. It is possible for only the *surplus number*, x_f, of surplus households to either actually search (Assumption 8) or be successful in that search (Assumption 7). The transition is then to a state with the CE allocation$\langle a_1^e, \ldots a_F^e \rangle$. This state in turn leads to CE in a number of weeks equal to the maximum difference between w_f and w_f^e across firms. Again by Assumption 7 or 8, this happens with positive probability. QED

Now I turn to the task of delineating the conditions under which this same convergence to CE occurs in an NMS governed by Assumption 5B.

Table 5.2.

w_i	1	2	3	4
$_fp_i$	0.25	0.25	0.25	0.25

Recall that this second household model has two parameters which determine for each household h the sequence of optimal reservation wages $w_1^*, w_2^*, \ldots, w_{N(h)}^*$. The parameters are a bound on the number of observations each week, $N(h)$, and the constant cost per observation, c_h. Some idea of the sensitivity of search to changes in these parameters is presented in Example 4.

Example 4. Assume a household at firm f can observe without recall at most three offers from a group of firms whose multinomial distribution is shown in table 5.2.

For various levels of c_h, the backward induction of (8a) and (8b) yields the sequences of reservation wages portrayed in the columns of table 5.3. Scanning across the rows, it is clear that as the cost of search, c_h, increases, the reservation wage at any position in the sequence declines. What is less clear, but nonetheless true, is that for any cost of search, the greater the number of observations, the greater the initial reservation wage. If only two offers could be observed, row w_2^* would contain the initial reservation wages. This follows from the fact that the calculations start with what is labeled row w_3^* and progress backwards until the bound on the observations is reached. From Lippman and McCall [14, p. 167], it is known that in general the sequence of reservation wages is nonincreasing. Thus the highest reservation wage and the greatest incentive to search are necessarily at the time of the first observation. In terms of raising this incentive to search, there is a potential tradeoff between lowering the search cost and raising the number of possible observations.

As $N(h)$ diverges to infinity, the initial reservation wage, w_1^*, approaches that value which is determined by (6) of Assumption 5A. As c_h approaches

Table 5.3. Reservation wages under Assumption 5b.

c_h	1/2	3/4	1	1–1/4	1–1/3	1–1/2	2	2–1/2
w_1^*	2–3/8	1–63/64	1–21/32	1–21/64	1–21/96	1	1/2	0
w_2^*	2–1/4	1–15/16	1–5/8	1–5/16	1–5/24	1	1/2	0
w_3^*	2	1–3/4	1–1/2	1–1/4	1–1/6	1	1/2	0

0, this value for w_1^* approaches W. Thus, the initial reservation wage can be driven up and search made advantageous for surplus households in every SW state except CE by an appropriate adjustment of $N(h)$ and c_h.

The question as to when the system converges is again the question of when the incentive to search is sufficient to prevent absorption of the NMS at *any* SW state other than CE. The task is to delineate limits on $N(h)$ and c_h which ensure this. In general, it is difficult to treat these parameters and their tradeoffs explicitly. Rather, I shall indicate the necessary effect these must have on the incentive to search. Define the *incentive to search* as the difference between the initial reservation wage and the current wage offer:

$$y_h(f,s) = w_1^*(f,s) - w_f. \tag{15}$$

This must be indexed by the household h, the firm f and the state s. The states with the *least* incentive to search are again the US states. The firms of concern are the surplus firms, $x_f = 1$. Although the surpluses are equal, these firms may vary in their offers, w_f, because of different curvature in their VMPs. The reservation wage varies with the parameters $N(h)$ and c_h of household h and the distribution of offers ${}_fp$. This probability mass function is in turn dependent upon the distribution of households across firms and thus the state s. The pairs of parameter values $\langle N(h), c_h \rangle$ across households must be such that the incentive to search is positive:

$$0 < y_{\min} = \min_{\substack{s \in US \\ f \text{ with } x_f = 1 \\ h \in \mathcal{H}}} (y_h(f,s)). \tag{16}$$

With this condition we can state Theorem 2, the proof of which is straightforward.

Theorem 2. An NMS satisfying Assumptions 5B, 6, and either 7 or 8 will reach CE with probability one in a finite number of periods if $y_{\min} > 0$.

The discussion of bounds on how easy—cheap and possible—search must be in order to assure convergence to CE naturally raises the question of what happens when these conditions are not met. By the way the proofs are laid out, it should be clear that in such a case additional SW states, starting with those in US, would become absorbing. The system would then exhibit multiple equilibria; the particular equilibrium which would be reached depends on the initial state of the system and would be a random event. The greater the impediments to search, the greater the number of these equilibrium states and the greater their possible divergence from CE in terms of surpluses and deficits. It is difficult to portray this with any rigor for an arbitrary NMS, but the general concept can be communicated through the use of simplifying assumptions. The pattern is particularly transparent if the following two assumptions are made.

Assumption 9. The VMPs are identical and linear over the relevant domain (i.e., $V_f = V$) all $f \in \mathcal{F}$ and:

$$H \leqslant M \tag{17}$$

$$V(a) = \begin{cases} w^e - J(a - a^e), & a < M, \\ 0, & a \geqslant M, \end{cases} \tag{18}$$

where J divides w^e and $M = w^e/J$. Equation (17) simplifies the analysis by insuring that no matter how large a given firm's work force grows, the marginal productivity does *not* fall to zero.

Assumption 10. All households have the same initial cost of search:

$$_h c_1 = c_1 \qquad \text{all } h \in \mathcal{H}. \tag{19}$$

It is now possible to simplify the discussion by reordering the firms in each SW state starting from those with the lowest offers (largest surpluses) and going to those with the highest offers (largest deficits). Consider an arbitrary SW state s; its allocation can be viewed equally well by the size of the surpluses and deficits:

$$\langle \underbrace{x_1, \ldots, x_m}_{m}, x_f, \underbrace{x_{f+1}, \ldots, x_{f+n}}_{n} \rangle$$

where $x_i \geqslant x_{i+1}$ and $F = m + n + 1$. By taking the right-hand side of (6) and summing over firms instead of wage offers, it is possible to show that the *expected gain from the first observation* for a household at firm f in state s is

$$EG(f,s) = \frac{J \cdot (n+1) \cdot x_f + J \cdot \sum_{i=1}^{m} x_i \cdot}{F - 1} \tag{21}$$

Because of the reordering, $EG(1,s) \geqslant EG(2,s) \geqslant \ldots \geqslant EG(F,s)$. As a special case of this formula,

$$EG(1,s) = \frac{J \cdot F \cdot x_1}{F - 1}. \tag{22}$$

Consider the following example.

Example 5. There are four households and four firms with common $V_f(a)=4-a$. Clearly, $J=1$ and $M=4 \geqslant H$. The five possible *types* of stationary wage states, ordered from largest surplus to largest deficit, and the expected gain from the first observation for households at firm 1 are as shown in table 5.4:

Table 5.4

SW states	$EG(1, s)$
1 $\langle 1,1,1,1;3,3,3,3\rangle = \text{CE}$	$(0+0+0)\cdot 1/3=0$
2 $\langle 2,1,1,0;2,3,3,4\rangle$	$(1+1+2)\cdot 1/3=4/3$
3 $\langle 2,2,0,0;2,2,4,4\rangle$	$(0+2+2)\cdot 1/3=4/3$
4 $\langle 3,1,0,0;1,3,4,4\rangle$	$(2+3+3)\cdot 1/3=8/3$
5 $\langle 4,0,0,0;0,4,4,4\rangle$	$(4+4+4)\cdot 1/3=12/3$

The reader can verify that these calculations conform to (21).

Resuming the general discussion, it is possible to define a sequence of *observation cost thresholds*:

$$T_n = \frac{J\cdot F\cdot n}{F-1}, \qquad n=0,1,\dots H-x^e, \tag{23}$$

and a sequence of classes of SW states:

$$K_n = \{s\in SW\colon x_1=n\}, \qquad n=0,1,\dots H-x^e. \tag{24}$$

Clearly, $K_0=\{\text{CE}\}$ and $K_1=\text{US}/\{\text{CE}\}$; the K_n are mutually exclusive.

Theorem 3. In an NMS satisfying Assumptions 5A, 6, 7 or 8, 9 and 10, if

$$T_n \leqslant c_1 < T_{n+1}, \qquad n=0,1,\dots,H-x^e, \tag{25}$$

then the set of absorbing states is

$$\bigcup_{i=1}^{n} K_i, \qquad n=0,\ 1,\dots,H-x^e,$$

and regardless of where the NMS begins, one of these absorbing states will be reached in finite time with probability one.

Proof. By (22), T_n is the maximum value of the expected gain from search across all households in the SW states whose largest surplus x_1 is n. The set $\cup_n K_i$ contains all SW states for which the largest surplus is n or less. By Assumption 5A, search will take place only if T_n exceeds the cost of the first observation for all households c_1. Equation (24) then sets the condition under which search will *not* take place in exactly the SW states $\cup_n K_i$.
QED

It is interesting to note that within a group of states K_n having the *same* observation cost threshold, there is in general *no* constancy as to the variance of the wage distribution. Example 5 shows this to a limited extent. States 2 and 3, with the same $EG(1, s)=4/3$, have variances in the distribution of wages of $\frac{1}{2}$ and 1, respectively. It can also happen that a state with a *lower* $EG(1, s)$ than another state has a *higher* variance in its wage offers.

For an NMS without simplifying Assumptions 9 and 10, a similar partitioning of the range on the cost of the first observation could be undertaken. However, there would no longer be any reason why groups of SW states with the same maximum surplus, x_1, would simultaneously become absorbing. Rather, there would potentially be a unique value of $EG(1, s)$ for every state, dependent upon precisely which households were currently employed at which firms. It seems reasonable to conjecture that as the level of search costs rises, there will be growth in that subset of SW states which do not provide an incentive to search and, thus, are absorbing.

5. Conclusion

The theory of search and the equilibrium of a nonauctioneered market has been presented in three theorems and several numerical examples. The theory as it stands is in no sense complete. It does provide a new and explicit view of the process of market interaction—price setting, the coming together of buyer and seller, price adjustment—as undertaken by households and firms themselves, without the aid of an auctioneer. Among the more promising avenues for research is the introduction of strategic or optimizing behavior on the part of the participants, particularly firms.

Appendix 1

Proof of Fact 2. The NMS satisfies the following conditions:

$$F \geqslant 4$$

and there are two firms f and g such that the slope of the demand curves are the same:

$$V_f(a_f^e + n) = V_g(a_g^e + n), \qquad n = n', n'+1, \ldots,,$$

where:

$$n' = -\min\,(a_f^e, a_g^e).$$

There are four possible relationships between f and g:

Case (1): $a_f = a_g$ and $w_f = w_g$,

Case (2): $a_f = a_g$ and $w_f < w_g$,

Case (3): $a_f \neq a_g$ and $w_f < w_g$,

Case (4): $a_f \neq a_g$ and $w_f = w_g$.

The inequalities are made possible by the arbitrariness of the labels. It must be shown that s leads to a state s^*, in which the conditions of Case 1 hold *and*:

$$V_f(a_f) = V_g(a_g) \leqslant V_{f'}(a_{f'}), \qquad \text{all other } f'. \tag{Al}$$

In such a state, the system possesses the inertia to reach SW. To separate this inertia from the lack of incentive to search, assume in the following any wage differential calls forth search.

The basic problem in transitions is that states may be reached in which a single firm has the lowest offer. Since households search, this firm will lose all of its work force. First consider state s in which Case 1, but not (Al) holds. Eventually there will be a week with some f' having $w_{f'} < w_f = w_g$. If $a_{f'}$ is an even integer, $a_{f'}/2$ households go each to f and g. If $a_{f'}$ is odd, then $(a_{f'} - 1)/2$ go each to f and g, and the odd household either stays at f' or goes to a fourth firm f'', depending on the relationship of the wage offers between f' and f''. The repeated application of this procedure leads to s^*. If either Case 2 or 3 holds, then firm f, with the lowest offer, first gives up all its households to firm g. Firm g in turn gives up all its households to a third firm f' as soon as $w_g < w_{f'}$. Bringing this about may require transferring households from f' to g and waiting. Once $a_f = a_g = 0$, these two firms will progress toward Case 1, with any activity contained among the other firms, and thence to s^*. The natural wage adjustment process will lead from Case 4 to Case 3, which has been covered:

References

[1] Arrow, K. J., "General economic equilibrium: purpose, analytic techniques, collective choice," *American Economic Review*, 64 (1974), 253–272.

[2] Arrow, K. J., "Limited knowledge and economic analysis," *American Economic Review*, 64 (1974), 1–10.

[3] Arrow K. J., and Hahn, F., *General Competitive Analysis*, Holden Day, San Francisco, 1971.

[4] Clower, R. W., (ed.), *Monetary Theory*, Penguin, Baltimore, 1969.

[5] Debreu, G., *Theory of Value*, Cowles Foundation Mono. 17, John Wiley, New York, 1959.

[6] DeGroot, M. H., *Optimal Statistical Decisions*, McGraw-Hill, New York, 1970.

[7] Doob, J. L., *Stochastic Processes*, John Wiley, New York, 1953.

[8] Ferguson, C. E., *Microeconomic Theory*, Irwin, Homewood, Illinois, 1966.

[9] Hicks, J., *Value and Capital*, Clarendon Press, Oxford, 1946.

[10] Jevons, W. S., *Theory of Political Economy*, (ed., Collinson Black, R. D.) Penguin, Baltimore, Maryland, 1970.

[11] Leftwich, R., *Price System and Resource Allocation*, Holt, Reinhart & Winston, New York, 1966.

[12] Leijonhufvud, A., *On Keynesian Economics and the Economics of Keynes,* Oxford University Press, New York, 1968.

[13] Leijonhufvud, A., The Varieties of Price Theory: What Micro Foundations for Macrotheory, UCLA Discussion Paper 44, January, 1974.

[14] Lippman, S. A., and McCall, J. J., "The economics of job search: a survey," Parts I and II, *Economic Inquiry,* 14 (1976), 155–189 and 347–368.

[15] McCall, J. J., "The economics of information and optimal stopping rules," *Journal of Business*, 38 (1965), 300–317.

[16] Mirman, L. J., and Porter, W. R., "A microeconomic model of the labor market under uncertainty," *Economic Inquiry*, 12, (1974), 135–145.

[17] Ostroy, J. M., "The informational efficiency of monetary exchange," *American Economic Review*, 63 (1973) 597–610.

[18] Rothschild, M., "Models of market organization with imperfect information: a survey," *Journal of Political Economy*, (1973) 1283–1308.

[19] Rothschild, M., "Searching for the lowest price when the distribution of prices is unknown," *Journal of Political Economy*, 82, (1974) 689–712.

[20] Sameulson, P., *Foundations of Economic Analysis*, Atheneum, New York, 1947.

[21] Smith, A., *Wealth of Nations*, (ed. Skinner A.), Penguin, Baltimore, Maryland, 1776, 1970.

[22] Stigler, G. J., "The economics of information," *Journal of Political Economy,* 69 (1961), 213–225.

[23] Stigler, G. J., "Information in the labor market," *Journal of Political Economy,* 70 (1962), 94–104.

[24] Stigler, G. J., *Theory of Price*, Macmillan, New York, 1966.

[25] Walras, L., *Elements of Pure Economics*, (trans. Jaffee, W.), Irwin, Homewood, Illinois, 1954.

[26] Wharton, J. B., "Search, competition and unorganized market equilibrium," unpublished PhD dissertation, UCLA, Los Angeles, 1976.

CHAPTER 6

On the role of consumption and decreasing absolute risk aversion in the theory of job search

JOHN P. DANFORTH*

Federal Reserve Bank of Minneapolis

1. Introduction

The agents in job search theories are different from the agents in most other microeconomic theories; and it isn't just that they are unemployed. In job search theories, individuals are typically assumed to maximize the expected utility of the present value of income net of search costs.[1] This contrasts with most other microeconomic models which assume individuals maximize the expected utility of lifetime consumption. It seems natural to ask whether or not this difference is of any consequence, but it is our impression that this question has been neither asked nor answered in the relevant literature.

Perhaps the question has been ignored because maximization of a utility of income function is not necessarily inconsistent with preferences being defined directly in terms of consumption. There are well known conditions which, if satisfied, allow income to be viewed as a composite good and included as the sole argument of an indirect utility function. However, if the direct utility function is not linear in consumption, these conditions are generally violated in models which, like job search, involve intertemporal utility maximization under uncertainty.[2] Thus, maximizing the expected utility of income is not necessarily (or even likely to be) equivalent to

*The views expressed herein are solely those of the author and do not necessarily represent the views of the Federal Reserve Bank of Minneapolis or the Federal Reserve System.

[1]See Kohn and Shavell [8] and Lippman and McCall [9] for comprehensive discussion of this literature.

[2]See Spence and Zeckhauser [14] or Danforth [5] for a discussion of why these conditions are generally violated.

maximizing the expectation of some reasonable utility of consumption function.[3]

Even granting this nonequivalence, though, one could still argue that the difference is inconsequential if the empirical content of the theory is not affected by the choice of objective function. But the empirical content is affected by this choice. If one assumes that individuals maximize the expected utility of consumption, then, as Sargent [13] and Hall [7] have demonstrated, consumption data can provide information on individual tastes and expectations. If, on the other hand, individuals are assumed to maximize the expected utility of income, consumption data lacks any such informational content.

These observations have prompted us to analyze a model of job search, wherein the job seeker's preferences are defined directly on random sequences of consumption. This basic approach is intrinsically more general than that found in conventional models of job search since, as argued above, it places fewer restrictions on preferences and it encompasses a wider set of economic decisions. We have, however, sacrificed some of this intrinsic generality in order to increase the number of testable hypotheses yielded by our theory. In particular, we restrict our attention to preferences that give rise to additively separable utility functions and which display decreasing absolute risk aversion (DARA). The first of these restrictions, separability, allows us to ignore past consumption levels in formulating a rule for current and future decisions.[4] The second restriction, DARA, captures the widely held (and empirically supported[5]) belief that individuals are willing to give up less in order to avoid a given amount of variability in consumption as their average level of consumption increases.

2. Plan of the paper and summary of results

The paper is divided into two sections. In the first section we present a finite horizon model of job search. In the second section we consider the infinite horizon analogue of that model.

We begin the first section with a presentation of the basic assumptions of the finite horizon model. The form of the optimal job search-cum-

[3] By "reasonable utility of consumption function" we mean one which is increasing in each period's consumption.

[4] Expected utility of income maximization implies separability.

[5] See Cohn, Lewellen, Lease and Schlarbaum [3] and Projector and Weiss [12] for such empirical support.

consumption allocation strategy is then deduced. This strategy specifies current consumption, next period's asset holdings, and a set of acceptable wage offers as a function of age and current asset endowments.

Two aspects of the unemployed individual's behavior can be inferred directly from our general solution. First, his strategy cannot, in general, be decomposed into separate expected income maximization and consumption allocation problems. Second, his decisions relating to job acceptability are sensitive to his current financial endowments.

The precise nature of this sensitivity is revealed in three propositions which follow from the DARA hypothesis. The first of these propositions may be referred to as "the rich are more selective" result. It asserts that an increase in initial wealth endowments induces a reduction in the set of wage offers which would be accepted in the current period if received. The second proposition is that "the rich search longer". That is, a *ceteris paribus* increase in assets leads to an increase in the expected duration of search unemployment for the individual. The last of these three results states that "the rich get richer". More precisely, this proposition observes that the expected present value of the returns from job search are directly related to current asset holdings.

In the fourth section we present an infinite horizon analogue of the model presented in section 3. While the propositions of section 3 remain valid for the model presented here, the influence of career length is not present in the infinite horizon setting. Thus, the only state variable for this model is asset holdings. We show that if the rate at which future utility is discounted is as large as the market discount rate for future income, then the job seeker will find it optimal to draw down his asset holdings and reduce his acceptance wage as time passes. This proposition reveals that one need not rely on an arbitrary deadline for terminating the search activity or a nonstationary distribution of wage offers in order to generate a declining acceptance wage.

3. A model of job search: the finite horizon version

In this section we present a model of optimal search with the following underlying structure. At each date the individual's current situation or state is completely described by his employment status (employed at some particular wage or unemployed) and his current asset holdings. He can exercise some control over movement between states through his choice of current consumption and his decision to accept or reject specific wage offers. Transition from one state to another is also influenced by which random wage offer is observed. The individual ranks alternative feasible control laws or strategies on the basis of the expected utility of the random consumption stream resulting from their adoption.

3.1. Assumptions[6]

We assume that the individual's satisfaction depends solely on his lifetime path of single-period consumption levels, $c(1), c(2), \ldots, c(N)$. His ordering of alternative consumption sequences is given by a von Nuemann–Morgenstern utility function, $V: R_+^N \to R^1$, having the intertemporally separable form:

$$V(c(1), c(2), \ldots, c(N)) = \sum_{i=1}^{N} \beta^i u(c(i)), \tag{1}$$

where u is assumed to be increasing, bounded, twice differentiable, and strictly concave.

Since u is strictly concave, the individual is, of course, risk averse. In the sequel we shall utilize the stronger condition on attitudes toward risk alluded to in the introduction, namely, decreasing absolute risk aversion. Mathematically we require[7] that $r_u \equiv -u''/u'$, the absolute risk aversion measure, is a decreasing function of $c(i), i = 1, 2, \ldots, N$. This assumption, the implications of which will be discussed in precise terms below, basically guarantees that in any period, the quantity of certain consumption the individual is just willing to exchange for a given random supplement to consumption increases as the nonrandom component of consumption increases.

Wage offers are the source of uncertainty in the model. We assume that the individual believes per-period wage offers to be identically and independently distributed random variables, $\mathcal{Y}_1, \mathcal{Y}_2, \ldots, \mathcal{Y}_N$. The subjective cumulative distribution function and density functions for each of these variables will be denoted by F and f, respectively.

On observing a per-period wage offer of y in period $i(<N)$ the individual may either accept it and receive y dollars in each of periods $i+1$,

[6]In Appendix 1 we indicate how these assumptions can be generalized without significantly altering the main conclusions of the section.

[7]The sense in which this mathematical condition is equivalent to DARA is made precise in Danforth [5].

$i+2,\ldots,N$, or reject it and sample again in period $i+1$, incurring a search cost of s dollars at that time.

The individual uses his labor income as well as his assets to finance consumption expenditures. We assume for convenience that each composite consumption good can be purchased at a price of one dollar per unit.

The individual is allowed to borrow and lend at a constant interest rate, r. We assume, however, that lenders do place limits on borrowing so as to ensure that the individual's outstanding debts at the end of period N do not exceed some fixed upper bound, B. The necessity of satisfying this terminal constraint then imposes limitations on the individual's consumption and savings which depend on his current employment status. In particular, if the individual has not accepted employment as of date $t-1 \leqslant N$, his asset holdings $A(t)$ at date t must satisfy

$$A(t)=[A(t-1)-c(t-1)-s](1+r), \tag{2}$$

and

$$A(t) \geqslant \sum_{i=t}^{N} s(1+r)^{t-i} - B(1+r)^{-(N+1-t)} \equiv B_{N-t+1}, \tag{2'}$$

where r is the one-period market rate of interest. Alternatively,

$$A(t)=[A(t-1)-c(t-1)+y](1+r), \tag{3}$$

and

$$A(t) \geqslant -\sum_{i=t}^{N} y(1+r)^{t-i} - B(1+r)^{-(N+1-t)} \equiv B_{N-t+1}^{y} \tag{3'}$$

if the individual is employed at wage y as of date $t-1 \leqslant N$. Equations (2) and (3) are just recursive budget equations, while (2′) and (3′) are the borrowing constraints imposed on the individual when he is unemployed and employed, respectively.

Finally, we assume that if the individual has not accepted a job prior to date $t=1,2,\ldots,N$, then $c(t)$ is chosen before the value of $\mathcal{Y}_t$ is observed.[8]

[8]This ordering is somewhat arbitrary in that reversing it leaves all of the implications of the analysis intact.

3.2. The optimal strategy

Our task now is to characterize the highest ranked or optimal feasible strategy. The technique we shall employ in obtaining this characterization is dynamic programming. Accordingly we define $J_{N-t}(A,y)$ as the maximal utility attainable in the $N-t$ periods between dates $t+1$ and $N+1$ when initial assets are A and the individual is employed at wage y. Then $J_0 \equiv 0$, and

$$J_n(A,y) = \max_{0 \leqslant c \leqslant A - B_n^y} \{u(c) + \beta J_{n-1}[(A-c+y)(1+r),y]\}. \tag{4}$$

Similarly, if the individual is unemployed at date $t+1$ with asset holdings equal to A, then let $S_{N-t}(A)$ be the maximal utility attainable in the $N-t$ periods between dates $t+1$ and $N+1$. Then $S_0 \equiv 0$, and

$$S_n(A) = \max_{0 \leqslant c \leqslant A - B_n} \left\{ u(c) + \beta \int_0^\infty \max\{S_{n-1}[(A-s-c)(1+r)]; \right.$$
$$\left. J_{n-1}[(A-s-c)(1+r),y]\} \mathrm{d}F(y) \right\}. \tag{5}$$

It is clear, given the definitions of J_n and S_n, that an offer of y will be accepted at date $N-n+1$ if

$$J_n(A,y) > S_n(A)$$

and will be rejected if

$$J_n(A,y) < S_n(A).$$

If neither inequality is satisfied, both acceptance and rejection are optimal. We thus define the continuous function $\hat{y}_n : [B_n, \infty) \to R_1$ by

$$\hat{y}_n(A) = \begin{cases} 0 \text{ if } J_n(A,0) \geqslant S_n(A), \\ y \text{ such that } J_n(A,y) = S_n(A) \quad \text{if} \quad J_n(A,0) < S_n(A). \end{cases} \tag{6}$$

Therefore, (5) may be rewritten as

$$S_n(A) = \max_{0 \leqslant c \leqslant A - B_n} \left\{ u(c) + \beta \int_{\hat{y}_{n-1}((A-c-s)(1+r))}^{\infty} J_{n-1}((A-c-s)(1+r), y) f(y) \mathrm{d}y \right.$$
$$\left. + \beta F(\hat{y}_{n-1}((A-c-s)(1+r))) S_{n-1}((A-c-s)(1+r)) \right\}^{9}. \tag{7}$$

Since $\hat{y}_n$ may not be a constant function, strict concavity of J_{n+1} and S_{n+1} need not imply concavity of (7). Indeed, one can easily construct examples where (7) is a locally convex function of A. The underlying reason nonconcavities can arise here, even though the individual's utility function is concave, is that the constraint set is nonconvex. That is, the individual can choose to accept employment or to remain unemployed but not a convex combination of the two.

The behavioral implications of this type of nonconcavity are twofold. First, there may be a multiplicity of expected utility-maximizing search strategies. Though each strategy yields the same expected utility, the consumption, savings and job acceptance decisions may differ among them. As we shall see below, no fundamental analytical difficulties result from such nonuniqueness.

Second, if the maximum expected utility of search is a nonconcave function of assets, the unemployed individual will be a risk preferrer for some levels of wealth holdings. Thus, while the individual would never think of accepting an actuarially unfair gamble so as to alter his assets when employed, he might be anxious to do so when unemployed.

Of course, the job search process itself may be viewed as a type of gamble or lottery. Each outcome is a particular income stream. The lottery evolves over time as various unacceptable job offers are encountered and terminates when a specific job is accepted. Given any level of asset holdings, there is some dollar amount, denoted $Y_n(A)$, which the individual would be just willing to accept when n periods remain rather than continue

[9]If one assumes that u and F each belongs to a particular finite parameter family of functions, (7) can be used in conjunction with data on consumption and acceptance wages to obtain maximum likelihood estimates of the parameters of those functions (see Sargent [13] and Hall [7] for worked examples of this type of procedure).

the job search lottery. When $J_n(A,0) \leqslant S_n(A)$, this amount is simply $\Sigma_{i=1}^n \hat{y}_n(A)/(1+r)^{i-1}$, the present discounted value of an "annuity" paying the period $t-1$ acceptance wage in periods t through N. When $J_n(A,0) > S_n(A)$, we solve for the $\bar{y}<0$ such that $J_n(A,\bar{y}) = S_n(A)$ and $Y_n(A) = \Sigma_{i=1}^n \bar{y}(1+i)^{i-1}$. By virtue of the continuity of S_n and J_n and the monotonicity of J_n, Y_n is a continuous function.

3.3. *Implications of DARA*

As was indicated in the introduction, there exists ample empirical evidence suggesting that consumers generally place higher dollar values on risky ventures as their wealth holdings are increased. Arrow [1] and Pratt [11] have shown that when the domain of an individual's utility function is the real line (i.e., V: $R^1 \to R^1$), such a positive correlation between wealth and risk value will obtain if and only if

$$r_V(x) = -V''(x)/V'(x) \tag{8}$$

is a decreasing function of x. When this condition is satisfied, we say that V displays or is characterized by DARA.

In Danforth [5] we have considered conditions which imply and are implied by a positive correlation between wealth and multidimensional risk value. One of the conclusions contained therein [5, Theorem 1, p. 58] was that if an individual's utility function is additively separable, as we have assumed in this paper, then the present dollar value of arbitrary multidimensional risks is positively correlated with wealth if and only if

$$r_u(x) = -u''(x)/u'(x)$$

is decreasing throughout, $i = 1, 2, \ldots, N$. Within the context of our search model, this result implies that Y_n is an increasing function of A since we have assumed r_u to be decreasing. In words, if the one-period utility function displays DARA, then the certain dollar value of job search is an increasing function of asset holdings. Furthermore, if the one-period utility function is strictly concave but does not display DARA, then the certain dollar value of job search can be a decreasing or constant function of asset holdings.

As an immediate consequence of the monotonicity of Y_n we have:

Theorem 1. If $\delta > 0$ and $A \geqslant B_n$, then $\hat{y}_n(A+\delta) \geqslant \hat{y}_n(A)$. ($\hat{y}_n(A+\delta) > \hat{y}_n(A)$ if $\hat{y}_n(A) \neq 0$).

Theorem 1 states that the acceptance wage is a monotone increasing function of asset holdings. Since the probability that an individual will no longer be unemployed in the next period is inversely related to the size of his current acceptance wage, Theorem 1 provides a link between asset holdings and state transition probabilities. One might suspect that this link could be easily extended to establish an empirically testable relationship between the expected duration of unemployment and wealth. The possible multiplicity of expected utility-maximizing strategies mentioned above, however, means that the expected duration of unemployment may depend on which expected utility-maximizing strategy is chosen. While this complicates our analysis to some extent, we are able to demonstrate that the expected duration of unemployment associated with *any* expected utility-maximizing strategy for asset holdings A is less than the expected duration of unemployment associated with *any* expected utility-maximizing strategy for asset holdings $A+\delta$.

First let $\Sigma(A,t)$ represent the individual's nonempty set of expected utility-maximizing, completely specified strategies when his state as of date $t=N-n+1$ is "unemployed with asset holdings $A \geqslant B_n$". Any $\sigma \in \Sigma(A,t)$ specifies a particular feasible sequence of consumption, asset stocks, and acceptance wages for each possible sequence of wage offers during the n periods between date t and date $N+1$. Of course, once an offer is accepted, no more wage offers are observed so that subsequent realizations of the wage offer process can have no effect on decisions. Furthermore, our assumptions of nonrecall and independent wage offer distributions imply that the level of previous unacceptable wage offers are irrelevant to current opportunities and utility. Thus, if the individual decides at date t to employ strategy $\sigma \in \Sigma(A,t)$, there is a unique level of wealth, denoted A^{σ}_{t+i}, which will be held at date $t+i$ if the wage offers realized in the intervening periods, $y(t), y(t+1), \ldots, y(t+i-1)$, have been unacceptable.[10]

The acceptance wage in period $(t+i)$, given that strategy $\sigma \in \Sigma(A,t)$ is being employed and that previous wage offers have been unacceptable, is $\hat{y}_{n-i-1}(A^{\sigma}_{t+i+1})$. The probability that the individual will be unemployed and searching at date j may, therefore, be expressed as

$$P^{\sigma}_{j} \equiv F(\hat{y}_{n-1}(A^{\sigma}_{t+1}))F(\hat{y}_{n-2}(A^{\sigma}_{t+2}))\ldots F\big(\hat{y}_{N+1-j}(A^{\sigma}_{j})\big). \tag{9}$$

The mathematical expectation of the duration of search unemployment

[10]Notice that since $c(t)$ is determined prior to the observation of $\mathcal{Y}(t)$, the level of assets held at date $t+1$ for strategy σ does not depend on wage offers observed subsequent to period $t-1$.

when strategy σ is employed, DS_n^σ, is then given by

$$DS_n^\sigma \equiv \sum_{i=t}^{N} (1+i-t)[P_i^\sigma - P_{i+1}^\sigma]. \tag{10}$$

Observing that $P_t^\sigma = 1$ and $P_{N+1}^\sigma = 0$, (10) may be rewritten in the more convenient form of

$$DS_n^\sigma = 1 + \sum_{i=t+1}^{N} P_i^\sigma. \tag{10'}$$

The next theorem observes that a *ceteris paribus* increase in the unemployed individual's current asset holdings will increase the expected duration of his search unemployment.

Theorem 2. If $\sigma^1 \in \Sigma(A^1, t), \sigma^2 \in \Sigma(A^2, t)$ and $A^2 > A^1$, then $DS_n^{\sigma^1} \leqslant DS_n^{\sigma^2}$; the inequality is strict if $\hat{y}_{n-1}(A_{t+1}^{\sigma^1}) > 0$ and $A_{t+1}^{\sigma^1} > B_{n-1}$.

Proof. A change in A affects expected duration of unemployment through the impact of such a change on future asset holdings and, consequently, on future acceptance wages. In particular, if increasing A increases asset holdings in future periods, then future acceptance wages will increase, thus increasing the probability of being unemployed in any future period.

Our proof will, therefore, be very nearly complete if it can be shown that asset holdings at dates $t+1$ through N are "normal goods" in the sense that increasing current asset holdings will lead to an increase in asset holdings in each subsequent period. Given that u is strictly concave, it is not surprising that in our model asset holdings are normal goods in this sense. The proof of this unsurprising fact is, however, rather lengthy due to the possible nonconcavities in and nondifferentiability of the S_{t+i}'s. We, therefore, refer the interested reader to Danforth [4, Lemma 9, pp. 46–49] wherein we establish that if

$$\sigma^1 \in \sum(A^1, t), \sigma^2 \in \sum(A^2, t), \quad \text{and} \quad A^2 > A^1,$$

then either

$$A_{j+1}^{\sigma^2} > A_{j+1}^{\sigma^1}$$

or

$$A_{j+1}^{\sigma^2}=A_{j+1}^{\sigma^1}=B_{j+1}, \qquad j=t,\ldots,N-1.$$

This result together with Theorem 1 ensures that each element of the product defining P_j is an increasing function of A for $j=t+1,\ldots,N$. Hence, $P_j^{\sigma^1}\leqslant(<)P_j^{\sigma^2}, j=t+1,\ldots,N$, and, therefore, by (10′), $DS_n^{\sigma^1}\leqslant(<)DS_n^{\sigma^2}$ (if $\hat{y}_{n-1}(A_{t+1}^{\sigma^1})>0$ and $A_{t+1}^{\sigma^1}>B_{n-1}$) and our proof is complete. QED

Job search is often described as a type of investment in human capital with the duration of search measuring the size of this investment. Theorem 2 establishes that if an individual is characterized by DARA, his demand for search, like his demand for other investments having risky returns, increases as his asset holdings increase. If, as I believe, the analogy between increased expected duration of search and increased participation in other risky investments is a good one, then the expected return to this increased search should be positive. The remainder of this section will be devoted to investigating the sign of the change in expected returns accompanying an increase in the expected duration of search unemployment.

Since the returns to search take the form of increases in lifetime earnings (net of search costs), the expected return of a particular search strategy is the expected present value of lifetime labor income less search costs resulting from the adoption of that strategy. It will prove convenient to have a recursive expression for this expected present value. Therefore, we define the expected present value of income less search costs as of date $t+i$ (where again $t=N-n+1$) if the individual is employing strategy $\sigma\in\Sigma(A,t)$ and has not accepted employment by

$$PVY_{n-i}^{\sigma}=-s+\int_{\hat{y}_{n-i-1}(A_{t+i+1}^{\sigma})}^{\infty}\sum_{j=t+i+1}^{N} y(1+r)^{i-j}f(y)\mathrm{d}y$$
$$+(1+r)^{-1}PVY_{n-i-1}^{\sigma}F(\hat{y}_{n-i-1}(A_{t+i+1}^{\sigma})), \tag{11a}$$

and

$$PVY_1^{\sigma}=-s. \tag{11b}$$

There are now two dollar figures to place on the individual's optimal search strategy, the certain dollar value of the strategy, $Y_n(A)$, and the expected present value of income less search costs resulting from the adoption of the strategy, PVY_n^σ. Since I have assumed the labor force participant to be risk averse (i.e., u strictly concave), one can easily verify that the difference,

$$PVY_n^\sigma - Y_n(A),$$

is nonnegative for $\sigma \in \Sigma(A,t)$. This difference can be interpreted as a risk premium.

In our model this risk premium is closely related to the marginal change in expected net income associated with an increase in the acceptance wage. To see this, observe that if a wage offer equal to the acceptance wage is received, $Y_n(A)$ is the present value of income if it is accepted and PVY_n^σ is the expected present value of income less search costs if it is rejected. Therefore, since an increase in asset holdings increases the expected duration of search by raising acceptance wages, it will also increase expected income less search costs if the risk premium is positive. This is the basis for our proof of

Theorem 3. If $\sigma^1 \in \Sigma(A^1,t)$, $\sigma^2 \in \Sigma(A^2,t)$ and $A^1 < A^2$, then $PVY_n^{\sigma^1} \leqslant (<) PVY_n^{\sigma^2}$ (if $\hat{y}_{n-1}(A_{t+1}^{\sigma^1}) > 0$ and $A_{t+1}^{\sigma^1} > B_{n-1}$).

Proof. Take as an induction hypothesis for date $t+i \leqslant N$

$$PVY_{n-i}^{\sigma^1} \leqslant PVY_{n-i}^{\sigma^2}.$$

Now recall from our proof of Theorem 2 that

$$\hat{y}_{n-i-1}\left(A_{t+i+1}^{\sigma^1}\right) \leqslant (<) \hat{y}_{n-i-1}\left(A_{t+i+1}^{\sigma^2}\right)$$

and hence

$$\int_{\hat{y}_{n-i-1}\left(A_{t+i+1}^{\sigma^1}\right)}^{\hat{y}_{n-i-1}\left(A_{t+i+1}^{\sigma^2}\right)} \left[Y_{n-i-1}\left(A_{t+i+1}^{\sigma^2}\right) - \sum_{j=t+i+1}^{N} y(1+r)^{i-j} \right] f(y)\,\mathrm{d}y \geqslant (>) 0 \tag{12}$$

$\left(\text{if } \hat{y}_{n-i-1}\left(A_{t+i+1}^{\sigma^1}\right) > 0 \quad \text{and} \quad A_{t+i+1}^{\sigma^1} > B_{n-i-1}\right).$

Also, since the "risk premium" is nonnegative,

$$\int_{\hat{y}_{n-i-1}(A^{\sigma^1}_{t+i+1})}^{\hat{y}_{n-i-1}(A^{\sigma^2}_{t+i+1})} \left[PVY^{\sigma^2}_{n-i-1} - Y_{n-i-1}\left(A^{\sigma^2}_{t+i+1}\right)\right] f(y)\,\mathrm{d}y \geqslant 0. \tag{13}$$

Our induction hypothesis implies

$$F\left(\hat{y}_{n-i-1}\left(A^{\sigma^1}_{t+i+1}\right)\right)\left[PVY^{\sigma^2}_{n-i-1} - PVY^{\sigma^1}_{n-i-1}\right] \geqslant 0. \tag{14}$$

Summing the LHSs of (12), (13) and (14) and referring to (11a), we conclude that

$$PVY^{\sigma^2}_{n-i} - PVY^{\sigma^1}_{n-i} \geqslant (>) 0 \quad \text{if} \quad \hat{y}_{n-i-1}\left(A^{\sigma^1}_{t+i+1}\right) > 0 \tag{15}$$

$$\text{and} \quad A^{\sigma^1}_{t+i+1} > B_{n-i-1}.$$

Since our induction hypothesis is clearly valid for $t+i+1=N$, the proof is complete. QED

Theorem 3 confirms the claim that there is a positive return to increased investment in job search. It is also worthwhile noting that this result provides a formal justification for Friedman's [6] statements regarding the existence of a "link between differences in natural endowments or inherited wealth and the realized distribution of wealth or income" which results from a systematic relationship between individual propensities to take risks and his initial endowments. Thus, if labor force participants are characterized by DARA and differ only as to their initial asset holdings, our model predicts that, on average, the rich will get richer.

4. A model of job search: the infinite horizon version

The model of this section differs in only one respect from the one considered in the previous section. The horizon is infinite rather than finite. The primary reason for this switch in horizons is that it allows us to isolate the effects of changes in asset holdings from changes in the length of the future as time passes.

The assumptions of the preceding section are easily altered to give rise to the infinite horizon analogue to our finite horizon model. First, the objective function given in (1) is changed to

$$V(c(1), c(2), \ldots) = \sum_{i=1}^{\infty} \beta^i u(c(i)). \tag{1'}$$

Second, jobs are assumed to last forever. Thus, when a wage offer of y is accepted, the individual will receive a "perpetuity" of y dollars per period. Finally, the borrowing constraints give in (2′) and (3′) become

$$A(t) \geqslant s(1+r)/r \equiv B \tag{2''}$$

and

$$a(t) \geqslant -y(1+r)/r \equiv B^y, \tag{3''}$$

respectively. Of course, $B = \lim_{n\to\infty} B_n$ and $B^y = \lim_{n\to\infty} B_n^y$.

The procedure employed in deriving an optimal strategy within this altered framework is a variant of Bellman's "method of successive approximations" discussed in [2]. First, a sequence of objective functions is specified which converges uniformly to V. For each element of this sequence, a strategy which maximizes its expected value is determined. Finally, the resulting sequence of maximizing strategies and expected values is used to characterize a strategy which maximizes the expected value of V.

Since the objective function and constraints of this model are the limits of those posited in the first section, it is not surprising to find that the sequence of functions which shall be used is $\{V_n\}$, where

$$V_n(c(1), c(2), \ldots) = \sum_{i=1}^{n} \beta^i u(c(i)). \tag{16}$$

Of course, we know a great deal about strategies which maximize the expected value of any particular V_n, since this is the utility function dealt with in the previous section.

Thus, if the labor force participant's state as of date 1 is "employed at wage y with asset holdings A", then the maximum attainable value of V_n from date 1 forward is $J_n'(A,y)$ where J_n' is defined as in (4), except that B_n^y is replaced by B^y. Similarly, if the individual's state as of date t is "unemployed with asset holdings A", then the maximum attainable expected value of V_n from date 1 forward is S_n' where S_n' is defined as in (5), except that B_n is replaced by B. Replacing J_n and S_n in (6) with J_n' and S_n' we obtain the definition of the acceptance wage function, $\hat{y}_n'$, for this truncated problem. J_n', S_n', and $\hat{y}_n'$ are easily shown to possess the same continuity, differentiability, monotonicity, and concavity properties as J_n, S_n, and $\hat{y}_n$, respectively.

Since u is bounded, there is no loss of generality in assuming that $u(0) \geqslant 0$, so that J_n' and S_n' are nondecreasing functions of n for any value of A. Also, since $0<\beta<1$ and u is bounded from above by some number $\bar{u}$, both J_n' and S_n' are uniformly bounded from above by $\bar{u}/(1-\beta)$ for all values of n. J_n' and S_n', therefore, converge uniformly to continuous and increasing functions, J and S, as n tends to infinity.

$J(A,y)$ is thus the maximum attainable value of V given the individual's state is "employed at wage y with asset holding A". $S(A)$ is the maximum attainable value of V given the individual's state is "unemployed with asset holdings A". The acceptance wage, $\hat{y}$, is, therefore, the solution to

$$J(A,\hat{y})-S(A)=0,$$

which depends on A but not on t.

Since the conditions under which employment will be accepted or rejected are completely summarized in the acceptance wage, all that remains to be said about the individual's strategy is how he chooses current consumption. Of course, this is no great mystery. If the individual's state is "unemployed with asset holdings A", he should choose $c, 0 \leqslant c \leqslant A-B$, to maximize

$$u(c)+\int_{\hat{y}((A-c-s)(1+r))}^{\infty} \beta J((A-c-s)(1+r),y)f(y)\,\mathrm{d}y$$
$$+\beta F(\hat{y}((A-c-s)(1+r)))S((A-c-s)(1+r)). \tag{17}$$

The maximized value of this sum is $S(A)$. Similarly, if the individual's state is "employed at wage y with asset holdings A", he should choose c, $0 \leqslant c \leqslant A-B^y$, so as to maximize

$$u(c)+\beta J((A-c+y)(1+r),y). \tag{18}$$

The maximized value of (18) is then $J(A,y)$.

Our model shares with standard models of consumption allocation over time the property that the intertemporal pattern of consumption and asset accumulation or deaccumulation is sensitive to the relationship between β, the psychological rate of time discount, and the interest rate r. For example, if $\beta(1+r)>1$, then the individual, having sold his resource, will increase his level of consumption and his financial asset holdings in each successive period without bound. Conversely, if $\beta(1+r)<1$, then the individual who has sold his resource will plan to consume less in future periods than in the present and will draw down his financial asset stock over time. If $\beta(1+r)=1$, the individual will neither increase nor decrease his asset holdings as time passes.

In this paper we are primarily interested in pre-job-acceptance asset dynamics so that the relationships cited in the preceding paragraph, while suggestive, are not directly applicable. In particular, the rate of change of financial asset holdings for an individual engaged in price search depends not only upon β and r but also upon the distribution F of wage offers. Although the addition of the wage distribution to our calculations makes it exceedingly difficult to determine conditions under which a job seeker will accumulate assets, restrictions which imply that financial asset holdings will be used up over time are straightforward. As the following theorem reveals, $\beta(1+r)\leqslant 1$ is a sufficient, though not necessary, condition to ensure that the job seeker's financial assets will decline over time.

Theorem 4. If $A(t)>B$, $\beta(1+r)\leqslant 1$, and c^* is the constrained maximizer for (17), then $A(t)>A(t+1)=(A(t)-c^*-s)(1+r)$.

Proof. This theorem can be proven in three steps. First, one can establish by induction that

$$\mathrm{d}S_n(A)/\mathrm{d}A \leqslant \partial J_n(x,0)/\partial x|x=A-B$$

$n=1,2,\ldots$, and therefore the derivatives of the limit functions satisfy

$$\mathrm{d}S(A)/\mathrm{d}A \leqslant \partial J(x,0)/\partial x|x=A-B.$$

Second, the relationship between the slopes of S and J together with the strict concavity of J (established in Appendix 2) can be shown to imply that the value of c which maximizes

$$u(c)+\beta J((A(t)-s-c)(1+r),0),$$

c°, is less than the value of c which maximizes (17), c^*. Third, one may easily verify that $\beta(1+r)\leqslant 1$ implies

$$A(t)\geqslant(A(t)-s-c^\circ)(1+r)$$

and thus

$$A(t) > (A(t) - s - c^*)(1 + r) = A(t + 1). \qquad \text{QED}$$

Our attention will be confined to search strategies which specify declining asset balances in our subsequent discussion. This emphasis can be justified on at least two grounds. First, conditions which are consistent with alternative savings behavior are illusive. Second, we believe asset deaccumulation by agents involved in price search is more plausible than asset accumulation. We, therefore, assume throughout the remainder of the paper that $\beta(1+r) \leqslant 1$.

Since utility, prices, and labor demand are all stationary in this infinite horizon model, the unemployed individual's optimal choice of controls (i.e., consumption and acceptance wage), will change over time solely in response to his declining asset holdings. We are, therefore, obliged to investigate the relationship which exists between the acceptance wage and asset holdings in this stationary setting if we are to infer anything about the dynamics of the first of these two variables. The nature of this relationship is partially revealed in the following lemma.

Lemma 1. The acceptance wage $\hat{y}$ is a nondecreasing function of the asset level A.

This result is a consequence of Theorem 1 of section 3, which asserts that the acceptance wage in a finite horizon optimal search strategy, $\hat{y}_n$, is an increasing function of A if $r_u'(c) < 0$. Since $J_n \to J$ and $S_n \to S$ uniformly as $n \to \infty$, $\hat{y}_n \to \hat{y}$ uniformly as $n \to \infty$ and the limit of a uniformly convergent sequence of increasing functions is nondecreasing.

Theorem 4 and Lemma 1 together imply that the acceptance wage will be nonincreasing as time passes. This, however, is not all that was promised in the introduction. We asserted that the acceptance wage would be declining over time. This distinction rules out the constant acceptance wage which is observed in an infinite horizon model of expected income maximizing job search.

In order to prove our stronger result, we must establish that $\hat{y}$ is a strictly increasing function. The main tool used in proving this is verifying that the indirect utility function U displays DARA, where U is given by $U(x) = J(x, 0)$.

Lemma 2. The indirect utility function has strictly decreasing risk aversion, that is, r_U is strictly decreasing.

The applicability of this proposition is in no way limited to models of job search. It says something quite general about the preservation of a property of direct utility functions, in the indirect utility function resulting from constrained maximization. Specifically the lemma observes that the indirect utility function associated with an infinite dimensional stationary direct utility function displays DARA if the single-period utility indicators $\beta^t u$ display DARA. The proof of Lemma 2 is technical and lengthy; accordingly, it is given in Appendix 2.

With the following theorem we conclude our analysis of the infinite horizon search problem. The theorem asserts that, so long as an individual's asset holdings have not been completely exhausted, his acceptance wage will decline with the passage of time. Thus, even though the labor force participant's decision rule $\hat{y}$ is stationary, the optimal decision $\hat{y}(A(t))$ at time t is not.

Theorem 5. If $A(t)>B$, then $\hat{y}(A(t))>\hat{y}(A(t+1))$.

Proof. As before, we shall denote by $\Sigma(A,t)$ the expected utility maximizing strategies available to the individual at date t when his state is "unemployed with asset holdings A". The acceptance wage, $\hat{y}(A)$, will then be a solution to

$$J(A,\hat{y}(A))=u(c_t^\sigma)+\int_{\hat{y}(A_{t+1}^\sigma)}^{\infty} J(A_{t+1}^\sigma,y)f(y)\,\mathrm{d}y + F(\hat{y}(A_{t+1}^\sigma))\beta J(A_{t+1}^\sigma,\hat{y}(A_{t+1}^\sigma))$$

for any $\sigma\in\Sigma(A,t)$.

It is easily demonstrated that

$$J(A,y)=J(A+y(1+r)/r,0)$$

so that

$$\max_{0<c<A^i+\hat{y}(A^i)(1+r)/r} u(c)+\beta J((A^i+\hat{y}(A^i)(1+r)/r-c)(1+r),0)$$

$$=u\left(c_t^{\sigma^i}\right)+\int_{\hat{y}(A_{t+1}^{\sigma^i})}^{\infty} J\left(A_{t+1}^{\sigma^i}+y(1+r)/r,0\right)f(y)\,\mathrm{d}y + F\left(\hat{y}\left(A_{t+1}^{\sigma^i}\right)\right)\beta J\left(A_{t+1}^{\sigma^i}+\hat{y}\left(A_{t+1}^{\sigma^i}\right)(1+r)/r,0\right)$$

for $i=1$, 2, and $\sigma^i \in \Sigma(A^i, t)$. Since r_u and r_J are decreasing, the conditions of Theorem 2 of [5], discussed in connection with our Theorem 1, are satisfied. We thus conclude that if $A^2 > A^1$, then

$$\hat{y}(A^2) > \hat{y}(A^1).$$

By Theorem 4, $A(t) > B$ implies $A(t) > A(t+1)$, completing the proof. QED

5. Summary and conclusions

The optimal labor market strategy of an unemployed expected utility of consumption-maximizing individual was investigated in this paper. In the first section we considered a finitely long-lived individual. We demonstrated that the individual has at least one optimal job search-cum-consumption allocation strategy, and that any such strategy consists of a decision rule which specifies current consumption, savings and acceptable wage offers as a function of current asset holdings and age.

Several testable hypotheses were generated under the assumption of decreasing absolute risk aversion. In particular, we proved that asset holdings are positively correlated with the acceptance wage, the expected duration of unemployment, and the expected present value of noninterest income.

These predicted correlations, especially the last one, are very much in the spirit of Friedman's comments cited in the text. If individuals are indeed characterized by decreasing absolute risk aversion, then the job search process has been shown to translate unequal nonhuman wealth endowments into unequal lifetime labor income. Thus, with the inclusion of bequests in the utility function, our analysis suggests that the apparently typical negative wealth-risk aversion relationship characterizing individuals acts as an inequality preserving factor in the dynamic determination of the personal distribution of income.

In the second section the job search-consumption allocation strategy of an infinitely long-lived individual acting in a stationary environment was derived. Here the strategy was shown to consist of a rule which specified current consumption, savings, and an acceptance wage for each level of financial asset holdings. Due to stationarity assumptions on wage expectations and preferences, this rule was also stationary (i.e., independent of date).

The stationarity of the rule did not, of course, imply that consumption, savings and acceptable wage offers would be the same in each period. In fact, it was shown that plausible restrictions on the relationship between the psychological discount rate and the market interest rate implied declining financial asset holdings (savings) before and after the culmination of the price search process.

The time path followed by financial asset holdings, the only quantitative state variable in the model, could be translated into a time path for the acceptance wage and consumption, the two control variables of the model. We found that if the individual satisfied the DARA hypothesis, the current financial asset holdings and current reservation price would be positively related to one another. When combined with our earlier result on the time path of financial asset holdings, we obtained a theorem which stated straightforward conditions under which the individual's acceptance wage would decline over time.

Appendix 1. Some generalizations of the finite horizon model

In a footnote to our discussion of the finite horizon model of job search, we suggested that several assumptions of that model could be relaxed without affecting our main results. We suggest five possible generalizations in this appendix. The reader wishing to see a rigorous analysis of the model when these more general assumptions are adopted should refer to [4].

First, we can assume that the individual believes wage offers to be generated as a fairly general stochastic process. This allows for the possibility of learning through sampling.

Second, the individual can be given the opportunity to recall previous offers for some specified number of periods. Thus, offers which were received in period t would be held open through period $t+s$.

Third, consumption good prices, interest rates, and search costs can be made period specific. So long as these prices and costs are known with certainty, they can have any intertemporal pattern one might care to assume and our analysis will be essentially unaffected.

Fourth, we can allow the individual a period of retirement.

Fifth, the utility function can have the more general form: $V(c(1),\ldots,c(N))=\Sigma_{i=1}^{N}u_i(c(i))$, where each of the u_i satisfies $u_i'>0$, $u_i''<0$, and $-u_i''/u_i'$ decreasing.

Aside from complicating our notation, the third through fifth of these generalizations have a negligible effect on our analysis and conclusions.

The first and second generalizations listed here, however, add more than notational complexity to our analysis. Each of these weakened assumptions has the effect of adding another state variable to our problem, namely, previously observed wage offers. Some difficult technical problems relating to the measurability of strategies arise when previous realizations of the stochastic process are state variables. Nevertheless, Theorems 2 and 3 are correct as stated even if each of these four generalizations is adopted.

On the other hand, Theorem 1 must be slightly modified since the set of acceptable wage offers at any particular date need not consist of all wage offers above some acceptance wage. That is, the set of acceptable wage offers may be disconnected. Our modified Theorem 1 asserts that the set of acceptable wage offers will shrink in response to an increase in asset holdings.

Appendix 2. Proof of Lemma 2

The requirements of our proof differ depending on whether

$$\lim_{c\to 0} u'(c) < \infty \quad \text{or} \quad \lim_{c\to 0} u'(c) = \infty,$$

so we shall consider these cases separately.

Case 1. $\lim_{c\to 0} u'(c) < \infty$. It is easy to verify that

$$J(x,0) = \max_{c_0, c_1, \dots} \sum_{i=0}^{\infty} \beta^i u(c_i)$$

subject to $c_i \geqslant 0$ and $\Sigma_{i=0}^{\infty} c_i/(1+r)^i = x$. Necessary conditions for this maximum are

$$u'(c_0) = (1+r)^i \beta^i u'(c_i) \quad \text{if} \quad c_i > 0 \tag{1}$$

and

$$u'(c_0) \geqslant (1+r)^i \beta^i u'(c_i) \qquad \text{if} \quad c_i = 0. \tag{2}$$

For any $x < \infty$ there exists an $n(x) < \infty$ such that the maximizing value of c_i is 0 for all $i > n(x)$. Since $u' < 0$, $n(x)$ is nondecreasing in x. Therefore, for any $M<\infty$ and $x<M$,

$$J(x,0)=\max_{c_0,\ldots,c_{n(M)}}\sum_{i=0}^{n(M)}\beta^i u(c_i)$$

subject to $c_i\geqslant 0$, $i=0,\ldots,\ n(M)$, and $\Sigma_{i=1}^{n(M)}c_i/(1+r)^i=x$.

Neave ([10] Lemma 1, page 46) has shown that if $-u''/u'$ is decreasing, then the assertion of Lemma 2 is valid for $x\in[0,M]$. Since M is an arbitrary real number, this establishes the lemma for Case 1.

Case 2. $\lim_{c\to 0}u'(c)=\infty$. The first-order conditions for this case are

$$u'(c_0)=(1+r)^i\beta^i u'(c_i),\qquad i=0,1,\ldots \tag{3}$$

Each of these conditions implicitly defines a twice differentiable function, g_i, with

$$u'(c_0)=(1+r)^i\beta^i u'(g_i(c_0)).$$

Since $\beta(1+r)<1$ and $-u''/u'$ is decreasing, $g_i(c)<c$ and $g_i'(c)<1$ for all $i=1,2,\ldots$. The budget constraint,

$$x=\sum_{i=0}^{\infty}g_i(c_i)/(1+r)^i, \tag{4}$$

therefore, gives rise to a twice differentiable function, h, such that (3) and (4) are satisfied when $c_i=g_i(h(x)), i=0,1,\ldots$. Given our assumptions on u, the necessary conditions are also sufficient, so that

$$J(x,0)=\sum_{i=0}^{\infty}\beta^i u(g_i(h(x))).$$

Differentiating this sum and making use of the first-order conditions, we obtain

$$r_J(x)=-u''(g_i(h(x)))g_i'(h(x))h'(x)/u'(g_i(h(x)))$$

for $i=0,1,\ldots$. This expression is decreasing in x since $g_i'>0$ and $h'(x)>0$ implies

$$-u''(g_i(h(x)))/u'(g_i(h(x)))$$

is decreasing in x for all i, and

$$g_i'(h(x))h'(x)$$

is nonincreasing in x for at least one i since differentiation of (4) implies

$$1=\sum_{i=0}^{\infty} g_i'(h(x))h'(x)/(1+r)^i.$$

This establishes the lemma for Case 2.

References

[1] Arrow, K. J., "Lecture II: Aspects of a theory of risk bearing", Yrjo Jahssonin Lectures, Helsinki, 1965.

[2] Bellman, R., *"Dynamic Programming"*, Princeton, New Jersey: Princeton University Press, 1957.

[3] Cohn, R. A., Lewellen, W. G., Lease, R. C., and Schlarbaum, G. G., "Individual investor risk aversion and investment portfolio composition", presented at the San Francisco American Finance Association Meetings, December 1974.

[4] Danforth, J. P., "Expected utility, mandatory retirement and job search", Discussion Paper Number 74–41, Center for Economic Research, University of Minnesota, June 1974.

[5] Danforth, J. P., "Wealth and the value of generalized lotteries", *Journal of Economic Theory*, 15 (1977), 54–71.

[6] Friedman, M., "Choice, change and the personal distribution of income", *Journal of Political Economy,* 61 (1953), 277–290.

[7] Hall, R. E., "Stochastic implications of the life cycle—permanent income hypothesis: theory and evidence", *Journal of Political Economy,* 86 (1978), 971–987.

[8] Kohn, M. G., and Shavell, S., "The theory of search", *Journal of Economic Theory*, 9 (1974), 93–124.

[9] Lippman, S. A., and McCall, J. J., "The economics of job search: a survey", Parts I and II, *Economic Inquiry*, 14 (1976), 155–189 and 347–368.

[10] Neave, E. H., "Multiperiod consumption, investment decisions and risk preference", *Journal of Economic Theory,* 3 (1971), 40–53.

[11] Pratt, J. W., "Risk aversion in the small and in the large", *Econometrica,* 32 (1964), 122–136.

[12] Projector, D. S., and Weiss, G. S., *Survey of Financial Characteristics of Consumers*, Board of Governors of the Federal Reserve System, 1966.

[13] Sargent, T. J., "Estimation of dynamic labor demand schedules under rational expectations", *Journal of Political Economy*, 86 (1978), 1009–1044.

[14] Spence, M., and Zeckhauser, R., "The effect of the timing of consumption decisions and the resolution of lotteries on the choice of lotteries", *Econometrica,* 40 (1972), 401–405.

CHAPTER 7

Expected utility maximizing job search

JEFFREY R. HALL, STEVEN A. LIPPMAN and JOHN J. McCALL

University of Santa Clara and University of California, Los Angeles

1. Introduction

Economic models of search and information have been proliferating at a rapid rate since Stigler's seminal work in the area [23, 24]. These models have been useful in explaining the phenomena of unemployed resources in the economy, most notably in providing a rationale for the Phillips curve relation (see [9] for a recent review of the literature). While the search literature represents a significant improvement over the earlier deterministic approaches, a standard assumption has been that the objective of the searcher is to maximize expected income. This conflicts with the traditional view that individuals maximize utility functions that are concave in income or wealth. It is the purpose of this paper to consider the implications of the introduction of a utility based objective into the search problem. The result is a significant restructuring of the qualitative properties of optimal search.

Section 2 reviews the basic search model, explicitly delineating its assumptions and implications, and sets forth the expected utility maximizing model that will be examined here. Section 3 derives the qualitative properties of expected utility maximizing search under conditions of recall. Section 4 then turns to the case of nonrecall.

2. The basic job search model

While Stigler's article [24] dealt with a consumer searching for the lowest price, the problem it addresses is present in a number of different contexts. Phrased in the paradigm of job search, the basic problem can be summarized as follows: An individual is seeking employment in a market in which jobs are homogeneous in all nonwage attributes. Since he does not know which wage is being offered by which prospective employer, but only the distribution function F of wages, he proceeds by randomly applying for positions, one at a time. For each application submitted there is a cost c incurred. The problem, then, is that of determining when to terminate the search process and accept a job offer in order to maximize the expected wage net of search costs. It should be noted that the term "wage" as it is used here may be thought of as the total lifetime earnings from the job (i.e., the wage rate times the duration of employment where the duration of employment is assumed the same for all jobs).

Stigler considered the case of recall, in which the searcher may accept any previously received offer (by contrast, in the case of nonrecall, an offer must either be accepted at the time it is presented or lost forever). The basic Stigler search model can be summarized by the following assumptions:

Assumption 1. A job offer X_i is presented in period i, where each X_i is a nonnegative random variable with cumulative distribution function $F(\cdot), E(X_i) < \infty$, and the X_i's are mutually independent. Furthermore, F has associated density f.

Assumption 2. The distribution F of wages is known to the searcher.

Assumption 3. The searcher pays a constant amount c for each offer received.

Assumption 4. The searcher may receive an unlimited number of offers.

Assumption 5. The searcher may, at any time, accept any offer received to date, so that recall is permitted.

Assumption 6. The searcher seeks to maximize the expected wage net of search costs.

The optimal strategy for this problem has a myopic sequential structure: after each offer is received, the decision is made whether to accept one of the offers received so far, or to search at least one more time. This decision is made by comparing the expected marginal return from soliciting one more offer with the marginal cost of receiving that offer. More formally, if

w is the best offer received to date, then $H(w)$, the expected gain from searching one more time, is given by

$$H(w)=\int_{w}^{\infty}(x-w)f(x)\mathrm{d}x.$$

The optimal rule is to stop searching and accept employment whenever w satisfies $H(w)\leqslant c$. Furthermore, the optimal rule is to accept any offer $w\geqslant\xi$ where ξ satisfies $H(\xi)=c$. The quantity ξ is referred to as the *reservation wage*, and it completely characterizes the optimal strategy.

The optimal strategy for this basic search problem has the following important properties:

Property 1. The optimal strategy is determined by a myopic policy; that is, the decision whether to accept a job is determined at each stage of the search process by considering the expected increase in income from observing one, and only one, more offer. The optimal strategy is then to search if and only if this quantity is positive.

Property 2. There exists a unique reservation wage ξ such that the optimal strategy is to accept a wage offer w if and only if $w\geqslant\xi$.

Property 3. The level of the reservation wage ξ depends only on the level of the search costs c and the distribution F of wages.

Property 4. The optimal strategy is the same under recall and nonrecall.

Property 5. The reservation wage increases with a mean preserving increase in the riskiness of the distribution of wages.[1]

Property 6. The reservation wage decreases as c increases.

While this particular model and concomitant results are neat and elegant, search theorists have considered various relaxations of the assumptions of the basic model so as to enhance the connection between

[1]A mean preserving increase in risk changes the distribution F by shifting mass toward the tails of the distribution while leaving the mean unchanged. The effect is to shift $H(w)$ upward for all w, thereby increasing the reservation wage (see n15).

the model and "reality".[2] It is, however, only recently that such modifications and in particular the implications of expected utility maximization have been considered.[3]

Nachman [13, 14] and Danforth [4] appear to be the first to study successfully the implications of utility maximization in the context of the basic search model. The resulting model is easy to analyze and serves to highlight the importance of the specific assumptions concerning the objective.

Henceforth, the model that will be used in this paper is the one framed in Assumption 1 through Assumption 6 with the important exception that Assumption 6 is altered as shown below:

Assumption 6. Let U be a twice continuously differentiable nondecreasing concave (utility) function (defined on the real numbers).[4] Denote the searcher's initial wealth by M.[5] The searcher seeks to maximize the expected utility of his wage plus initial wealth minus search costs.

[2]For example, Lippman and McCall [8] have considered the case of a distribution of wages changing over time; Rothschild [20] has dealt with the problem facing a searcher who doesn't know the distribution F with certainty, but rather has a prior over the set of all possible distributions; Burdett [2] and Lippman and McCall [9] have considered a searcher who can receive only a finite number of offers, and other changes such as discounting, variable search intensity, and on-the-job search have also been considered (see [9]).

[3]Kohn and Shavell [7] specifically consider the problem of utility maximizing search, but because search costs are assumed constant when measured in utility and possible wealth effects are neglected, their model is equivalent to the basic Stigler model; the problem is the same, the only difference is that the term "utility" has been substituted for the term "wages".

It should be noted that Danforth in two essays [3,4] has introduced a utility based objective into a search model in a very meaningful and innovative way. Danforth makes utility a function of consumption over time, and hence draws an essential link between the consumption decision and the job acceptance decision. In addition, the search environment he constructs is very general; for example, there is the possibility of partial recall in which any of the last k offers may be accepted, variable search costs, variable interest rates, uncertainty as to the actual distribution of wages, and unemployment benefits. Because of the generality of his model, it is difficult to isolate the effect of the introduction of expected utility maximization; nevertheless, his independent work contains a number of the results presented in this paper.

[4]For the analysis that will follow, it will be convenient to have the utility function defined for all real numbers. Thus, if $\lim_{z\to b^+} U'(z)=\infty$, we define

$$U(z)=-\infty \quad \text{for all} \quad z<b \quad \text{and} \quad U(b)=\lim_{z\to b^+} U(z).$$

This says that infinite disutility results from having net worth less than b. Thus, an individual will not search if the search results in a net worth less than or equal to b with positive probability.

While wealth (possibly negative) is being explicitly introduced into the model, there is no explicit use of a budget constraint. This corresponds to the Stigler model where there is no limit to the number of offers one may receive, even though there is a positive cost for each offer. Also, we shall use the symbol M to stand for the searcher's current wealth.

We shall demonstrate in section 3 that Property 1 through Property 5 can all fail when the recall option is permitted and U is strictly concave. In particular, it is shown that there may be no reservation wage in the sense that the acceptance set has gaps (Example 1), myopic policies need not be optimal (Example 2), the acceptance set depends on the individual's wealth (Theorem 2), the recall option may be utilized (Example 1), an increase in the riskiness of F may increase the acceptance set (Example 3).

3. Expected utility maximizing search with recall

In our analysis, we utilize dynamic programming techniques as well as several of Pratt's [16] concepts and results concerning risk aversion. For ease of reference, we present all of definitions and notation at this point.

To begin, we say that the searcher is in state (M,w) if his current wealth (initial wealth minus search costs accumulated to date) is M and the best wage offer received to date is w. Let the random variable $Y(M,w,U,i)$ be the individual's final (accepted) wage less search costs associated with taking one more observation and thereafter following an optimal strategy corresponding to the utility function U and state (M,w) when at most $i(\leqslant +\infty)$ more offers can be received. For notational simplicity we will abbreviate and write Y_i, Y_U, or Y_M in place of $Y(M,w,U,i)$ when the nonsubscripted variables are being held constant and no confusion can arise.

Next, define $V_i(M,w)$ to be the maximum expected utility that can be achieved when the searcher is in state (M,w) and at most i more offers can be received. Then $V_i(M,w)$ satisfies the recursive equation $[V_0(M,w)= U(M+w)]$

$$\begin{aligned} V_i(M,w) &= \max\{U(M+w);\ EU(M+Y(M,w,U,i))\} \\ &= \max\{U(M+w);\ EV_{i-1}(M-c,w\vee X_1)\} \qquad (1) \end{aligned}$$

where $x\vee y\equiv\max(x,y)$ and $Y(M,w,U,0)\equiv w$ so that we have $EU(M+Y(M,w,U,0))=U(M+w)$ as desired.

It is clear upon reflection that

$$EU(M+Y(M,w,U,i))\geqslant EU(M+Z(w,i)) \qquad (2)$$

for all random variables Z that represent the individual's final wage less search costs associated with taking one more observation and thereafter following any strategy when the initial state is (M,w) and at most i more offers can be received. From (2) we can immediately conclude that $EU(M+Y_i) \geqslant EU(M+Y_{i-1})$ so that

$$V_{i+1}(M,w) \geqslant V_i(M,w). \tag{3}$$

In view of $E(X_1)<\infty$, U concave, and (3), we see that $V(M,w)$, the maximum expected utility attainable when the searcher is in state (M,w) and able to solicit an unlimited number of offers, satisfies[6]

$$V(M,w)=\lim_{i\to\infty} V_i(M,w) \tag{4}$$

and

$$\begin{aligned} V(M,w) &= \max\{U(M+w);\ EU(M+Y(M,w,U))\} \\ &= \max\{U(M+w);\ EV(M-c,w\vee X_1)\}. \end{aligned} \tag{5}$$

Furthermore, this formulation of the optimal return informs us which wage offers to accept via (1) or (5); viz., accept w when wealth is M if and only if

$$U(M+w) \geqslant EU(M+Y(M,w,U,i)). \tag{6}$$

Equation (6) merely says that the individual should search only if the expected utility from continued search is greater than the utility from accepting the best offer to date.

Given M, U, and i, any wage w that satisfies (6) is referred to as an acceptable wage. Denote the set of acceptable wages by $\mathscr{W}(M,U,i)$ if $i<\infty$ and $\mathscr{W}(M,U)$ otherwise. (When no confusion can arise, we will simply write $\mathscr{W}(M)$ or $\mathscr{W}(M,i)$ as appropriate.)

We now investigate the behavior of $\mathscr{W}(M,U,i)$ as we vary each of the three arguments. Toward this end, let r_U be the Arrow–Pratt measure of absolute risk aversion:

$$r_U(x) \equiv -U''(x)/U'(x), \qquad \text{all} \quad x. \tag{7}$$

If r_U is nonincreasing, then we say that the searcher has decreasing

[6]Robbins [17] has given a very clever proof to demonstrate that the optimal return is finite (and equal to ξ) if U is linear and $E(X_i)<\infty$. By the concavity of U, there are integers n and m such that $U(x)\leqslant n+mx$. Hence, (i) $V(M,w)\leqslant n+m(M+w+\xi)$ by Robbins' result. Now by $E(X_1)<\infty$ and (i) we can conclude that (ii) $V(M-c,w\vee X_1)$ is integrable. Coupling (3) and (i) yields (4), whereas (5) follows from (1), (4), and (ii).

absolute risk aversion, and a searcher with utility function $\mathcal{U}$ is said to be more risk averse than a searcher with utility function U if $r_{\mathcal{U}} \geqslant r_U$.

For a concave utility function u, Pratt [16] defines the (nonnegative) risk premium $\pi(x, Z, u)$ associated with initial wealth x and the random variable Z by

$$Eu(x+Z) = u(x+E(Z)-\pi(x,Z,u)). \tag{8}$$

Of course, the risk premium $\pi \geqslant 0$ is simply chosen so that an individual is indifferent between receiving the certain amount $x+E(Z)-\pi$ and receiving the random amount $x+Z$. Pratt's Theorems 1 and 2 assert that[7]

$$\pi_{\mathcal{U}} \geqslant \pi_U \quad \text{if} \quad r_{\mathcal{U}} \geqslant r_U \tag{9}$$

and

$$\pi_y \leqslant \pi_x \quad \text{if} \quad y \geqslant x \quad \text{and} \quad r_U \quad \text{is decreasing.} \tag{10}$$

Furthermore, the inequalities in (9) and (10) are strict if $r_{\mathcal{U}} > r_U$ and r_U is strictly decreasing, respectively.

As a direct consequence of (3), (4) and (6) we see that the searcher is more selective the greater his opportunities for search.

Theorem 1. The acceptance sets satisfy

$$\mathcal{W}(M,1) \supset \mathcal{W}(M,2) \supset \cdots \supset \mathcal{W}(M), \qquad \text{all} \quad M. \tag{11}$$

The next result validates intuition in its assertion that the more risk averse individual searches less (i.e., stops sooner) and, equivalently, is less selective in that he accepts all offers the less risk averse individual accepts in addition to some that the less risk averse individual does not accept. Nachman was the first to rigorously derive this result (see Theorem 11 of [13] and Theorem 6 of [14]). He did so by developing a number of properties of stopping times in a broad setting. His method entails a rather sophisticated approach, whereas our proof merely utilizes the fact that, *ceterus paribus*, the more risk averse individual has a higher risk premium. (Additionally, our version does not require $E(X_1^2) < \infty$ as does Nachman's [13, p. 18].)

[7] Again we abbreviate the notation both for convenience and to highlight the parameter of interest. More formally, (9) reads

$$\pi(x, Z, \mathcal{U}) \geqslant \pi(x, Z, U) \qquad \text{for all} \quad x \quad \text{and} \quad Z \quad \text{whenever} \quad r_{\mathcal{U}} \geqslant r_U.$$

Theorem 2. If $r_{\mathfrak{U}} \geqslant r_U$, then the acceptance sets satisfy

$$\mathfrak{W}(M,U,i) \subset \mathfrak{W}(M,\mathfrak{U},i), \qquad \text{all} \quad M, \quad \text{all} \quad i \leqslant +\infty. \tag{12}$$

Proof. Fix M and $i \leqslant +\infty$ and select $w \in \mathfrak{W}(M,U,i)$ so that $U(M+w) \geqslant EU(M+Y_U)$. Then

$$\begin{aligned}\mathfrak{U}(M+w) &= \mathfrak{U} \circ U^{-1} \circ U(M+w) \\ &\geqslant \mathfrak{U} \circ U^{-1}(EU(M+Y_U)) \\ &\geqslant \mathfrak{U} \circ U^{-1}(EU(M+Y_{\mathfrak{U}})) = \mathfrak{U} \circ U^{-1} \circ U(M+EY_{\mathfrak{U}} - \pi_U) \\ &\geqslant \mathfrak{U} \circ U^{-1} \circ U(M+EY_{\mathfrak{U}} - \pi_{\mathfrak{U}}) = \mathfrak{U}(M+EY_{\mathfrak{U}} - \pi_U) \\ &= E\,\mathfrak{U}(M+Y_{\mathfrak{U}}),\end{aligned}$$

where the inequalities follow from $\mathfrak{U} \circ U^{-1}$ nondecreasing, (2) and (9), respectively. Hence, $w \in \mathfrak{W}(M,\mathfrak{U},i)$. QED

Because $r_U \geqslant 0$ for a concave nondecreasing utility function and $r_U = 0$ for a linear utility function, an immediate consequence of Theorem 2 is that regardless of the searcher's wealth or the number of additional observations that can be taken the acceptance set for a concave utility function contains the acceptance set for a linear utility function, that is[8]

$$[\xi, \infty) \subset \mathfrak{W}(M,i), \qquad \text{all} \quad i \leqslant +\infty. \tag{13}$$

While the acceptance set under utility maximization contains the acceptance set under income maximization, it is not as well behaved. In particular, the next example shows that the reservation wage property will not hold in general, that is, the optimal strategy at each stage of the search process cannot be represented by a single critical number such that all offers greater than or equal to it will be accepted and all others rejected. This means that the acceptance set may have "gaps".

Example 1. There may be no reservation wage. Let the distribution F of wages be given by $P(X_1=0.5) = P(X_1=2) = 0.1$ and $P(X_1 = e+0.5) = 0.8$.

[8]Under recall, the reservation wage ξ_n when n periods (observations) remain and the individual is maximizing a linear utility function satisfies $\xi_n \equiv \xi$ (see p. 170 of [9]).

Let $c=0.5$, $M=0$ and

$$U(x)=\begin{cases} \ln(z) & \text{for} \quad z>0, \\ -\infty & \text{for} \quad z\leqslant 0. \end{cases}$$

Regardless of what search strategy is adopted, if $w=0.5$ there is a positive probability that continued search will result in a negative net worth, so that

$$EV(-0.5, 0.5\vee X_1)=-\infty<\ln(0.5)=U(0.5).$$

Thus, an offer of 0.5 will be accepted.

On the other hand, if $w=2$ a strategy of searching once more and then stopping yields an expected utility of $0.20\ \ln(1.5)+0.80\ \ln(e)$ which exceeds $\ln(2)$, the return from accepting $w=2$ immediately. Consequently, it is optimal to continue to search when $w=2$. Thus, a wage of 0.5 is accepted but a wage of 2 is rejected. QED

The explanation of this phenomenon lies in the fact that when searching with recall, the best offer received to date serves as a form of insurance against unsuccessful search in the future. If the searcher has a reasonably good wage offer to which he can return, then the loss in utility from unsuccessful continued search is limited. If, however, the maximum wage offer to date is poor, then searching for one more period and failing to get a better offer might entail a large loss of utility. A high wage offer, in effect, raises the searcher's wealth to the point that he can afford to be more selective.

That there might not be a reservation wage when sampling with recall is due, at least in part, to the fact that if the current wealth is M and an offer of w has been made, then $M+w$ is the "true wealth" with w representing the accrued but as yet unclaimed portion of the searcher's true wealth. In view of this, let μ and w denote the true wealth (as defined above) and the maximum offer received to date, respectively, and define $\mathscr{Q}(\mu,i)$ to be the set of acceptable offers when μ is the true wealth and at most $i(\leqslant +\infty)$ additional offers can be received. The next result[9] establishes the existence of numbers $\xi_{\mu,i}$ such that $\mathscr{Q}(\mu,i)=[\xi_{\mu,i},\infty)$. In this sense the reservation wage property is preserved and $\xi_{\mu,i}$ is the reservation wage.

[9]Theorems 3 and 5 have appeared in [9].

Theorem 3. Given μ and i there is a number $\xi_{\mu,i}$ with the property that

$$\mathcal{A}(\mu,i)=[\xi_{\mu,i},\infty). \tag{14}$$

Moreover,

$$\xi_{\mu,i}\leqslant\xi_{\mu,i+1}, \qquad i=1,2,\ldots,+\infty \tag{15}$$

Proof. Let $\tilde{V}_n(\mu,w)$ be the optimal return when n observations remain. Clearly $\tilde{V}_n$ satisfies $[\tilde{V}_0(\mu,w)=U(\mu)]$

$$\begin{aligned}\tilde{V}_{n+1}(\mu,w)&=\max\left\{U(\mu);\ F(w)\tilde{V}_n(\mu-c,w)\right.\\&\qquad\left.+\int_w^\infty\tilde{V}_n(\mu-c+x-w,x)\,\mathrm{d}F(x)\right\}\\&\equiv\max\{U(\mu);\ \bar{V}_n(\mu,w)\}.\end{aligned} \tag{16}$$

Since $\bar{V}_0(\mu,w)=F(w)U(\mu-c)+\int_w^\infty U(\mu-c+x-w)\,\mathrm{d}F(x)$, the fact that U is a nondecreasing function implies that $\bar{V}_0(\mu,w)$ is nonincreasing in w and nondecreasing in μ. Assume it to be true for $\bar{V}_{n-1}(\mu,w)$ so that $\tilde{V}_n(\mu,w)$ is nonincreasing in w and nondecreasing in μ. Then

$$\begin{aligned}\bar{V}_n(\mu,w)&=F(w)\tilde{V}_n(\mu-c,w)+\int_w^{w+\varepsilon}\tilde{V}_n(\mu-c+x-w,x)\,\mathrm{d}F(x)\\&\quad+\int_{w+\varepsilon}^\infty\tilde{V}_n(\mu-c+x-w,x)\,\mathrm{d}F(x)\\&\geqslant F(w)\tilde{V}_n(\mu-c,w+\varepsilon)+\int_w^{w+\varepsilon}\tilde{V}_n(\mu-c+x-w,w+\varepsilon)\,\mathrm{d}F(x)\\&\quad+\int_{w+\varepsilon}^\infty\tilde{V}_n(\mu-c+x-w,x)\,\mathrm{d}F(x)\\&\geqslant F(w+\varepsilon)\tilde{V}_n(\mu-c,w+\varepsilon)+\int_{w+\varepsilon}^\infty\tilde{V}_n(\mu-c+x-w,x)\,\mathrm{d}F(x)\\&\geqslant\bar{V}_n(\mu,w+\varepsilon),\end{aligned}$$

which completes the induction step. This establishes the existence of a reservation wage $\xi_{\mu,n}$ for the n-period problem. Since $\tilde{V}_{n+1}\geqslant\tilde{V}_n$, the optimal return function $\tilde{V}$ satisfies $\tilde{V}(\mu, w) = \lim_{n\to\infty} \tilde{V}_n(\mu, w) = \max\{U(\mu), \bar{V}(\mu, w)\}$, whence the existence of ξ_μ follows. The monotonicity of $\xi_{\mu,i}$ in i stems from $\tilde{V}_{n+1} \geqslant \tilde{V}_n$. QED

As was noted earlier, expected income maximizing search has the property that the optimal strategy is myopic. A myopic policy is, of course, particularly attractive, since the reservation wage and optimal value functions are rather easy to deal with, both computationally and analytically. In expected utility maximizing search, the myopic policy is defined in terms of $\Delta U(M, w)$, the expected increase in utility from searching exactly once more; that is,

$$\Delta U(M,w) = EU[M - c + (w \vee X_1)] - U(M + w). \tag{17}$$

The myopic decision rule accepts any wage w that makes $\Delta U(M,w)$ nonpositive. Example 2 reveals the unfortunate fact that in general the myopic policy is not optimal.

Example 2. The myopic policy may not be optimal. Let the parameters be as in Example 1, but set $M = 2\times 10^{-7}$. Compare the expected utility when in state $(M, w) = (2\times 10^{-7}, 0.5)$ under the following three strategies:

Strategy (a) Search exactly once more.
Strategy (b) Search once more; then stop if an offer of 0.5 or $e+0.5$ is received, but search exactly once more if an offer of 2 is received.
Strategy (c) Do not search.

Denoting the expected utility from using strategy α when in state (M, w) by E_α, we have

$$E_a \approx 0.10\ln(2\times 10^{-7}) + 0.10\ln(1.5) + 0.80\ln(e) \approx -0.7019,$$

$$E_a U(-0.5, 2) \approx 0.2\ln(1.0) + 0.80\ln(e - 0.5) \approx 0.6374,$$

$$E_b \approx 0.10\ln(2\times 10^{-7}) + 0.10\, E_a V(-0.5, 2) + 0.80\ln(e) \approx -0.6788,$$

$$E_c \approx \ln(0.5) \approx -0.6931.$$

Since $E_b > \max(E_a, E_c)$, the myopic policy is not optimal. (The failure of the myopic policy to be optimal in this example is a direct consequence of the existence of gaps in the acceptance set.) QED

Example 1 indicated that an individual tends to be more selective in job search the higher his best offer to date. Similarly, one would expect that if the individual's wealth also acts as insurance against unsuccessful search, then the set of acceptable wages would shrink as wealth increases. To ensure that wealth offers such insurance, we assume that the absolute risk aversion function r_U is decreasing.

Theorem 4. If r_U is decreasing, then the set of acceptable wage offers is decreasing in wealth, that is,

$$\mathcal{W}(M+\varepsilon,i)\subset\mathcal{W}(M,i), \qquad \text{all} \quad M,i\leqslant+\infty, \quad \varepsilon>0. \tag{18}$$

Proof. Fix $M,i\leqslant+\infty$, $\varepsilon>0$ and pick $w\in\mathcal{W}(M,i)$. From (6) and then (2) we obtain

$$U(M+w)\geqslant EU(M+Y_M)\geqslant EU(M+Y_{M-\varepsilon}). \tag{19}$$

From (19) we see that there is a $\gamma\geqslant0$ such that

$$U(M+w)=EU(M+Y_{M-\varepsilon}+\gamma). \tag{20}$$

Coupling (8) and (20) yields

$$M+w=M+\gamma+EY_{M-\varepsilon}-\pi_{M+\gamma}. \tag{21}$$

Utilizing (21), (10), and $U'\geqslant0$ yields

$$\begin{aligned} U(M-\varepsilon+w) &= U(M-\varepsilon+\gamma+EY_{M-\varepsilon}-\pi_{M+\gamma}) \\ &\geqslant U(M-\varepsilon+\gamma+EY_{M-\varepsilon}-\pi_{M-\varepsilon+\gamma}) \\ &= EU(M-\varepsilon+\gamma+Y_{M-\varepsilon}) \\ &\geqslant EU(M-\varepsilon+Y_{M-\varepsilon}). \end{aligned}$$

Hence, $w\in\mathcal{W}(M-\varepsilon,i)$. QED

Decreasing absolute risk aversion also yields an increasing reservation wage with respect to true wealth.

Theorem 5. If r_U is decreasing, then

$$\xi_{\mu+\varepsilon,i}\geqslant\xi_{\mu,i}, \qquad \text{all} \quad i\leqslant+\infty, \quad \varepsilon>0. \tag{22}$$

Proof. Fix $\mu, i \leqslant +\infty$, and $\varepsilon>0$. If $\xi_{\mu+\varepsilon}<\xi_{\mu}$, then $\xi_{\mu+\varepsilon}\in\mathcal{A}(\mu+\varepsilon)$ and $\xi_{\mu+\varepsilon}\notin\mathcal{A}(\mu)$. Equivalently, $\xi_{\mu+\varepsilon}\in\mathcal{W}(\mu+\varepsilon-\xi_{\mu+\varepsilon})$ and $\xi_{\mu+\varepsilon}\notin\mathcal{W}(\mu-\xi_{\mu+\varepsilon})$. But this contradicts (18). QED

As search proceeds, the individual's wealth decreases by c with each offer received. Accordingly, an immediate consequence of Theorem 4 is the fact that the individual's acceptance set grows as search continues. This is in marked contrast to the standard case of search with a linear utility function (Assumption 6) where the set of acceptable wages remains unchanged regardless of the duration of search or the individual's wealth.[10]

In the case of adaptive search wherein the distribution function F is not known with certainty, the optimal strategy also entails an adjustment of the acceptance set as the search process proceeds. Under adaptive search, however, the specific values of all rejected offers influence the acceptance set whereas in our model the acceptance set only depends upon the current level of wealth and thus on the number of searches to date.

More striking than the searcher's changing acceptance set is the fact that the recall option will, on occasion, be utilized.[11] For instance, the optimal strategy in Example 1 is to search from state (2,0), but after three consecutive unsuccessful searches it is optimal to accept the previously bypassed offer of 2. Again, this fact distinguishes the general model from the linear case where the recall option is never used.

If there is a level of final net worth which is unacceptable in the sense of having utility equal to minus infinity, then not only will the search process be finite with probability 1, it will be bounded in length. We make this notion precise in the next theorem.[12]

Theorem 6. If $E(X_1^2)<\infty$ and there is a constant b such that $\lim_{x\to b^+}U'(x)=+\infty$, then the search process is bounded. That is, given M there is an integer B_M such that one of the first B_M wage offers will be accepted.

Proof. Let Z be a random variable having the same distribution as $\sup Y_n$, where $Y_i=\max(X_1,X_2,\ldots,X_i)-ic$. A direct application of the Borel–Cantelli lemma in conjunction with $E(X_1^2)$ establishes that $E(|Z|)<\infty$. We

[10]There are variants of the standard model which yield decreasing reservation wages. For example, the reservation wage drops if there is systematic search (see [22]).

[11]In the finite horizon model with recall and linear utility function, the recall option is, on occasion, exercised; however, it is exercised only after receipt of all offers.

[12]A similar result is contained in Rothschild [20].

shall now demonstrate that the return from any state (M,w) with $M+w<b-E(Z)$ is minus infinity. To begin, note that the final net worth from optimal search when the state is (M,w) is bounded above by $M+w+Z$, which in turn is less than $b-E(Z)+Z$. Because Z is not degenerate (otherwise $Z=Y_1$ and X_1 is degenerate in which case all offers are accepted), we have

$$P(M+w+Z \geqslant b) \leqslant P(Z-E(Z) \geqslant 0) < 1.$$

Thus, there is a positive probability that the final net worth will be less than b so that the expected utility associated with state (M,w) is minus infinity.

From (13) we know that any offer of ξ or more will be accepted. Therefore, at most $B_M=[M+\xi-(b-E(Z))]/c$ offers can be received until: (i) a state with $M+w<b-E(Z)$ is reached, or (ii) an offer of ξ or more is received. QED

Using Theorem 6, it is an easy matter to verify that $V(M,w)$ is jointly continuous on the set of states with $M+w>b-E(Z)$ where Z is defined in the proof of Theorem 6.[13] If all wages are not acceptable (i.e., $\mathcal{W}(M) \neq [0,\infty)$), then the continuity of $V(M,w)$ and $U(M+w)$ in w yields the existence of an "indifference wage",[14] that is, a wage w_M satisfying $U(M+w)=EU(M+Y_{M,w})$.

In the next example, we make use of the existence of an indifference wage to show that increasing the riskiness of the distribution F does not necessarily lead to a smaller set of acceptable wages as is true for linear utility functions [7].[15] Increasing the riskiness of F can lead to an increase or to a decrease in the set of acceptable wages.

[13]To do so, note that the continuity of U yields that of V_1, and a simple induction argument establishes that V_i is continuous for each i. But now the finiteness of the search process implies that $V(M,w)=V_{B_M}(M,w)$ which, in view of the fact that the integer B_M jumps by at most one on any $(M-)$ interval of length c, allows us to assert the continuity of V.

[14]Because $\mathcal{W}(M) \neq [0,\infty)$, there is a w_0 such that $E(M+Y_{M,w_0})>U(M+w_0)$. On the other hand, we know from Theorem 2 that $U(M+\xi) \geqslant EU(M+Y_{M,\xi})$. Thus, the continuous function $g(w) \equiv EU(M+Y_{M,w})-U(M+w)$ is positive at w_0 and nonpositive at ξ, yielding existence of a wage satisfying $g(w)=0$ as desired.

[15]Let ξ_g and ξ_f be the reservation wages corresponding to the random variables G and F having densities g and f, where $g=f+s$ and s is a mean preserving spread as per (23). As is clear upon inspection from (23), we have

$$H_g(x)=\int_x^\infty (y-x)g(y)\,dy$$

$$=H_f(x)+\int_x^\infty (y-x)s(y)\,dy \geqslant H_f(x), \qquad \text{all } x.$$

Before demonstrating that both changes are possible, we note that we are using the term riskiness in the sense of Rothschild and Stiglitz [21]. To wit, a distribution function G with density g is said to be riskier than F with density f if there is a mean preserving spread[16] s such that $g = f + s$, where

$$s(x) \begin{cases} \alpha & \text{for} \quad a < x < a + t, \\ -\alpha & \text{for} \quad a + d < x < a + d + t, \\ -\beta & \text{for} \quad b < x < b + t, \\ \beta & \text{for} \quad b + e < x < b + e + t, \\ 0 & \text{otherwise,} \end{cases} \tag{23}$$

$\alpha > 0, \beta > 0, 0 \leqslant a \leqslant a + t \leqslant a + d \leqslant a + d + t \leqslant b \leqslant b + t \leqslant b + e \leqslant b + e + t$, and $\beta e = \alpha d$.

Example 3. Let U have strictly decreasing absolute risk aversion (so U' is strictly decreasing), and choose M, c, F, and U so that $\mathscr{W}(M) \neq [0, \infty)$. Then there is an indifference wage w_M. Now define $V(M, w, f_1, f_2)$ to be the expected utility associated with initial state (M, w_M) and continued search when f_1 is the density of the wage offer distribution but the searcher has adopted a search strategy that would be optimal if in fact f_2 were the density of the wage offer distribution.

First we show that if s is a mean preserving spread with $g = f + s$, then $\mathscr{W}_g(M)$ may not contain w_M even though $\mathscr{W}_f(M)$ does, where $\mathscr{W}_k(M)$ is used to denote the acceptance set when the underlying distribution has density k. It suffices to demonstrate that

$$V(M, w_M, g, f) > V(M, w_M, f, f), \tag{24}$$

for with (24) we would then have

$$V(M, w_M, g, g) \geqslant V(M, w_M, g, f) > V(M, w_M, f, f) = U(M + w_M), \tag{25}$$

which reveals the desired conclusion that $w_M \notin \mathscr{W}_g(M)$.

But too, $H_f(\xi_f) = c = H_g(\xi_g) \geqslant H_f(\xi_g)$ so the decreasing nature of H_f yields $\xi_f \leqslant \xi_g$.

An alternative proof could be based on second order stochastic dominance as follows. Define C_x by $C_x(y) = 0$ for $y \leqslant x$ and $C_x(y) = (y - x)$ for $y > x$. Hence C_x is convex. Consequently,

$$H_g(x) = EC_x(G) \geqslant EC_x(F) = H_f(x), \qquad \text{each } x.$$

[16]Note that a random variable with density g has the same mean as one with density f and that its variance is larger since $\int_0^\infty s(x)\,\mathrm{d}x = 0$ and $\int_0^\infty x^2 s(x)\,\mathrm{d}x > 0$.

By virtue of Theorem 3, $w_M \in \mathcal{W}_f(M-c)$ so if f is thought to be the density of the wage offer distribution and one more offer must be taken, then the searcher will stop with the next offer. Thus, if s is selected so that $b+e=w_M$, we obtain

$$\begin{aligned} V(M,w_M,g,f)-V(M,w_M,f,f) &= E_g U(M-c+(X_1 \vee w_M)) \\ &\quad - E_f U(M-c+(X_1 \vee w_M)) \\ &= \int_0^{w_M} U(M-c+w_M)s(x)\,\mathrm{d}x \\ &\quad + \int_{w_M}^{\infty} U(M-c+x)s(x)\,\mathrm{d}x \\ &= -\beta t U(M-c+w_M) \\ &\quad + \beta \int_{b+e}^{b+e+t} U(M-c+x)\,\mathrm{d}x > 0, \end{aligned}$$

where the inequality follows from the fact that U is strictly increasing. This verifies (24) and, hence, the fact that $w_M \notin \mathcal{W}_g(M)$.

To demonstrate the more striking possibility, *viz.* $w \in \mathcal{W}_g(M)$ and $w \notin \mathcal{W}_f(M)$, requires a more delicate argument. We begin by selecting s so that $a=w_M$ and verifying that (24) holds. To do so necessitates the use of the following inequalities which are an immediate consequence of $U'>0$ and $U''<0$:

$$(y-x)U'(y) < U(y)-U(x) < (y-x)U'(x), \qquad \text{for} \quad y>x \tag{26}$$

and

$$\begin{aligned} (y-x)[U(y+z)-U(y)] &< \int_{x+z}^{y+z} U(v)\,\mathrm{d}v - \int_x^y U(v)\,\mathrm{d}v \\ &< (y-x)[U(x+z)-U(x)], \end{aligned}$$

$$\text{for} \quad y>x \quad \text{and} \quad z>0. \tag{27}$$

Utilizing (27), (26), $b>a+d+t$, and $\beta e=\alpha d$ yields[17]

$$V(M,w_M,g,f)-V(M,w_M,f,f)$$

$$=\int_0^{w_M} U(M-c+w_M)s(x)\,\mathrm{d}x+\int_{w_M}^{\infty} U(M-c+x)s(x)\,\mathrm{d}x$$

$$=\alpha\int_a^{a+t} U(M-c+x)\,\mathrm{d}x-\alpha\int_{a+d}^{a+d+t} U(M-c+x)\,\mathrm{d}x$$

$$+\beta\int_{b+e}^{b+e+t} U(M-c+x)\,\mathrm{d}x-\beta\int_b^{b+t} U(M-c+x)\,\mathrm{d}x$$

$$<-\alpha t\left[U(M-c+a+d+t)-U(M-c+a+d)\right]$$

$$+\beta t\left[U(M-c+b+e)-U(M-c+b)\right]$$

$$<-\alpha tdU'(M-c+a+d+t)+\beta teU'(M-c+b)$$

$$<(-\alpha td+\beta te)U'(M-c+a+d+t)$$

$$=0.$$

Thus,

$$V(M,w_M,g,f)<U(M+w_M). \tag{28}$$

Without loss of generality we can assume that w_M is the largest indifference wage; hence, $[w_M,\infty)\subset\mathcal{W}_f(M)$. Consequently, we can employ (28) and the continuity of U and V to assert that there is an $\varepsilon>0$ such that

$$V(M,w,g,f)\leqslant U(M+w),\qquad \text{for all}\quad w\geqslant w_M-\varepsilon. \tag{29}$$

[17]A simpler argument than the one based on (26) and (27) relies on the fact that if X is riskier than Y in the sense of second order stochastic dominance, then $Eu(X)\leqslant Eu(Y)$ for all concave increasing functions u.

Equation (29) states that stopping is preferable to taking exactly one more observation. Unfortunately this is not enough to imply that $w \in \mathcal{W}_g(M)$ for all $w \geqslant w_M - \varepsilon$, for Example 2 shows that myopic policies need not be optimal. However, (29) is equivalent to

$$EU(X-c+(y \vee X_1)) \leqslant U(x+y) \qquad \text{for} \quad x \leqslant M \quad \text{and} \quad y \geqslant w_M - \varepsilon, \tag{30}$$

where X_1 has density g. The fact that (30) holds for $x<M$ stems from Theorems 4 and 6.

Now define $V_i(x,y)$ as in (1) but with X_1 having density g rather than f. The virtue of (30) is that it enables us to begin an induction argument to verify that

$$V_i(x,y) = U(x+y), \qquad \text{for} \quad x \leqslant M \quad \text{and} \quad y \geqslant w_M - \varepsilon. \tag{31}$$

To begin, note that (31) holds for $i=1$ by (30). Assume (31) holds for i. Then by hypothesis and (30),

$$\begin{aligned} V_{i+1}(x,y) &= \max\{U(x+y), EV_i(x-c, y \vee X_1)\} \\ &= \max\{U(x+y), EU(X-c+(y \vee X_1))\} = U(x+y). \end{aligned}$$

This completes the induction. Consequently,

$$V(M,w) = \lim_{i \to \infty} V_i(M,w) = V(M+w) \qquad \text{for} \quad w \geqslant w_M - \varepsilon.$$

Thus, we see that it is optimal to stop from state (M,w) if $w \geqslant w_M - \varepsilon$ when X_1 has density g. That is, $w \in \mathcal{W}_g(M)$ if $w \geqslant w_M - \varepsilon$. QED

We conclude this section by noting that the optimal return V need not inherit the properties of U. For example, V is not necessarily concave in the level of wealth. This raises the possibility that an individual pursuing an optimal strategy will accept some actuarially fair or even unfair gamble even though he is strictly risk averse (i.e., $U'' < 0$). In the next example we demonstrate that this can indeed occur.

Example 4. Unfair gambles may be accepted. Let the utility function, search costs, and distribution over wage rates be as in Example 1. Let wealth be zero and the best wage offer to date be 0.5. Suppose that the searcher is offered a bet such that he wins or loses the amount 2×10^{-7} with probability of $\frac{1}{2}$ for each outcome. If the bet is not accepted then the searcher will accept the wage offer of 0.5 and will have the utility level $\ln(0.5)\approx -0.6931$ with certainty. On the other hand, if the offer is accepted then with probability $\frac{1}{2}$ he will: (a) win, whence the expected utility will be at least -0.6788 (see Example 2); and (b) lose and accept the offer of 0.5 for a utility level of $\ln(0.5-2\times 10^{-7})\approx -0.6931$. Consequently, the expected utility from accepting the bet is at least -0.6860 as opposed to -0.6931 from rejecting it. The searcher will accept an actuarially fair gamble even though his utility function is strictly concave. QED

4. Expected utility maximizing search without recall

In this section we assume that the recall option is not available. As will soon be revealed, this simplifies the analysis and induces the existence of reservation wages.

When we say that the searcher is in state (M,w), we mean that his current wealth is M and the *last* offer (as opposed to the best so far) received is still available and equal to w. The random variable $Y(M,w,U,i)$ is defined as in section 3. Because w represents the value of the currently available offer and recall is not allowed, $Y(M,w,U,i)$ does not depend upon w.

Next, define $V_i^*(M,w)$ to be the maximum expected utility that can be attained when the searcher is in state (M,w) and at most i more offers can be received. Then $V_i^*(M,w)$ satisfies $[V_0^*(M,w)=U(M+w)]$.

$$\begin{aligned} V_i^*(M,w) &= \max\{U(M+w);\ EU(M+Y(M,U,i))\} \\ &= \max\{U(M+w);\ EV_{i-1}^*(M-c,X_1)\} \\ &\equiv \max\{U(M+w);\ V_{i-1}(M)\}. \end{aligned} \tag{32}$$

Because the obvious analogs of (2) and (3) hold, we can employ the concavity of U and the finiteness of $E(X_1)$ to ensure V^*, defined by

$$V^*(M,w)=\lim_{i\to\infty} V_i^*(M,w), \tag{33}$$

exists and that V^* satisfies the functional equation

$$V^*(M,w)=\max\{U(M+w);\ EV^*(M-c,X_1)\}$$
$$=\max\{U(M+w);\ V(M)\}. \tag{34}$$

Furthermore, a straightforward application of the Lebesgue Dominated Convergence Theorem enables us to assert that

$$V(M)=\lim_{i\to\infty} V_i(M). \tag{35}$$

Denote the set of acceptable wages by $\mathscr{W}^*(M,U,i)$ for $i<\infty$ and by $\mathscr{W}^*(M,U)$ when the number of additional offers that can be received is unlimited. The monotonicity of $V_i(M)$ in i and the fact that $V_i(M)$ is not a function of the wage offer allows us to obtain sharper results than those in Theorem 1.

Theorem 7. There are numbers $W^*(M)$ and $W^*(M,i), i=1,2,\ldots,$ referred to as reservation wages, which satisfy

$$\mathscr{W}^*(M,i)=[W^*(M,i),\infty), \tag{36}$$

$$\mathscr{W}^*(M)=[W^*(M),\infty) \tag{37}$$

$$W^*(M,i)\leqslant W^*(M,i+1), \qquad i=1,2,\ldots, \tag{38}$$

and

$$W^*(M)=\lim_{i\to\infty} W^*(M,i). \tag{39}$$

A point of considerable interest is the relationship between the acceptance sets $\mathscr{W}(M,i)$ and $\mathscr{W}^*(M,i)$. As anticipated, the reservation wage when recall is not permitted is no greater than the smallest acceptable wage when recall is allowed, that is, $\mathscr{W}(M,i)\subset\mathscr{W}^*(M,i)$. All that is needed to obtain this result is

$$V_i(M,w)\geqslant V_i^*(M,w), \tag{40}$$

which can be established with a simple induction argument.

Theorem 8. Given M,

$$W^*(M,i)\leqslant w_{M,i}, \qquad i=1,2,\ldots, \tag{41}$$

and

$$W^*(M) \leqslant w_M, \tag{42}$$

where

$$w_{M,i} = \inf\{w : w \in \mathscr{W}(M,i)\}, \qquad i = 1,2,\ldots \tag{43}$$

and

$$w_M = \lim_{i\to\infty} w_{M,i} = \inf\{w : w \in \mathscr{W}(M)\}. \tag{44}$$

Proof. Fix M and $i < \infty$ and pick $w \in \mathscr{W}(M,i)$. Then by (40),

$$U(M+w) \geqslant V_i(M,w) \geqslant V_i^*(M,w). \tag{45}$$

This establishes (41). Next, pick $w \in \mathscr{W}(M)$ so $w \in \mathscr{W}(M,i)$ for all i by (11). This last fact coupled with (45) shows that $w \geqslant W^*(M,i)$ for all i, whence $w \geqslant W^*(M)$ by (39). QED

The proof of Theorem 2 suffices to establish:

Theorem 9. If $r_{\mathscr{U}} > r_U$, then the reservation wages satisfy

$$W^*(M,\mathscr{U},i) \leqslant W^*(M,U,i), \qquad \text{all } M \quad \text{and} \quad i \leqslant +\infty. \tag{46}$$

Denote by ξ_i and ξ_i^* the reservation wage when at most i more offers can be received in the presence of a linear utility function, with and without recall, respectively. It has been shown [9, pp. 167 f] that

$$\xi_i^* \nearrow \xi \quad \text{and} \quad \xi_i \equiv \xi. \tag{47}$$

Notice that (12), (41), (42), (46) and (47) spell out the relationship between the set of acceptable wages under expected income maximization, expected utility maximization with recall, and expected utility maximization without recall; namely,

$$[\xi_i, \infty) \subset \mathscr{W}(M,i) \subset \mathscr{W}^*(M,i), \qquad i \leqslant +\infty, \tag{48}$$

and

$$[\xi_i^*, \infty) \subset \mathscr{W}^*(M,i), \qquad i \leqslant +\infty. \tag{49}$$

Alternatively, $W^*(M,i) \leqslant w_{M,i} \leqslant \xi_i$ and $W^*(M,i) \leqslant \xi_i^*$. Evidently, we need not have a relationship which always holds between $[\xi_i^*, \infty)$ and $\mathcal{W}(M,i)$.

The proof of Theorem 4 suffices to verify monotonicity of the reservation wage as a function of wealth in the presence of decreasing absolute risk aversion.

Theorem 10. If r_U is decreasing, then the acceptance sets $\mathcal{W}^*(M,i)$ are nonincreasing in M; in particular [18]

$$W^*(M,i) \leqslant W^*(M+\varepsilon,i), \qquad \text{all } M, \varepsilon > 0, \quad i \leqslant +\infty. \tag{50}$$

In the presence of recall, we saw that increasing the riskiness of f via adding a mean preserving spread s could lead to a smaller or to a larger set of acceptable wages. It is easy to verify that both changes can occur without the recall option. We do so in a heuristic manner. First, from the argument immediately preceding (28) we obtain $E_g U(M-c+Y) - E_f U(M-c+X) < 0$ if $U'' < 0$, where X has density f and Y has density $g = f+s$. Consequently, the reservation wage when only one more offer can be received is higher under f. Clearly this result can be extended by selecting U and M so that even without any restriction on the number of offers that can be received from (M,w) it is optimal to accept w under g and take exactly one more offer under f. Conversely, if U is nearly linear, then it will be optimal to be more selective under g than under f.

Finally, we note that typically the myopic policy will not be optimal. This results from the fact that $EV^*(M-c, X_1)$ can be significantly larger than $EU(M-c+X_1)$, so that basing the acceptance decision on the sign of $U(M+w) - EU(M-c+X_1)$ (which is what the myopic policy does) leads to an overly conservative decision rule. That is, the myopic policy's acceptance sets are too large.

References

[1] Arrow, K. J., *Essays in the Theory of Risk Bearing*, Markham Publishing Company, Chicago, 1971.

[2] Burdett, K., "Theories of search in a labor market", unpublished manuscript, Northwestern University, October 1973.

[3] Danforth, J. P., "Expected utility, infinite horizon and job search", Discussion Paper No. 74–42, Center for Economic Research, University of Minnesota, June 1974.

[18] It is somewhat surprising that (50) obtains in spite of the fact that $V_2(\cdot, w)$ is not concave even if we assume $U''' \geqslant 0$. The assumption that U has a convex derivative implies that (50) holds when $i=1$ as well as that r_U is decreasing.

[4] Danforth, J. P., "Expected utility, mandatory retirement and job search", Discussion Paper No. 74-41, Center for Economic Research, University of Minnesota, June 1974. (Also presented orally at various universities in 1971 and 1972.)

[5] Danforth, J. P., "Wealth and the value of generalized lotteries", *Journal of Economic Theory*, 15 (1977), 54–71.

[6] Diamond, P. A. and Stiglitz, J. E., "Increases in risk and in risk aversion", *Journal of Economic Theory*, 8 (1974), 337–360.

[7] Kohn, M. G., and Shavell, S., "The theory of search", *Journal of Economic Theory*, 9 (1974), 93–124.

[8] Lippman, S. A., and McCall, J. J., "Job search in a dynamic economy", *Journal of Economic Theory*, 12 (1976), 365–390.

[9] Lippman, S. A., and McCall, J. J., "The economics of job search: a survey", Parts I and II, *Economic Inquiry*, 14 (1976), 155–189 and 347–368.

[10] McCall, J. J., "The economics of information and optimal stopping rules", *Journal of Business*, 38 (1965), 300–317.

[11] McCall, J. J., "Economics of information and job search", *Quarterly Journal of Economics*, 84 (1970), 113–126.

[12] McCall, J. J., "Probabilistic microeconomics", *Bell Journal of Economics and Management Science*, 2 (1971), 403–433.

[13] Nachman, D. C., "On risk aversion and optimal stopping", unpublished paper, Northwestern University, 1972.

[14] Nachman, D. C., "Risk aversion, impatience, and optimal timing decisions", *Journal of Economic Theory*, 11 (1975), 196–246.

[15] Nelson, P., "Information and consumer behavior", *Journal of Political Economy*, 78 (1970), 311–329.

[16] Pratt, J. W., "Risk aversion in the small and in the large", *Econometrica*, 32 (1964), 122–136.

[17] Robbins, H., "Optimal stopping", *The American Mathematical Monthly*, 77 (1970), 333–343.

[18] Ross, S. M., *Applied Probability Models with Optimization Applications*, Holden-Day, San Francisco, 1970.

[19] Rothschild, M., "Models of market organization with imperfect information: a survey", *Journal of Political Economy*, 81 (1973), 1283–1308.

[20] Rothschild, M., "Searching for the lowest price when the distribution of prices is unknown", *Journal of Political Economy*, 82 (1974), 689–712.

[21] Rothschild, M., and Stiglitz, J., "Increasing risk I: a definition", *Journal of Economic Theory*, 2 (1970), 225–243.

[22] Salop, S. C., "Systematic job search and unemployment", *Review of Economic Studies*, 40 (1973), 191–201.

[23] Stigler, G. J., "Information in the labor market", *Journal of Political Economy*, 70 (1962), 94–104.

[24] Stigler, G. J., "The economics of information", *Journal of Political Economy*, 69 (1961), 213–225.

CHAPTER 8

Search, leisure and individual labor supply

KENNETH BURDETT*

University of Wisconsin, Madison

1. Introduction

The purpose of this study is to make some progress in integrating the standard analysis of an individual worker's labor supply decision with the job search approach to this topic. This will be achieved by allowing workers to make allocation of time decisions within the context of a labor market with imperfect information about the wages available. Alternatively, the model constructed can be perceived as a job search model in which workers can vary their search intensity. It will be shown that this leads to new and empirically relevant insights into the labor supply choice. Only the short-run labor supply model will be considered in this study. Nevertheless, the framework developed appears general enough to contemplate analyzing the long-run labor supply decision in a later study.

The most commonly presented theory of an individual's labor supply decision analyzes the percentage of a period a worker will elect to work, given there is a known, fixed wage rate associated with working. The well known single period version of this class of models involves a worker whose utility is a positive function of the leisure time consumed and the income earned. The problem for a worker is to choose the percentage of the period to spend working when faced with a given wage rate. It has been shown many times that a utility maximizing worker will select leisure and work times such that the ratio of the marginal utilities of leisure time

*I would like to thank Dale Mortensen and the anonymous referees for their helpful comments. They are, of course, not responsible for the remaining errors. This research was supported by funds granted to the Institute for the Research on Poverty at the University of Wisconsin-Madison by the Department of Health, Education, and Welfare pursuant to the Economic Opportunity Act of 1964.

and income equals the wage rate faced.[1] Hence, given the usual convexity assumptions are made about an individual's preferences, there is a unique utility maximizing choice of leisure time and work time for any given wage rate. The individual labor supply function can then be derived by determining the effects on work time supplied of changes in the known wage rate. Of course, at low wage rates a worker may decide to supply no work time in the period.

The majority of job search studies presented to date have considered the following basic model.[2] Suppose an unemployed worker knows the probability of receiving a job offer in each period. A job offer is perceived as a random draw from a known, nondegenerate distribution of wage offers in the market. A worker who accepts an offer from a firm earns the offered wage each period until employment is terminated. A worker, however, receives no job offers while employed. Workers are assumed to maximize their own expected discounted lifetime incomes. It has been shown many times that the best strategy for an unemployed worker can be characterized by an optimal reservation wage in each period of unemployment. A job offer is accepted if and only if the wage offered is at least as great as the relevant optimal reservation wage.

Workers envisaged in the standard analysis of labor supply elect not to work at a given wage because of a preference for leisure. Workers portrayed in job search models turn down job offers because the wage offered implies an income less than the expected income from receiving at least one more job offer. In the present study a worker is assumed to face a labor market similar to that utilized in job search studies. There are two important differences. First, a worker is assumed to maximize expected lifetime utility, which is "a function of leisure time and of income earned" in each period. Second, a worker is assumed capable of increasing the probability of receiving a job offer by sacrificing leisure in that period.

In Section 2 the utility maximizing strategy of an unemployed worker is characterized for any given length of unemployment. It will be shown that this involves the selection of a reservation wage and leisure choice in the next period. Further, it is shown how these choices change as the duration of unemployment increases.

[1]To demonstrate this result let $u(y,l)$ denote the single period utility accruing to a worker who earns income y and enjoys leisure l. As a worker can only work or enjoy leisure, $y=w(1-l)$, where w is the wage rate faced by that worker. Maximizing $u(y,l)$ subject to $y=w(1-l)$ yields the result stated in the paper.

[2]Lippman and McCall [4] have produced a good survey of the job search literature. Most of the assumptions made in the present study are discussed in detail in this survey.

In a recent study Lippman and McCall [4] have developed a variable job search intensity model somewhat similar to that presented in this paper.[3] There are two differences. First, in this paper some attempt will be made to relate the job search model to the standard labor supply model. Hence it is assumed that individuals maximize expected lifetime utility and the cost of increasing search intensity is the extra leisure sacrificed. Lippman and McCall assume workers maximize lifetime incomes and do not specify why the cost of search increases with intensity. Second, Lippman and McCall [4] demonstrate that an unemployed worker's search intensity will change if and only if the distribution of wage offers changes. In the present study it is shown that an unemployed worker will vary search intensity as the duration of unemployment increases, even if the distribution of wage offers remains constant through time.

Most job search models presented to date assume workers do not look for another job while employed. Recently it has been shown that this restriction can only be justified if the cost of search while employed is great relative to the cost when unemployed; and this is not the case in many actual labor markets.[4] In the present study workers will be allowed to look for a job while employed. Employed workers select the percentage of a period to spend (a) working, (b) enjoying leisure and (c) looking for another job. The more time allocated to work, the greater the current income. The more time spent in leisure, the greater the current utility. Nevertheless, a worker may be willing to sacrifice some work and leisure time to look for another job because of the possible future gains in that a better wage rate may be offered. It will be shown in Section 3 that the utility maximizing choices of these uses of time are functions of the wage rate faced by the worker.

2. The search and leisure decisions of unemployed workers

In this section a model of a labor market is described that is similar in most respects to many others used in the job search literature. This framework, plus new assumptions about worker behavior, will be used to analyze the time an unemployed worker assigns to (a) looking for a job,

[3] I am grateful to an anonymous referee for pointing out this contribution to the literature.

[4] Burdett [2] and Lippman and McCall [4] have considered a model of job search where workers are allowed to look for a job while employed. Tobin [7] was the first to point out the weakness of job search models that do not allow employee job search. Previous models of job search have not allowed workers to vary their search intensity.

and (b) enjoying leisure. Further, it will be shown how these choices change as the duration of unemployment increases. Other aspects of an unemployed worker's optimal search strategy will be specified.

Suppose time can be divided into periods of equal length, termed search periods. Assume an unemployed worker receives at most one job offer in each period. A job offer is envisaged as a random draw from a known distribution of wage rate offers in the market. Let W denote the random variable of wage rate offers in the market and F the distribution function associated with this random variable. Two restrictions will be imposed on this distribution function. First, assume it has an associated density function f. Second, assume there exists a maximum and minimum wage rate offer in the market, and the density function is strictly positive between these wage rates. Hence $F(w)$ denotes the proportion of job offers in any period with a wage rate less than w. A worker who accepts a job offer faces the offered wage rate in each future period of employment at the firm. All the above is included in the majority of previously presented job search models. Two other commonly used assumptions will also be made. First, workers are assumed to have infinite working lives. Second, a worker is incapable of returning to an offer previously rejected by that worker. Alternatives to these last two assumptions can be used, but the two selected much simplify the exposition.[5]

Suppose a worker can influence the probability of receiving a job offer in a period by sacrificing leisure. Let s and l denote the proportion of a period an unemployed worker spends looking for a job and enjoying leisure respectively and assume $s+l=1$. The greater the proportion of a period spent looking for a job the greater the probability a job offer is received. Specifically, let $\pi(s)$ denote this probability if (100) s per cent is spent looking for a job, and assume

$$\pi(0)=0, \pi'(s)>0, \quad \text{and} \quad \pi''(s)\leqslant 0 \quad \text{for any} \quad 0\leqslant s\leqslant 1. \tag{1}$$

Note that it is assumed the rate of increase in the above probability declines as s increases. It follows that $\pi(s)(1-F(w))$ denotes the probability an unemployed worker who elects to look for a job for s per cent of a period obtains a job offer with a wage rate at least as great as w in that period.

To highlight the issues under consideration only the simplest possible preference structure for each worker is assumed. Specifically, suppose the

[5]The consequences of utilizing alternative assumptions to the two stated are discussed in the study by Lippman and McCall [4].

lifetime utility of a worker is the discounted sum of each future period utility, and the form of each single period utility function is the same. Let $v(y,l)$ indicate the single period utility accruing to a worker who selects to spend l per cent of a period enjoying leisure and receives income y in the period. Suppose this function is unique up to a linear combination, and assume

$$v_y > 0,\ v_l > 0,\ v_{yy} < 0,\ v_{ll} < 0, \quad \text{and} \quad v_{yy}v_{ll} - (v_{yl})^2 > 0. \tag{2}$$

The restrictions imposed by (2) ensure the single period utility function is strictly concave. The precise results obtained in this section depend on the nature of this function. Nevertheless, similar results can be obtained if any separable (by search period) lifetime utility function is assumed which satisfies the usual restrictions.

A worker is assumed to receive unemployment insurance (UI) payment x_t in search period t of a spell of unemployment. The most commonly used UI scheme implies a worker receives a fixed amount in each of the first τ periods of a spell of unemployment. No UI payments are received by workers who have been unemployed more than τ consecutive periods. Formally, let

$$x_t = \begin{cases} u > 0 & \text{if} \quad t \leqslant \tau, \\ 0 & \text{if} \quad t > \tau. \end{cases} \tag{3}$$

Assume in the environment described above a worker attempts to maximize expected discounted lifetime utility. Let $\psi(w)$ denote the expected lifetime utility to a worker who accepts a job offer with wage rate w. Although the precise form of this function will be discussed in a later section, it follows directly that $\psi'(w) \geqslant 0$. Suppose a worker chooses to remain unemployed at least one more period after $t-1$ consecutive periods of unemployment. Let μ_t indicate the maximum expected discounted lifetime utility to a worker who selects to be unemployed at least one more period after $t-1$ periods in a spell. From the assumptions made above it is straightforward to show that the optimal strategy for an unemployed worker involves the selection of a reservation wage rate and leisure choice in each period. A reservation wage rate is defined as the minimum acceptable wage rate offer to a worker. Hence μ_t can be written as

$$\mu_t = \max_{\substack{0 < l < 1, \\ w}} \{ v(x_t, l) + \beta\pi(1-l)(1-F(w))E[\psi(W) | W \geqslant w] + \beta[1 - \pi(1-l)(1-F(w))]\mu_{t+1} \}, \tag{4}$$

where β is the discount rate. Let w_t^* and l_t^* denote the utility maximizing choices in period t of a spell of unemployment. Assumptions have been made that imply the calculus can be used to determine the first order conditions for the optimal choice of leisure time and reservation wage rate. These conditions for an interior solution imply

$$\beta\pi(1-l_t^*)f(w_t^*)\{\mu_{t+1}-\psi(w_t^*)\}=0, \quad \text{and} \tag{5}$$

$$v_l(x_t,l_t^*)-\beta\pi'(1-l_t^*)\int_{w_t^*}^{\infty}(\psi(w)-\mu_{t+1})f(w)\mathrm{d}w=0 \tag{6}$$

for any $t>0$.[6] Assuming an interior solution (i.e., $\pi(1-l_t^*)f(w_t^*)\neq 0$), we have

$$\psi(w_t^*)=\mu_{t+1}, \quad \text{and} \tag{7}$$

$$v_l(x_t,l_t^*)=\beta\pi'(1-l_t^*)T(\psi(w_t^*)), \tag{8}$$

where $T(x)=\int_x^{\infty}(\psi(w)-\psi(x))f(w)\mathrm{d}w$. Equation (7) implies that, given an interior solution, the expected payoff to accepting an offer with wage rate w_t^* in period t of a spell of unemployment is equal to the maximum expected payoff to remaining unemployed at least one more period. The second condition (8) implies that, given an interior solution, the worker will select a search time in the period such that the marginal utility of leisure equals the marginal expected gain to search time. If an interior solution does not hold, one of three situations will hold. First, a worker may elect zero search time in the period and hence receive no job offers in the period. Second, a worker may choose to spend all of the period looking for a job. Finally, it is possible that a worker could select a reservation wage such that all possible offers in the market would be accepted. In the rest of this study it will be assumed that an interior solution does exist. The results to be obtained can be easily extended to include the noninterior solution case. This will not be done as little insight would be gained.

So far the optimal search strategy of a worker in any given period has been considered. It will now be shown how these optimal choices of leisure time and reservation wage rate change as the duration of unemployment increases. Suppose a worker has been unemployed at least τ periods in a spell. This worker is faced with the same problem in each future period until a job is found. This follows as the number of possible job offers a worker can receive is unbounded and no UI payments are received after τ

[6]It is straightforward to check the second order conditions for a maximum are satisfied.

consecutive periods of unemployment. This is not the case if a worker has been unemployed less than τ consecutive periods. Here the expected payoff to a given search strategy will depend on the number of periods remaining until UI payments are stopped. In the proof following Proposition 1 it is shown that μ_t declines as t increases, if $t \leqslant \tau$. This fact and (5) imply that the optimal choices of leisure time and reservation wage rate change as the duration of unemployment increases in the way specified below.

Proposition 1
(a) $w_{t-1}^* > w_t^*$, if $t \leqslant \tau$,
(b) $w_{t-1}^* = w_t^*$, if $t > \tau$,
(c) $l_{t-1}^* > l_t^*$, if $t \leqslant \tau$,
(d) $l_\tau^* > l_{\tau+1}^*$, if $v_{yl} > 0$,
(e) $l_{t-1}^* = l_t^*$, if $t > \tau + 1$.

The proof of Proposition 1 is presented in Appendix 1.

Proposition 1 implies the optimal reservation wage and leisure choice decline in each of the first τ periods of unemployment. These optimal choices then remain constant each period after $\tau + 1$ periods of unemployment. Hence a worker increases job search intensity in each of the first τ periods of unemployment. Search intensity then remains the same each period until a job is found. The form of the UI scheme assumed in the model plays a significant role in establishing the results presented in Proposition 1. If a worker is allowed to receive the same UI payment in each period of unemployment, it is straightforward to show the optimal reservation wage and leisure time choice will be the same in each period. Nevertheless, the form of the UI scheme assumed above is a reasonable representation of the UI schemes used in most so-called modern economies. Further consequences of embedding this form of UI scheme in a job search model are discussed in a recent study by Burdett [2].

So far only the problems faced by unemployed workers have been considered. In the next section the problems faced by employed workers will be analyzed. The same basic framework as used in this section will be followed.

3. The work, search and leisure decisions of employed workers

In the previous section $\psi(w)$ was used to denote the expected discounted lifetime utility to a worker who accepts a job with wage rate w per period. In this section this payoff will be discussed in some detail. It will be shown that a worker's choice of work, search and leisure time in each period are related to the wage rate faced by that worker.

Suppose a worker is employed at wage rate w per period. Assume firms will not tolerate a worker supplying less than α work time in a period, where $0<\alpha<1$. This appears to be a reasonable institutional assumption. If this assumption is not made, there is no difference between a worker who turns down a job offer after t periods of unemployment and one who accepts an offer but supplies no work time at the firm.

Each period an employed worker must choose the percentage of a period to spend (a) working ($h>\alpha$), (b) searching for another job (s) and (c) enjoying leisure (l), subject to $h+s+l=1$. As it has been assumed that a worker's working life is unbounded, the optimal choices in a period will remain the same as long as the wage rate faced remains the same. Hence $\psi(w)$ can be interpreted as the expected lifetime utility accruing to a worker employed at wage rate w, given the optimal choices of work, search and leisure times are made in each future period. The objective in what follows is to determine the consequences of assuming a worker works for at least α per cent of a period at any particular wage rate. Of course, a worker may prefer to be unemployed rather than work at low wage rates. The option of remaining unemployed will not be discussed until the end of this section.

If an employed worker spends a strictly positive percentage of a period looking for another job, it is possible that a job offer with a better wage is received. It is assumed there are no fixed costs to changing jobs. Hence a worker employed at wage rate w will accept any job offer with a wage greater than w, and reject all other offers. Employed workers who look for a job in a period do so to increase their expected future utility at the cost of reducing their current utility by a reduction of income and/or leisure in that period.

Utilizing the assumptions made above, the expected payoff $\psi(w)$ can be written as

$$\psi(w)=\max_{\substack{0\leq l\leq 1,\\ 0\leq s\leq 1,\\ y}}\{v(y,l)+\beta\pi(s)(1-F(w))E[\psi(W)|W>w] + \beta[1-\pi(s)(1-F(w))]\psi(w)\} \tag{9}$$

subject to

$$y=w(1-s-l) \tag{10}$$

and

$$1-s-l \geqslant \alpha. \tag{11}$$

Let $\hat{y}$, $\hat{s}$ and $\hat{l}$ indicate the utility maximizing choices of income, search time, and leisure time respectively for a given wage rate. Assumptions have been made that guarantee the calculus can be used to characterize these optimal choices. The first order conditions, given $\hat{s}>0$, $\hat{l}>0$, and $1-\hat{s}-\hat{l}>\alpha$, can be written as

$$v_y(y,\hat{l})-\lambda=0; \tag{12a}$$

$$\beta\pi'(s)T(\psi(w))-w\lambda=0; \tag{12b}$$

$$v_l(\hat{y},l)-w\lambda=0; \tag{12c}$$

and (10), where λ is the multiplier associated with the income constraint (10). Hence, given an interior solution, a worker will choose leisure and work times such that the ratio of the marginal utilities of income and leisure equals the wage rate w. Further, the worker selects a search time such that the marginal utility of leisure equals the expected marginal gain to search time. The second order conditions for a maximum are guaranteed from the assumptions made about the individual period utility function in (2), and the restrictions placed on the expected gain to search time in (1).

Of course, an interior solution to the above problem may not exist. For example, a worker may elect to spend no time in the period enjoying leisure, or a worker may choose to work for only α per cent of the period. The consequences of these special cases can be analyzed relatively easily. A noninterior solution of special interest is where a worker elects not to look for another job while employed. This situation is considered below.

When will a worker choose to look for another job when employed? To answer this question consider $\eta(w)$, the maximum expected payoff to a worker employed at wage rate w, given search time is forced to be zero in the next period. It follows that

$$\eta(w)=\max_{\substack{0\leqslant l\leqslant 1,\\ y}}\{v(y,l)+\beta\psi(w)\} \tag{13}$$

given $y=w(1-l)$ and $1-l\geqslant\alpha$. Let $\tilde{y}$ and $\tilde{l}$ indicate the optimal values of income and leisure time respectively in this case. Given an interior solution, we have

$$\frac{v_l(\tilde{y},l)}{v_y(y,\tilde{l})}=w. \tag{14}$$

Note that $\psi(w)\geqslant\eta(w)$ for any w and $\psi(w)>\eta(w)$ if and only if the unrestricted choice of search time, $\hat{s}$, is strictly greater than zero. Let the wage z be defined as the smallest wage rate such that

$$\psi(w)=\eta(w) \quad \text{for any} \quad w\geqslant z. \tag{15}$$

It is straightforward to show that z exists. For example, suppose a worker is employed at a wage rate at least as great as any other in the market. In this case the worker will choose not to spend any time looking for another job as there is no hope of an offer with a better wage rate being received. Of course, z may be less than the maximum wage rate in the market. Without further restriction being made, it is possible that a worker may elect not to look for another job even if the wage rate faced is less than z. Specifically, there can exist two wage rates w_1 and w_2 such that $w_1<w_2<z$, $\psi(w_1)=\eta(w_1)$, and $\psi(w_2)>\eta(w_2)$ (i.e., the set of wage rates that imply an employed worker will not search is not connected).

Proposition 2 states conditions that guarantee the set of wage rates that imply an employed worker will elect to work but not search is connected. These restrictions do not appear to be overly restrictive.

Proposition 2. If $v_{yl}\geqslant 0$ and $\hat{s}>0$, then (a) $\mathrm{d}\hat{h}/\mathrm{d}w\geqslant 0$ only if $\mathrm{d}\hat{s}/\mathrm{d}w<0$, and (b) $\mathrm{d}\hat{s}/\mathrm{d}w\geqslant 0$ implies $\mathrm{d}\hat{h}/\mathrm{d}w<0$ and $\mathrm{d}\hat{l}/\mathrm{d}w>0$.

The proof of Proposition 2 is presented in Appendix 1.

Proposition 2 establishes that, given an employed worker elects to look for another job, an increase in the wage rate faced reduces the amount of time allocated to looking for a job if the hours of work function is positively related to the wage rate. Further, if the amount of time allocated to search increases as the wage rate faced increases, the hours of work function is negatively related to the wage rate and leisure time increases with the wage rate faced. Proposition 3 follows directly from Proposition 2 and (15), and consequently no proof is presented.

Proposition 3. If an individual's supply of work time function is nonnegatively related to the wage rate faced and $v_{yl} \geqslant 0$, then that individual will elect to look for a job when employed if and only if the wage rate faced is less than z, where z is defined in (15).

In the remainder of this section it will be assumed that the hypotheses made in Proposition 3 hold true. This guarantees an employed worker will only choose to look for another job if he/she is employed at a job with a wage rate less than z. So far in this section it has been assumed that the worker selected to be employed at the wage rate w. From (7), however, we know an unemployed worker in period t of a spell of unemployment will only elect to become employed in the next period if the wage offered is at least as great as the relevant optimal reservation wage. In terms of the notation developed in Section 2 an unemployed worker in period t of unemployment will accept a job offer if and only if the wage rate offered is at least as great as w_t^*, where w_t^* is defined in (5).

It was shown in Proposition 1 that the optimal reservation wage declines in each of the first τ periods of unemployment, and then remains constant. Proposition 4 uses this fact and Proposition 3 to completely characterize the strategy of a worker with respect to wage rates and job search.

Proposition 4

(a) There exists a $\bar{t}$ such that $w_t^* \geqslant z$ if and only if $t \leqslant \bar{t}$ ($\bar{t}$ may equal zero or infinity).

(b) If an acceptable offer is found in the first $\bar{t}$ periods of unemployment, a worker will elect not to look for a job while employed.

(c) If an acceptable offer is found after $\bar{t}$ periods of unemployment, a worker will choose to look for another job if and only if the wage rate faced is less than z.

The value of $\bar{t}$ will depend on (i) the distribution of wage rate offers, (ii) the UI payments relative to the wage rates in the market, and (iii) a worker's preferences. Other consequences of Proposition 4 can easily be derived. For example, it is straightforward to check that the higher the wage rate faced by an employed worker the less likely that worker is to quit a job. This claim follows as a worker will search for another job less intensely when employed at a higher wage rate, and a better wage rate is more difficult to find.

Appendix 1

Proof of Proposition 1. To establish the claims of Proposition 1 it is first shown that (i) $\mu_t = \mu_{t+1}$ if $t > \tau$, and (ii) $\mu_t > \mu_{t+1}$ if $t \leqslant \tau$, and an interior solution exists. The proof of claim (i) has been presented many times in the literature, and will therefore not be repeated here. Let

$$\gamma_t(\bar{w}, \bar{l}) = v(x_t, \bar{l}) + \beta\pi(1-\bar{l})(1-F(\bar{w}))E[\psi(W)|W \geqslant \bar{w}] + \beta[1-\pi(1-\bar{l})(1-F(\bar{w}))]\mu_{t+1}. \tag{A1}$$

It follows that $\mu_t = \max_{\bar{w},\bar{l}} \gamma_t(\bar{w}, \bar{l})$. From Assumption 1 we have

$$\gamma_t(\bar{w}, \bar{l}) - \gamma_{t+1}(\bar{w}, \bar{l}) = [1-\pi(1-\bar{l})(1-F(\bar{w}))]\{\mu_{t+1} - \mu_{t+2}\} + \delta_t[v(u, \bar{l}) - v(0, \bar{l})]$$

where

$$\delta_t \begin{cases} 1 & \text{if} \quad t = \tau, \\ 0 & \text{if} \quad t \neq \tau. \end{cases}$$

Hence if $\pi(1-\bar{l})(1-F(\bar{w})) \neq 0$,

$$\mu_{t+1} - \mu_{t+2} > 0 \qquad \text{implies} \quad \gamma_t(\bar{w}, \bar{l}) - \gamma_{t+1}(\bar{w}, \bar{l}) > 0.$$

It is straightforward to show $\mu_\tau - \mu_{\tau+1} \geqslant v(u, l^*_{\tau+1}) - v(0, l^*_{\tau+1}) > 0$. Therefore $\gamma_{\tau-1}(\bar{w}, \bar{l}) - \gamma_\tau(\bar{w}, \bar{l}) > 0$. This implies $\mu_{\tau-1} - \mu_{\tau-2} > 0$. Continuing in the same way claim (ii) can be established.

Claims (a) and (b) of Proposition 1 follow directly from the above claims (i) and (ii) and (7). To demonstrate claims (c)–(e) note that from (8) we have

$$v_l(x_t, l^*_t) - v_l(x_{t-1}, l^*_{t-1}) = \beta\pi'(1-l^*_t)T(w^*_t) - \beta\pi'(1-l^*_{t-1})T(w^*_{t-1}). \tag{A2}$$

From (2) it follows that

$$v_l(x_t, l^*_t) \gtreqless v_l(x^*_{t-1}, l^*_{t-1}) \quad \text{as} \quad l^*_t \gtreqless l^*_{t-1} \quad \text{if} \quad x_t = x_{t-1}, \tag{A3}$$

whereas from (1) we have

$$\pi'(1-l^*_t) \gtreqless \pi'(1-l^*_{t-1}) \quad \text{as} \quad l^*_t \gtreqless l^*_{t-1}. \tag{A4}$$

Further, note that

$$\frac{\mathrm{d}T(z)}{\mathrm{d}z} = (F(z)-1)\psi'(z) < 0,$$

and therefore

$$T(w_t^*) \gtreqless T(w_{t-1}^*) \quad \text{as} \quad w_t^* \gtreqless w_{t-1}^*. \tag{A5}$$

From claim (a) we know that if $t \leqslant \tau$, $w_{t-1}^* > w_t^*$. Suppose $l_{t-1}^* \leqslant l_t^*$ for some $t \leqslant \tau$. Using (A3), (A4) and (A5) it follows that the left hand side of (A2) is negative, whereas the right hand side is strictly positive, a contradiction. Thus, $l_{t-1}^* > l_t^*$ if $t \leqslant \tau$. Claim (e) can be proved in a similar manner. For $t = \tau + 1$ (A2) becomes

$$v_l(0, l_{\tau+1}^*) - v_l(u, l_\tau^*) = \beta T(w_\tau^*)\{\pi'(1-l_{\tau+1}^*) - \pi'(1-l_\tau^*)\},$$

as $w_\tau^* = w_{\tau+1}^*$. Given $v_{ly} > 0$ it follows that this equation can be satisfied only if $l_\tau^* > l_{\tau+1}^*$. This establishes claim (d). QED

Proof of Proposition 2. Substituting into the equations of (12) yields

$$wv_y = \beta\pi'(s)T(\psi(w)) \quad \text{and} \quad v_l = \beta\pi'(s)T(\psi(w))$$

where the superscripts have been dropped to simplify the exposition. Taking the total derivative of the above with respect to w yields

$$wv_{yy}\frac{\mathrm{d}y}{\mathrm{d}w} + wv_{yl}\frac{\mathrm{d}l}{\mathrm{d}w} - \beta\pi''(s)T(\psi(w))\frac{\mathrm{d}s}{\mathrm{d}w} = \beta\pi'(s)T'(\psi(w)) - v_y,$$

$$v_{yl}\frac{\mathrm{d}y}{\mathrm{d}w} + v_{ll}\frac{\mathrm{d}l}{\mathrm{d}w} - \beta\pi''(s)T(\psi(w))\frac{\mathrm{d}s}{\mathrm{d}w} = \beta\pi'(s)T'(\psi(w)).$$

Substituting $\mathrm{d}y/\mathrm{d}w$ from the second equation into the first equation and manipulating yields

$$\frac{\mathrm{d}l}{\mathrm{d}w} = \frac{\beta\pi'(s)T'(\psi(w))[wv_{yy} - v_{yl}] + v_y v_y}{w[v_{yy}v_{ll} - (v_y)^2]} + \frac{\pi''(s)\beta T(\psi(w))[wv_{yy} - v_{yl}]}{w[v_{yy}v_{ll} - (v_y)^2]}\,\frac{\mathrm{d}s}{\mathrm{d}w}.$$

Going through the above expression term by term it can be checked that

$$\frac{dl}{dw} = \theta + \Delta \frac{ds}{dw}, \quad \text{where} \quad \theta > 0 \quad \text{and} \quad \Delta > 0.$$

Hence

$$\frac{dl}{dw} > 0, \quad \text{if} \quad \frac{ds}{dw} \geqslant 0.$$

From (10) we have

$$\frac{dy}{dw} + w\frac{dl}{dw} + w\frac{ds}{dw} = (1 - s - l).$$

Substituting and using the fact $dy = h dw + w dh$ yields

$$\frac{dh}{dw} = -\theta - (\Delta + 1)\frac{ds}{dw}.$$

Therefore

$$\frac{dh}{dw} > 0 \quad \text{implies} \quad \frac{ds}{dw} \leqslant 0$$

and the claims made in Proposition 2 are established. QED

References

[1] Burdett, K., "Theories of search in a labor market," Technical Analysis Paper No. 13, Office of Evaluation, ASPER, Dept. of Labor, Washington, D.C., 1973.
[2] Burdett, K., "Unemployment insurance payments as a search subsidy: a theoretical analysis", Institute for Research on Poverty Discussion Paper, University of Wisconsin-Madison, 1977.
[3] Lippman, S. A., and McCall, J. J., "Job search in a dynamic economy," *Journal of Economic Theory*, 12 (1976), 365–390.
[4] Lippman, S. A., and McCall, J. J., "The economics of job search: a survey", *Economic Inquiry*, 14 (1976) 155–189.
[5] McCall, J. J., "Economics of information and job search", *Quarterly Journal of Economics*, 84 (1970), 113–26.
[6] Mortensen, D. T., "Unemployment insurance and the labor supply decision", paper presented at the Department of Labor/University of Pittsburgh Conference on Unemployment Insurance, 1976.
[7] Tobin, J., "Inflation and unemployment", *American Economic Review*, 62 (1972), 1–18.

CHAPTER 9

Estimation of wage offer distributions and reservation wages

NICHOLAS M. KIEFER and GEORGE R. NEUMANN*

University of Chicago

1. Introduction

Though theoretical work on job search and the theory of reservation wages has attracted considerable attention, very little empirical work along the lines suggested by theory has been done. Empirical work in this context is potentially useful not only for better understanding of unemployment but for measuring the effects of diverse labor-market programs. For example, the provision of contingency payments such as unemployment insurance may have effects on observed market phenomena such as earnings or unemployment, but these effects are transmitted indirectly through the effect of unemployment insurance (UI) on reservation wages. To evaluate the effects of UI on market phenomena it is necessary to examine the transmission mechanism directly. Similarly, if one wishes to measure the displacement effect of a minimum wage, it is necessary to estimate the number of individuals who have reservation wages less than the minimum wage.

In this paper we begin the econometric analysis of job search models. We specify an appropriate econometric model and discuss several issues which arise in its estimation and interpretation. We then apply the model to a sample of workers who were permanently separated from previous employment. Throughout the paper we discuss the model in the context of a labor market, though the empirical model is more general.

*We thank James Heckman, Roger Kormendi, Robert E. Lucas, Jr., Tom Macurdy, Melvin Reder and Sherwin Rosen for helpful comments on earlier versions. We benefited from the help of two anonymous referees who detected a flaw in a previous version of the paper.

The lack of empirical work along the lines suggested by theory is largely due to the identification problems which cloud the issues. Central to all sequential search models is the choice of a reservation wage — and the implications of search theory for empirical phenomena follow from the effects of reservation wages on such phenomena.

In using the term reservation wage we note that the concept is intrinsically different from the normal meaning of the term in labor economics. In the theory of labor supply the term reservation wage has come to mean the critical value of the wage rate which will make an individual indifferent between participating in market activities or engaging in nonmarket work. In this framework the reservation wage is determined solely by "tastes", or in the spirit of the new economics of consumption, by productivity in nonmarket alternatives. It is not affected by market wages, at least not directly. By contrast, the term reservation wage as we use it and as is generally used in the search literature denotes the critical value which equates the marginal gain from an additional search with the marginal cost of one more search. Since the marginal gain from search depends upon the distribution of wages, it is clear that the reservation wage must also depend upon the wage distribution. It is this dependence, reflecting the investment nature of search activity, that differentiates the two concepts of reservation wages.

Reservation wages are not, however, directly observable; this makes it difficult to test the implications of search theory directly. Consequently, one must rely heavily on restrictions implied by the theory. In this paper we describe a method for estimating the wage offer distribution facing individuals from incomplete data — that is, from information on accepted wage offers. We then examine the conditions under which this information enables one to identify reservation wages. We present one method of identification based on an implication of the underlying theoretical model. The plan of the paper is as follows.

In section 2 we set out the model to be estimated and discuss its implications. Section 3 introduces the data source we use and presents the estimation technique and the estimates of the wage offer distribution (which do not depend on the crucial identification assumption). Section 4 discusses the identification and estimation of reservation wage functions and presents a discussion of the results and potential applications. Section 5 is the conclusion.

2. The model

In the simplest form of job search model studied by McCall [6] and Mortensen [8], the decision problem which the individual faces is that of wealth maximization with uncertain wage offers generated by a known wage offer distribution. Denoting wage offers by w^0 and reservation wages by ξ, the reservation wage which maximizes wealth is found as the solution to the following necessary condition:

$$(1-F(\xi))\{h(\xi)-\xi\}=m+\theta\xi \tag{1}$$

where $F(\xi)=\int_{-\infty}^{\xi} f(w^0)\mathrm{d}w^0$ is the distribution function of wage offers,

$$h(\xi) = \frac{\int_{\xi}^{\infty} w^0 f(w^0)\,dw^0}{\int_{\xi}^{\infty} f(w^0)\,dw^0}$$

is the mean of w^0, given that $w^0 \geqslant \xi$, θ is the rate of discount, and m is the direct costs of search per period.

Under the assumptions of the models in [6] and [8]—risk neutrality, no capital constraints and agelessness—the value of ξ which solves (1) is constant across time but varies with θ and m across individuals. Although (1) can in principle be solved, empirical testing is made difficult since ξ is unobservable; thus one cannot proceed directly to estimating the determinants of ξ. An alternative is to use the implications of (1) for analyzing observed employment and earnings patterns across individuals. If two otherwise identical individuals differ in their costs of search, then their expected probability of finding a job in any number of periods will differ as will their expected earnings upon reemployment, and these will both differ in a systematic way. Hence, one can in principle use these implications to test the theory. To use these implications requires not only that the sources of differences in cost of search be specified, but also that the manner in which these differences affect observed phenomena be specified as well. This necessarily involves some assumptions about the distribution $F(w^0)$, but, as we indicate below, these assumptions can themselves be tested.

Let the wage offer distribution facing the ith individual be:

$$\ln w_i^0 = x_i'\beta + \epsilon_i^0 \tag{2}$$

with

$$\epsilon_i^0 \sim N(0,\sigma_0^2).$$

The vector $x_i'=(x_{1i},\ldots,x_{ki})$ contains all characteristics of the worker and the labor market which affect the job search process. The reservation wage of the ith individual is generated by:

$$\ln \xi_i = Z_i' \gamma + \epsilon_i^r \tag{3}$$

with

$$\epsilon_i^r \sim N(0, \sigma_r^2).$$

The independent variables Z_i are again worker and labor market characteristics. We further assume that the error terms are jointly distributed as bivariate normal with covariance $\sigma_{0,r}$.

This characterization of the reservation wage function merits comment. If (3) is viewed as the exact solution of (1), then no error should be contained in it. An alternative interpretation is that ϵ_i represents inter-individual variation in ξ_i which is not captured by Z_i. We will maintain this latter interpretation throughout.

An individual accepts a job if and only if $S_i \equiv \ln w_i^0 - \ln \xi_i$ is greater than zero. which from (2) and (3) is:

$$\begin{aligned} S_i &= x_i' \beta - Z_i' \gamma + \epsilon_i^0 - \epsilon_i^r > 0 \\ &= x_i' \beta - Z_i' \gamma + \epsilon_i > 0 \end{aligned} \tag{4}$$

with

$$\epsilon_i \sim N(0, \sigma_0^2 - 2\sigma_{0,r} + \sigma_r^2).$$

Since the condition for observing an individual's wage is that (4) hold, it is clear that the distribution of observed wages is truncated—offers below ξ_i are not accepted and therefore not observed. The observation on the wage offer distribution comes from a conditional distribution where the condition is that (4) holds. If w_i^{0*} is the logarithm of a drawing from the observed wage offers, then it is distributed with:

$$E(w_i^{0*}) = x_i' \beta + \rho \sigma_0 \lambda_i. \tag{5}$$

$$\operatorname{var}(w_i^{0*}) = \sigma_0^2 (1 + \rho^2 r_i \lambda_i - \rho^2 \lambda_i^2) \tag{6}$$

where:

$$\text{(a)} \quad \lambda_i = \frac{\phi(-r_i)}{1 - \Phi(-r_i)}, \tag{7}$$

$$\text{(b)} \quad r_i = \frac{x_i' \beta - Z_i' \gamma}{\sigma},$$

$$\text{(c)} \quad \rho = \frac{\sigma_0^2 - \sigma_{0,r}}{\sigma_0 \sigma},$$

$$\text{(d)} \quad \sigma = (\sigma_0^2 + \sigma_r^2 - 2\sigma_{0,r})^{\frac{1}{2}}.$$

Here ϕ and Φ are the standard normal density and distribution function respectively. If λ_i were known, the regression:

$$w_i^{0*} = x'\beta + \rho\sigma_0\lambda_i + \epsilon_i \tag{8}$$

could be run and β and $\rho\sigma_0$ estimated. Heckman [3] shows that probit estimates of the normalized version of (4), that is

$$\begin{aligned} S_i^* = \frac{S_i}{\sigma} &= \frac{x_1'\beta - Z_i'\gamma}{\sigma} + \frac{\epsilon_i}{\sigma} \\ &= x_i'\beta^* - Z_i'\gamma^* + \epsilon_i^*, \end{aligned} \tag{4'}$$

can be used to estimate λ_i consistently, which in turn provides consistent estimates of β and $\rho\sigma_0$. Generalized least squares can be used to improve efficiency.

This framework is useful for interpreting two issues which arise in previous work on wage offer distributions, [1], [2]. Suppose λ is omitted from (6), but instead some elements of Z' are included. To the extent that truncation is important, these variables will serve as an approximation to λ and thus may become significant for that reason alone.[1] Thus variables which affect an individual's reservation wage but not his wage offer in the market, such as variables representing the level of UI payments, may appear significant in a wage equation. The significance of UI variables in a wage equation is correctly interpreted as evidence of misspecification. The second issue concerns the requirements for an observation to be included in a sample. Most studies use observations only for completed spells of job search, which eliminates any information from (4) because (4′) is always greater than zero. Since individuals with long spells of job search are likely to have the highest reservation wages, relative to potential earnings, selection by employment status results in a truncation of the reservation wage distributions.

Collecting equations with observable or partially observable dependent variables, we have:

$$w_i^{0*} = x_i'\beta + \epsilon_i \quad \text{(wage offer function)} \tag{2}$$

[1]For example, some elements of x_i may also be elements of Z_i; in this case their coefficients in a regression which does not include λ will confound market wage effects with reservation wage effects.

and

$$S_i^* = x_i'\beta^* - Z_i'\gamma^* + \epsilon^* \quad \text{(employment function)}, \tag{4'}$$

where the sign of S_i^* is observed and w_i^0 is observed if S_i is positive. In the following sections we provide estimates of the parameters of these equations.

3. The data and the wage offer distribution

The data are from a survey of workers in 14 states conducted by the Institute for Research on Human Resources of the Pennsylvania State University. The data were collected under contract to the Department of Labor for a study of the effects of the Trade Adjustment Assistance program (TAA); full details of the survey are reported in [8]. The individuals sampled had all become unemployed within the four year period 1969–1973. The survey took place in October of 1975. In this paper we restrict attention to male workers. Summary statistics for this subsample are reported in table 9.1.

The sample consists of workers who were permanently displaced from their jobs during the period 1969–1973. Over half of the sample (54 per cent) were recipients of unemployment benefits under TAA, which was considerably more liberal in terms of benefits than existing state programs. The remaining individuals were permanently separated from jobs in the same labor market but were not recipients of TAA. Because individuals were separated in different years, earnings are expressed in 1967 dollars. As a glance at table 9.1 indicates, this sample of workers is not typical; in general, they are older, less educated and more heavily unionized than the

Table 9.1. Sample characteristics of male workers.

	Mean	Maximum	Minimum
Education/years	10.2	21.0	0.0
Number of dependents	1.7	9.0	0.0
Per cent married	83.6		
Per cent union members	70.4		
Local unemployment rate (per cent) at layoff	5.30	9.00	2.20
Age	47.8	75.0	19.0
Unemployment benefits per week ($1967)	62.7	117.11	0.0
Maximum benefit period, weeks	41.5	65.6	0.0
Previous weekly earnings ($1967)	149.0	457.0	19.20

entire male population. Since our interest is primarily methodological, this lack of representativeness is not a serious drawback. The value of this particular sample for our purpose is that it excludes all individuals on temporary layoff.

In order to estimate the parameters of the wage offer distribution, we first estimate (4′) by probit, then use the estimated probit coefficients to calculate a series on λ, the adjustment for the truncation in the observed wage offers. Then, conditioning on our series for λ, we estimate (8) by GLS. Estimates of the employment equation are presented in column 1 of table 9.2. The dependent variable is a 0–1 variable which takes the value 1 if the originally unemployed individual has become employed within 65

Table 9.2. Employment equations.[a]

	1	2
Constant	0.781	−2.18
	(0.494)	(1.02)
Education	−0.112	−0.222
	(1.08)	(1.82)
Dependents	−0.058	−0.049
	(1.08)	(0.917)
Married	0.248	0.227
	(1.44)	(1.32)
Unemployment rate	−0.166	−0.200
	(3.80)	(4.09)
Age	0.115	0.064
	(2.44)	(1.25)
Age × Ed	0.0019	0.0035
	(0.962)	(1.63)
Age**2	−0.002	−0.0017
	(4.85)	(4.07)
Unemployment benefit	−0.0052	−0.0062
	(1.27)	(1.47)
Maximum duration of benefits	0.0059	0.0056
	(0.977)	(0.923)
Tenure on previous jobs	−0.014	
	(2.32)	
Wage at previous job	0.0018	
	(1.32)	
Expected W^0		1.15
		2.04
χ^2	114	111
lnL	−281.45	−282.59

[a]Probit estimates of (4′) and (12′) in the text. The χ^2 test is a test against a binomial specification, df = 11 in 1, 10 in 2. Numbers in parentheses are asymptotic t-statistics. There are 517 observations.

weeks and zero otherwise. Note that the choice of 65 weeks is arbitrary under this specification of the job search model. Since reservation wages for each individual are assumed constant across time, as is the wage offer function, it makes no difference (asymptotically) what cut-off point is chosen. The equation is significant as measured by a chi-squared test against the binomial model (analogous to the F-statistic in an ordinary regression model).

The coefficient estimates obtained are "reduced form" coefficients; that is, they represent the net effect of the wage offer distribution and the reservation wage. Thus, being married increases the probability of employment, age has a positive but decreasing effect on employment, and the size of unemployment benefit payments reduces the probability of employment. Surprisingly, the effect of education is estimated to be negative and the maximum potential duration of unemployment benefits has a positive effect. Neither of these effects is significant, however. The local unemployment rate has a strongly negative effect on the probability of employment — a finding which is intuitively reasonable (the "discouraged worker" hypothesis) but which has implications about the appositeness of the simple job search model. These implications and a detailed interpretation of these coefficients are discussed in section 4. For now we turn to the wage offer distribution.

Table 9.3. Wage equation.[a]

	OLS	GLS
Constant	1.42	1.54
	(2.25)	(2.55)
Education	0.106	0.097
	(2.96)	(2.80)
Age	0.036	0.034
	(1.59)	(1.57)
Age**2	−0.00016	−0.00016
	(0.594)	(0.659)
Age × Ed	−0.0016	−0.0014
	(2.21)	(2.02)
Unemployment	0.027	0.023
rate	(1.32)	(1.22)
Tenure on	−0.0068	−0.006
previous job	(2.60)	(2.55)
(Log of)	0.319	0.316
previous wage	(4.46)	(4.51)
λ	−0.056	−0.050
	(0.679)	(0.793)
R^2	0.199	0.438
N	327	327

[a]The dependent variable is the log of weekly wages.

Table 9.3 reports the estimates of the parameters of the wage equation estimated by ordinary least squares and generalized least squares. The equation is estimated over the sample of individuals who were employed and the series on λ constructed from the employment probit was entered as a regressor. The dependent variable was the logarithm of weekly wages. The strongest effect seems to be that of previous wages—the coefficient of the logarithm of lagged weekly wages is 0.32. The local unemployment rate has a positive (though insignificant) effect on the mean of the wage offer distributions facing individuals in the local labor market. This is somewhat difficult to interpret; in part the high unemployment rate could reflect queuing for the higher paying jobs, but then supply pressures could be expected to reduce the market wage. In the job search context there is no reason to believe that higher mean wage offer distributions will lead to higher unemployment—this depends on the response of reservation wage functions to changes in the wage offer distribution. Below we present evidence that this response is not complete (i.e., that reservation wages do not fully adjust to changes in the wage offer distribution). Tenure on an individual's previous job has a negative effect on the wage the individual subsequently faces in the market. This can be interpreted as, holding previous earnings constant, an individual with greater job tenure has more firm-specific capital and less general capital. Consequently, the wage offer function facing such individuals is lower because the firm-specific capital is now worthless. Age, age squared and education have the usual effects.

The coefficient on λ is small, negative and insignificant. Recall from (5) and (7c) that this coefficient is

$$\frac{(\sigma_0^2-\sigma_{0,r})}{(\sigma_0^2-2\sigma_{0,r}+\sigma_r^2)^{\frac{1}{2}}},$$

therefore $\sigma_{0,r}$ is greater than σ^2. Thus, the error terms in the wage equation and in the employment equation are slightly negatively correlated, although the correlation between the "errors" in the wage offer equation and the reservation wage equation are positively (and substantially) correlated.

Although a high positive correlation between reservation wages and market productivity seems intuitively reasonable, there is no *a priori* reason why this should be so. One plausible explanation runs along the following lines. Suppose that there is an omitted variable $\tilde{x}$, call it ability, uncorrelated with all other exogenous variables, which affects both market wages and reservation wages. Then if the true $\sigma_{0,r}$ were zero, the estimated σ_{0r} would be positive. It is straightforward to show under this specification that our estimate of the coefficient on λ is biased upwards if ability affects market wages more than or the same as reservation wages, and biased downwards if ability has a greater effect on reservation wages.

4. Reservation wages

An individual's reservation wage is assumed to be a function of the wage offer distribution faced and the costs of searching. In our model

$$E(\ln\xi_i)=f(x_i'\beta,\text{costs}_i)=Z_i'\gamma \tag{9}$$

since the higher moments of the wage offer distribution are assumed to be the same for everybody.

This formulation requires then that all elements of X be contained in Z, necessarily because they affect w^0, (i.e., through $x_i'\beta$), and possibly because they affect the costs of search as well—e.g., more educated individuals may need less time to read the help wanted section of the newspaper. Define x_i^j as the set of variables which affect wage offers and costs of search, x_i^k as the set of variables which affect wage offers but not costs of search, and Q_i as the set of variables which affect costs of search but not wage offers. Thus

$$Z_i'=\left[x_i'^j,x_i'^k,Q_i'\right]. \tag{10}$$

By employing a Taylor series expansion on the middle expression in (9), the parameter vector γ can be decomposed as

$$\gamma=(f_1B_j+\gamma_j,f_1B_k,\gamma_Q) \tag{11}$$

where

$$f_1=\frac{\partial\xi_i}{\partial x_i'\beta}.$$

Using (10) and (11) the employment equation (4) can be rewritten in normalized form as:

$$S_i^*=\frac{\ln(w_i^0)-\ln(\xi_i)}{\sigma}=x_i'^j\left(\frac{(1-f_1)B_j-\gamma_j}{\sigma}\right)+x_i'^k\frac{(1-f_1)B_j}{\sigma}-Q_i'\frac{\gamma_Q}{\sigma} \tag{12}$$

or, equivalently,

$$S_i^* = \frac{\ln(w_i^0) - \ln(\xi_i)}{\sigma} = (x_i'\beta)\frac{(1-f_1)}{\sigma} - x_i'^j\frac{\gamma_j}{\sigma} - Q_i'\frac{\gamma_Q}{\sigma}. \tag{12'}$$

The question is, can we identify separately, σ, $1-f$, and γ? The estimate in (12), which we shall call the reduced form estimates, are obviously of no help. The structural estimates of (12′) provide some possibility, however. Since consistent estimates of $x_i'\beta$, the mean of each individual's wage offer function, can be obtained, it is possible to enter it separately into a probit model. This raises the central identification problem referred to in section 1. If all variables which affect earnings also affect the costs of search, then (12′) will be perfectly collinear. In order to identify the parameters of the reservation wage function it is necessary that some elements of x_i' affect reservation wages solely through their effect on wage offers. *A priori* restrictions are thus required on x_j'. These restrictions permit identification of $(1-f_1)/\sigma$, (γ_j/σ), and γ_Q/σ, but except in the degenerate case of $f_1=0$, they are not sufficient to separately identify the remaining parameters. However, information on f_1 is available from at least two other sources; one is the requirement that the estimated error covariance matrix be positive semidefinite (this restricts f_1 because it restricts σ and we can estimate $(1-f_1)/\sigma$). From the coefficient on λ in (5) and the definition (7c) and the interpretation of the coefficient on expected wages in (12′) (denote this k) we find that feasible $(f_1, \sigma_{0,r})$ pairs lie along the line

$$f_1 = -kw^{-1}\sigma_0^2 + kw^{-1}\sigma_{0,r}$$

where w is the coefficient on λ in (5). Only points with $f_1 < 1$ satisfy the requirement that the estimated standard deviation σ is positive (for positive k; $f_1 > 1$ for negative k). The only other constraint arising from the consideration of definiteness which will ever be binding is the requirement that $\hat{\sigma}_r > 0$. The set of points $(f, \sigma_{0,r})$ for which $\sigma_r = 0$ is given by:

$$\left(\frac{1-f}{k}\right)^2 - \sigma_0^2 + 2\sigma_{0,r} = 0; \tag{13}$$

feasible $(f, \sigma_{0,r})$ pairs lie to the right of this curve.

The second source of additional information is given in the following proposition.

Proposition 1. Let g, the wage offer density, be differentiable, with finite mean, and let u be a translation of the wage offer density. Then, $0 \leqslant \partial\xi/\partial u \leqslant 1$.

Proof.[2] Define the necessary condition (1) as:

$$H(\xi,u)=\int_{\xi}^{\infty}(w^0-\xi)g(w^0+u)\,\mathrm{d}w^0-\theta[\xi+m]=0$$

and note that

$$\frac{\mathrm{d}\xi}{\mathrm{d}u}=-\frac{\dfrac{\partial H}{\partial u}}{\dfrac{\partial H}{\partial \xi}}.$$

We have

$$\frac{\partial H}{\partial u}=\int_{\xi}^{\infty}(w^0-\xi)g'(w^0+u)\,\mathrm{d}w^0.$$

Integrating by parts yields

$$\begin{aligned}\frac{\partial H}{\partial u}&=(w^0-\xi)g(w^0+u)\Big|_{\xi}^{\infty}-\int_{\xi}^{\infty}g(w^0+u)\,\mathrm{d}w^0\\&=-[1-G(\xi+u)]\end{aligned}$$

where the first term on the right hand side vanishes if (1) has a solution. Also

$$\begin{aligned}\frac{\partial H}{\partial \xi}&=-\int_{\xi}^{\infty}g(w^0+u)\,\mathrm{d}w^0-\theta\\&=-[1-G(\xi+u)+\theta].\end{aligned}$$

Therefore

$$\frac{\partial\xi}{\partial u}=\frac{(1-G(\xi+u))}{(1-G(\xi+u))+\theta}=\frac{\alpha}{\alpha+\theta}\leqslant 1.$$ QED

[2]We are indebted to Roger Kormendi for correcting and generalizing an earlier version of this point.

This result bounds $f_1(=\partial\xi/\partial u)$ to the $[0,1)$ interval, since α is necessarily contained in the interval $[0,1]$, and θ is assumed to be positive; this implies that our estimate of k must be greater than zero. It can be shown that α is equal to the inverse of expected duration; consequently, data on duration can be combined with *a priori* values of θ to yield estimates of f_1. This allows estimation of the entire reservation wage function.

Proceeding to its application, we assume that two variables which enter the wage offer function do not affect the cost of search: an individual's tenure on his previous job and his previous wage. Both of these variables significantly affect the mean of the wage offer distribution. The advantage of imposing more than one restriction is that a test of the (overidentifying) restrictions can be made.

The second row of table 9.2 reports probit estimates of (3) with the zero restrictions imposed. The variables in Q, which are assumed to affect costs of search but not the wage offers, are: the number of dependents, marital status, potential unemployment benefits and the maximum potential duration of benefit payments. The coefficient of the mean of the wage offer distribution, which up to a positive constant is $1-f$, is of particular interest. *A priori* we expected f_1 to be nearly one, however, the estimates show that f_1 is significantly less than one. Thus, when the wage offer distribution shifts, reservation wages do not shift by as much.

This is consistent with observed patterns of unemployment over the business cycle, which are usually "explained" by sticky wages. However, an alternative interpretation, consistent with our evidence, is that wages are not sticky but that reservation wages are. In this view, changes in average observed wages will not fully reflect changes in market wage offers.

A check on the appropriateness of the identifying restrictions can be made on the basis of a likelihood ratio test between (1) and (2) of table 9.2. The resulting χ^2 (1) statistic is 1.14, thus the restrictions cannot be rejected under usual standards of significance. This is a test of whether the two variables, tenure on previous job and previous wage, enter the reservation wage function in the same relative amounts (i.e., the same linear combination up to a constant) that they enter the wage offer function. To the extent that these variables do affect costs of search in the same relative proportion that they affect the offer distribution, our test would be misleading. The procedure tests only the overidentifying restriction. Note that this likelihood ratio test is conservative; if the test were done without conditioning on the estimated β vector (i.e., if the wage offer equation and the employment equation were estimated simultaneously), the resulting test statistic would take a lower value.

Table 9.4. Reservation wage function[a] $\theta=0.1$.

	Structural equation	Reduced form equation
Constant	0.113	1.56
Education	0.0115	0.103
Dependents	0.0025	0.0025
Marital status	−0.012	−0.012
Unemployment rate	0.0104	0.032
Age	−0.0033	0.0286
Age × Ed	−0.00018	−0.0015
Age**2	0.0000088	−0.00006
Unemployment benefits	0.00032	0.00032
Maximum duration	−0.00029	−0.00029
Expected[b] wage	0.94	
Tenure previous job		−0.0056
Wage previous job		0.297

[a]Derived using $f=0.94$, corresponding to a discount of 0.10.
[b]The mean of the wage offer distribution.

A further check on the appropriateness of our division of variables into those affecting costs only and those affecting the costs of search and the wage offer distribution is available. The coefficients γ, those variables which affect only cost, should be the same under both versions of the employment equation (with and without the predicted wage). From table 9.2 we see that the coefficients on dependents, marital status, unemployment benefits and maximum duration of benefits are practically the same for the two versions of the equation. Consequently we are reasonably confident about our classification of variables.

In order to estimate f_1 and, therefore, interpret our model in more detail we must obtain estimates of α and θ.[3] A natural estimate of α is the inverse

[3]The variance restriction noted in the text above was not binding for these data (i.e., the only f_1 violating the $\hat{\sigma}_r>0$ constraint were greater than one).

of mean duration of unemployment in our sample. The mean duration in our sample is 34 weeks. We present estimates of the reservation wage function based on a value of θ of 0.1, a traditional value for discount rates. The implied value of f_1 is 0.94. The estimated parameters of the structural and reduced forms of the reservation wage equations corresponding to this value of f_1 is given in table 9.4. Comparing the structural and reduced form estimates is of interest and shows, for example, that age and education affect reservation wages primarily through their effect on the wage offer distribution facing an individual.

To estimate the variance structure note that the coefficient on expected wage, $X\hat{\beta}$, in the structural employment probit is equal to $\sigma^{-1}(1-f_1)$. Consequently, for $\theta=0.25$

$$\sigma^2=\sigma_0^2-2\sigma_{0,r}+\sigma_r^2=0.148 \tag{14}$$

and since the coefficient on λ in the GLS regression in table 9.3 has interpretation

$$\frac{(\sigma_0^2-\sigma_{0,r})}{\sigma} \tag{15}$$

we have

$$(\sigma_0^2-\sigma_{0,r})=0.006. \tag{16}$$

An estimate of σ_0^2 is available (and was used in constructing the GLS estimators, following Heckman [3]) from the squared residuals from (1). The estimate is $\sigma_0^2=0.1866$. Consequently, $\sigma_{0,r}=0.193$ and σ_r^2 can be obtained from (14). The resulting variance–covariance matrix for the joint distribution of ϵ^0 and ϵ^r is

$$V=\begin{bmatrix} 0.187 & 0.193 \\ 0.193 & 0.214 \end{bmatrix}, \tag{17}$$

which implies a correlation of 0.97 between the errors in the wage offer distribution and those in the reservation wage function.[4]

[4]The corresponding variance–covariance matrix for the errors in the offer and employment equations are

$$\begin{bmatrix} 0.187 & -0.006 \\ -0.006 & 0.015 \end{bmatrix},$$

which implies a correlation between the errors in the offer equation and the employment equation of -0.116.

The high correlation between errors in the wage offer function and those in the reservation wage function indicates that the amount of "pure" wage variation is not as large as one would have expected merely from looking at the unexplained variation in the wage offer function. Taken literally the amount of unexplained variation would be 56.2 per cent of the total—a degree of randomness that is difficult to accept. If 97 per cent of this is accounted for by unmeasured factors—that is, if the correlation between reservation wages and market offers is due solely to omitted productivity factors—then obviously the amount of pure wage variation is considerably less. An interesting research question is how to appropriately decompose the observed variance into unmeasured individual specific components and pure wage variation. We defer this topic to a later paper.

A central assumption used in estimating this model of search activity is that the distribution of wage offers is distributed log-normally. This assumption greatly facilitates the computation of the estimates, since the conditional mean of a normal variable can be easily estimated. Alternative distributions could be considered, but their use would require full maximum likelihood estimation. It is beyond the scope of the present paper to pursue this approach; instead we employ a direct test of the distributional assumption. Distributional tests are not usually performed on cross-section data, in part because the large number of observations available usually means that some peculiar outlier will occur. In the present context, however, the nature of the distribution, in particular the appropriate truncation point, suggests that such a test be applied. Although the failure to pass such a test will not indicate the appropriate area in which further work needs to be done, the passing of such a test would be fairly persuasive evidence in favor of the model.

We note here that the distribution of the errors in the equation for observed wages does not have a simple form. Although these errors are independently distributed, conditional on the parameters being known, they are not identically distributed. The density of the errors can be derived as follows. Let $p(\epsilon^0,\epsilon)$ be the joint density of the errors in the earnings and employment equations. This is assumed to be bivariate normal with zero means, variances σ_0^2 and σ^2 and covariance $\rho\sigma_0\sigma$. If the distribution is truncated so that only points for which $\epsilon > -s$ are observed the joint density becomes (Johnson and Kotz [4])

$$\left[1-\Phi\left(-\frac{s}{\sigma}\right)\right]^{-1} p(\epsilon^0,\epsilon) \qquad \begin{cases} -\infty<\epsilon^0<\infty, \\ -s<\epsilon<\infty. \end{cases}$$

To find the marginal density of ϵ^0 we integrate ϵ out of this density. Write the joint density as the product of the conditional and the marginal

$$p(\epsilon^0,\epsilon)=p(\epsilon|\epsilon^0)p(\epsilon^0).$$

Using properties of the normal distribution it is clear that

$$p(\epsilon|\epsilon^0)=\phi\left(\frac{\epsilon/\sigma-\rho(\epsilon^0/\sigma^0)}{\sqrt{(1-\rho^2)}}\right)(\sigma\sqrt{(1-\rho^2)})^{-1}$$

and

$$p(\epsilon^0)=\phi(\epsilon^0/\sigma^0)\sigma_0^{-1}.$$

Therefore,

$$f(\epsilon^{0*})=\frac{\int_{-s}^{\infty}}{\sigma}\left[1-\Phi\left(-\frac{s}{\sigma}\right)\right]^{-1}p(\epsilon^0,t)\,\mathrm{d}t$$

$$=f_i(\epsilon^{0*})=\frac{\sigma_0^{-1}\phi\left(\frac{\epsilon_i^{0*}}{\sigma^0}\right)\left[1-\Phi\left(\frac{(-s_i/\sigma)-(\rho\epsilon_i^{0*}/\sigma^0)}{\sqrt{(1-\rho^2)}}\right)\right]}{1-\Phi\left(\frac{-s_i}{\sigma}\right)}, \tag{18}$$

where ϕ is the standard normal density function and Φ is the corresponding cumulative distribution function. It is clear that the density of ϵ_i^{0*} depends on s_i unless ρ is zero. The first two moments of this density were given above. The implication of having nonidentically distributed errors is that the residuals cannot be used directly to form a simple test of the distributional hypothesis such as the Kolmogorov–Smirnov test. However, a transformation which makes the errors identically distributed is available. Let $F_i(x)$ be the distribution function corresponding to the density $f_i(x)$, that is

$$F_i(x)=\int_{-\infty}^{x} f_i(t)\,\mathrm{d}t.$$

Then the random variables

$$y_i=F_i(x) \tag{19}$$

are distributed according to the uniform distribution on [0, 1]. To show this let $g(y)$ denote the density of y and standard formulae give:

$$g(y)=f_i(F_i^{-1}(y))\frac{\mathrm{d}F_i^{-1}(y)}{\mathrm{d}y},$$

but from (19),

$$\begin{aligned}\mathrm{d}y_i&=\mathrm{d}F_i(F_i^{-1}(y))\,\mathrm{d}F_i^{-1}(y)\\&=f_i(F_i^{-1}(y))\,\mathrm{d}F_i^{-1}(y),\end{aligned}$$

so

$$g(y)=1, \qquad 0\leqslant y\leqslant 1.$$

This property of probability distributions is discussed in, for example, Kendall and Stuart [5]. In order to test our distributional hypothesis we transform the residuals to independently identically distributed uniform random variables using the above transformations.[5] Under the null hypothesis that the underlying error distribution is bivariate normal these transformed residuals will have the uniform distribution. A Kolmorogov–Smirnov test can be performed to test whether the observed distribution is significantly different from the uniform.

To perform this test we need the integral of $f_i(\epsilon)$ from minus infinity to ϵ. Since a closed form solution to the integral of (18) does not exist, numerical methods were required. We evaluated the integral over the range -11 to ϵ by a 24-point Gaussian quadrature.[6] The Kolmorogov–Smirnov test is based on the statistic $\sqrt{N}\cdot D$ where D is defined as

$$D=\max\left|\frac{i}{N}-S_N(y_i)\right|$$

and S_N is the empirical CDF. The value of the K–S statistic obtained was 1.86 which exceeds the 90 per cent critical value of 1.32. Thus the data in this sample do not completely support this specification of the model. The source of this discrepancy is not clear; the K–S statistic tests the full specification of the model—both distributional assumptions and the functional form of the equations. Thus, although the model yields results which

[5]This method of constructing identically distributed random variables is quite general and can be used to test distributional assumptions other than that used in this paper.

[6]In practice this procedure was fast and efficient.

are plausible and intuitively appealing, the rejection by the K–S test indicates that further investigation is necessary.

5. Conclusion

In this paper we have examined the econometric issues involved in estimating a simple job search model, and presented some preliminary econometric work on the topic. Subject to the identification problems discussed—that some variables must effect wages but not costs of search, and conditional on the value of θ, the average rate of time preference—it is possible to estimate the determinants of reservation wages. The advantage which this approach possesses is that a broader set of questions about labor market behavior can be asked, and more accurate estimates of the quantitative effects of various policy measures can be obtained. For example, it is possible in this framework to analyze exactly how unemployment insurance payments affect wages or duration of unemployment. Although this paper represents a start, there is clearly much more that needs to be done. Our investigation was in the context of a simple job search model, and the empirical results obtained, while generally consistent, indicate that more complex models may be required.

References

[1] Classen, K., "The effects of unemployment insurance: evidence from Pennsylvania", CNA mimeo, April 1975.

[2] Ehrenberg, R., and Oaxaca, R., "Unemployment insurance, duration of unemployment, and subsequent wage gain", *American Economic Review*, 66, (1976), 754–766.

[3] Heckman, J., "Sample selection bias as a specification error", forthcoming in *Econometrica*.

[4] Johnson, N., and Kotz, S., *Distributions in Statistics*: *Volume Four*, *Continuous Multivariate Distributions*, John Wiley, New York, 1972.

[5] Kendall, M., and Stuart, A., *The Advanced Theory of Statistics*, Vol. II, 2nd edition, Hafner Publishing Company, New York, 1967.

[6] McCall, J. J., "Economics of information and job search", *Quarterly Journal of Economics*, 84, (1970), 113–126.

[7] Mohabbat, K. A., and Simos, E. O., "Consumer horizon: further evidence", *Journal of Political Economy*, 85 (1977), 851–858.

[8] Mortensen, D. T., "Job search, the duration of unemployment and the Phillips curve", *American Ecconomic Review*, 60 (1970), 847–862.

[9] Neumann, G., "The direct labor market effects of the trade adjustment assistance program", in (ed. Dewald, W. G.), *The Impact of International Trade and Investment on Employment*, GPO, Washington, DC, 1978, pp. 100–122.

CHAPTER 10

Unemployment insurance and job search

KATHLEEN P. CLASSEN*

Center for Naval Analyses

1. Introduction

The growing body of theoretical work on optimal job search characterizes the unemployed individual as an income-or utility-maximizing searcher in an environment in which there are significant costs of obtaining information about job opportunities.[1] Some of the specific behavioral predictions of the various search theory models differ according to the assumptions made about the nature of the search environment and individual preferences, but the general framework places the job seeker squarely on center stage. He no longer waits in the wings to be propelled into a job by the whims of aggregate demand.

This recasting has important implications because it highlights the productive aspects of unemployment that were not apparent in previous models. The search–theoretic framework has also focused attention on the factors that influence search behavior and, consequently, on the potential government role in many areas in which public policy affects the job search environment.

One way in which the government can influence the job search environment is through unemployment insurance (UI). Since benefit payments lower the cost of unemployment, they may increase the duration of unemployment. This hypothesized relationship between the duration of unemployment and UI has received a great deal of attention recently for two reasons. First, the initial impetus came from empirical work on

*The author is indebted to the editors of this volume and to Frank Brechling, Glen Gotz and James Hosek for their very valuable comments on an earlier draft of this paper.

[1]For a survey of this literature see Lippman and McCall [16].

unemployment that was motivated by theoretical models of job search. The response of the unemployed to UI is an indication of the extent to which job seekers actively weigh the costs and benefits of remaining unemployed and, hence, it serves as an empirical test of the validity of the search–theoretic characterization of unemployment. The relationship between UI-induced unemployment and earnings following unemployment is of particular interest since a major contribution of search theory has been to point out that unemployment can represent time that is devoted to obtaining a better job.

Second, the UI program has also received considerable attention recently because of a growing suspicion that changes in the unemployment rate may not always measure changes in the health of the economy. Many people feel that at least some unemployment is due to the incentives provided by UI and that the "natural" rate of unemployment has risen in the last three years because of liberalizations in the UI program, particularly the December 1974 legislation that increased the duration of benefits and the number of workers covered by the program. If UI has raised the "natural" rate, then fiscal and monetary policies may only buy a temporary reduction in unemployment at a cost of higher inflation. The long term result could be higher inflation with no mitigating reductions in unemployment.

This paper presents empirical estimates of the effects of UI on the duration of unemployment and earnings following unemployment. The empirical results are preceded by a brief discussion of the theoretical effects of unemployment insurance in job search models. The conclusion provides a summary of the results and comments on the usefulness of the results in formulating public policy.

2. Job search models and unemployment insurance

Early models of job search, including those of McCall [18] and Mortensen [19] led to the prediction that an increase in UI causes an increase in the expected duration of unemployment and an increase in expected wages following unemployment. The job seeker in these models maximizes his expected income through an optimal stopping rule that determines a set of acceptable wages during each period of a sequential search process. The search process is sequential because there is a positive probability that it will terminate (an acceptable wage will be encountered) in any period that contains search activity.[2]

In the standard search model, the optimal set of acceptable offers can frequently be described by a single number–the reservation wage.[3] Any offer equal to or above the reservation wage is accepted. An increase in the reservation wage means that more offers will be rejected and therefore, that the expected duration of unemployment will be longer. The marginal cost of raising the reservation wage is the expected forgone income plus search costs associated with the expected increase in duration. The reservation wage equates this marginal cost with its expected, discounted marginal benefit (i.e., the gain in lifetime earnings that would result from a higher reservation wage). Since unemployment insurance lowers the forgone earnings costs of unemployment, an increase in the level of benefit payments leads to a higher reservation wage and to a longer expected duration of unemployment. If the reservation wage (ξ) is constant over the duration of unemployment, an increase in UI will also lead to a higher expected post-unemployment wage ($E(\overline{W})$). This can be seen from the facts that $\mathrm{d}E(\overline{W})/\mathrm{d}\xi > 0$ and ξ is an increasing function of UI benefits.

Early models of search behavior generated constant reservation wages and, hence, the positive relationship between UI and the two observable outcomes of the optimal search strategy: the duration of search and post-unemployment wages. The constant reservation wage feature was a result of assumptions made in characterizing the search environment, specifically, that the searcher faces the same environment in every period that he is unemployed. The searcher's remaining life in these models is not shorter after each search period (infinite horizon), nor does he come closer to the day that his UI benefits end. Since he was assumed to be risk neutral, neither wealth nor risk aversion has any influence. In addition, he has complete information about the offer distribution. In this environment, a reservation wage that is optimal in period t is also optimal in period $t+1$.

Although this simple model of search behavior has motivated a number of empirical tests of search theory (see Ehrenberg and Oaxaca [6]), the predictions of the model are not robust with respect to the assumptions made when it comes to the effects of UI. Almost all models predict a

[2]Stigler's [26] pioneering work postulated a non-sequential stopping rule that optimized the number of offers collected. His major concern was demonstrating that a rational job seeker does not always accept the first offer. Subsequent work on optimal search strategies demonstrated the superiority of sequential search.

[3]Rothchild [23] is responsible for the best counter-example. A low wage is accepted and a higher wage is rejected because of the information that the offer conveys about the unknown distribution of wage offers. In the standard model the distribution is known and this problem does not arise.

positive relationship between UI and expected durations but the relationship between UI and expected post-unemployment wages depends crucially on the constant reservation wage property of the early models. The following is a simple example that illustrates the effects of UI on duration and post-unemployment wages in an environment where optimal reservation wages decline over the period of unemployment. It also illustrates the dynamic programming methodology that is used in sequential search models.

Example 1. Suppose an unemployed searcher, who had five periods left in his working life, faces the following distribution of three possible wage offers: $(\pi(\$60), \pi(\$30), \pi(\$10)) = (0.1, 0.3, 0.6)$. Suppose also that the searcher receives one offer per period to begin work the following period and he must accept or reject the offer when it is made. He cannot search while he is employed and he gets UI benefits if he is unemployed only for the first three periods. A zero discount rate and no search costs are assumed for simplicity. If our searcher is unemployed at the beginning of period t, and he sets an income-maximizing reservation wage ($\xi^*(t)$) each period, the expected value of his total income for the remainder of his working life is Y_t where:

$$E(Y_t) = \max_{\xi(t)} \left[\pi(W \geqslant \xi(t)) \cdot E(W | W \geqslant \xi(t)) \cdot (5-t) + \pi(W < \xi(t)) [Y_{t+1} + UI_{t+1}] \right] \quad (1)$$

If the searcher is unemployed in period 4, he will accept any offer for period 5 since there is no return to search in the last period before retirement. Thus, $\xi^*(4) = 10$. The reservation wages for the other periods can be calculated by substituting $\xi^*(4) = 10 = \xi^*(t+1)$ into (1) and solving iteratively for $\xi^*(3), \xi^*(2)$ and $\xi^*(1)$. The resulting values of $\xi^*(t)$ are given in table 10.1 for three levels of UI.

Each time-path of reservation wages is associated with an expected post-unemployment wage, $E(\overline{W})$, and an expected duration of unemployment, $E(D)$. If π_t is the probability of starting work at the beginning of period t, then

$$\pi_t = \pi[W \geqslant \xi^*(t-1)] \left(1 - \sum_{i=1}^{i=t-1} \pi_i \right), \qquad \pi_1 = 0, \quad (2)$$

$$E(\overline{W}) = \sum_{t=1}^{5} \pi_t \cdot E(W | W > \xi^*(t-1)), \quad (3)$$

$$E(D) = \sum_{t=1}^{5} \pi_t \cdot (t-1). \quad (4)$$

Table 10.1

UI for periods 1,2,3	Reservation wage $\xi^*(t)$ (π_t in parentheses) 1	2	3	4	5	Expected post-unemployment wage	Expected duration of unemployment
0	30	30	30	.10		33.94	2.2
		(0.40)	(0.24)	(0.144)	(0.216)		
40	60	30	30	10		34.40	2.8
		(0.10)	(0.36)	(0.216)	(0.324)		
50	60	60	30	10		33.76	3.2
		(0.10)	(0.09)	(0.324)	(0.486)		

The last two columns of table 10.1 list the expected post-unemployment wages and the expected durations for reservation wage paths associated with three levels of unemployment insurance. Note that although $E(D)$ is increasing with UI, there is a nonmonotonic relationship between $E(\overline{W})$ and UI. An increase in UI does not always lead to an increase in expected post-unemployment wages. When a searcher sets a high reservation wage in the early period of search because of UI payments, he increases the probability that he will be out of work in later periods when the reservation wage is low. The probability that our hypothetical searcher is still out of work in the last search period more than doubles when benefits are increased from 0 to \$50. An increase in UI always leads to an increase in the expected value of income (which includes UI) but it may lead to a decrease in expected post-unemployment wages when reservation wages decline over time.

In all search models, if t^* is the length of the benefit period and the offer distribution is continuous and positive on $[0, \infty]$, the effects of an increase in the level of weekly benefit payments (WBA) *on newly unemployed UI recipients* can be summarized as follows:[4]

$$\text{(a)}\quad \mathrm{d}\xi^*(t)/\mathrm{d}WBA > 0, \text{ if } t^* > 0, \text{ and } t < t^*, \tag{5}$$

thus

$$\text{(b)}\quad \mathrm{d}E(D)/\mathrm{d}WBA > 0, \tag{6}$$

[4]The second effect–(b)–that UI increases the expected duration–is a weaker than necessary prediction. Duration is stochastically increasing with the level of unemployment insurance. This means that the probability that any given number of weeks of duration is exceeded is a positive function of UI. This stronger condition implies (b) but (b) does not imply stochastic superiority.

but

$$\text{(c)}\quad \mathrm{d}E(\overline{W})/\mathrm{d}WBA > 0 \text{ or } < 0 \text{ if } \xi(t) > \xi(t+1). \tag{7}$$

The length of the benefit period is another parameter of the UI system that affects search behavior. An increase in t^* increases reservation wages and, hence, the expected duration of unemployment. Again, if reservation wages decline over time, the effect of an increase in t^* on the expected wage is ambiguous. Our hypothetical searcher can be used here also to demonstrate the ambiguity. For each level of UI listed in table 10.1, $t^*=3$. We can also hold the UI payment per period constant and let t^* vary. It can be shown by straightforward computation that if the level of UI is set at \$40 per period and the $\xi^*(t)$'s are computed for $t^*=2,3$ and 4, the reservation wage paths are the same (reading downward in order) as the three paths shown in table 10.1. Since the paths are the same, they lead to the same expected durations, and the same nonmonotonic relationship between t^* and $E(\overline{W})$. In all search models, an increase in the number of periods that benefits are available increases the expected duration of unemployment. The same increase may, however, either increase or decrease expected post-unemployment wages.

The important feature of the example above is that optimal reservation wages decline. There is a good deal of empirical evidence that reservation wages do decline over the period of unemployment.[5] They decline in the example partly because of approaching retirement (finite horizon) but largely because UI benefits are not available indefinitely.

There are other reasons why optimal reservation wages decline with time and these reasons have been explored by more recent work in search theory. This work has investigated the theoretical implications of relaxing the assumptions of the standard model. The simplifying assumptions of this search model, which helped to expose the basic character of optimum sequential search, were relaxed to incorporate more realistic features of the decision-making process faced by an unemployed worker. These added features often lead to declining optimum reservation wages. The inclusion of risk aversion in a search model is just one example of a change in assumptions that leads to declining reservation wages.[6] When the utility

[5]Kasper [13] is one of the earliest studies. Katz [14] presents additional evidence and reviews several other studies of reservation wage flexibility.

[6]See Nachman [21] and Hall, Lippman and McCall [8].

function is characterized by decreasing absolute risk aversion, reservation wages decline as wealth decreases. Wealth declines as unemployment lengthens even in an infinite horizon model because of search costs and effective wealth declines in finite horizon models because of search costs and because the expected working life shortens with lengthening unemployment.

In addition to the effect that declining wealth has on risk aversion and thus, upon reservation wages, the threat of approaching bankruptcy may also cause a decline in reservation wages. If assets fall below some critical level (the bankruptcy point), the searcher may be forced to take the next job offered. Since continuing unemployment reduces wealth, it increases the chances that bankruptcy will occur, and hence, the threat of bankruptcy has the same effect as the mandatory retirement in the numerical example above–reservation wages decline.

The new wrinkle in models with risk aversion and the threat of bankruptcy is that asset levels affect a searcher's reservation wage. This feature plays a role in determining the theoretical effects of UI in two ways. First, asset sensitive models lead to declining reservation wages, and the affect of UI on post-unemployment wages is ambiguous when reservation wages decline. Second, UI has a direct affect on assets so an increase in UI has the same effect as an increase in assets. In the above summary of the effects of UI, the positive effect of UI on reservation wages (a) was restricted to the duration of benefits. In an asset-sensitive model, the effect of UI on reservation wages can linger past the end of benefits because an increase in UI increases assets, and if the utility function exhibits declining absolute risk aversion, reservation wages will be higher with an increase in UI even after benefits end.

Other search models have concentrated on relaxing the assumption in the standard model that searchers sample randomly from some known, fixed wage distribution. Salop [24], for instance, has modeled an environment where searchers can rank firms according to likely wage offers and they proceed from higher to lower firms (systematic search). In this environment, reservation wages decline. Another assumption that can be made is that searchers do not know the actual distribution of wages, but that they form priors and update them with the information contained in successive job offers. Initially, over-optimistic job searchers have high reservation wages that they will revise downward. Since their pessimistic counterparts are plucked out of the cohort early because of their low but rising reservation wages, an adaptive search process can lead to observed reservation wages that are, on average, declining.

In the example presented above, there is no distinction between time not working and search time. The search environment is characterized by assuming that the searcher has some fixed probability of receiving an offer each period. Given that the individual chooses to participate in the labor force, the amount of search per period (search intensity) is not controlled by the searcher. More recent contributions to the search theory literature have modeled not only the setting of the reservation wage but also the determinants of job search intensity.[7] The inclusion of search intensity as a choice variable introduces another factor that may lead to a negative relationship between the level of UI payments and expected post-unemployment wages. The optimal search intensity equates the marginal value of time in search and the marginal utility of time in the home, since both have the same price, namely, forgone earnings. If UI increases the marginal utility of time in the home (leisure and goods are complements) then not only will the reservation wage increase with an increase in UI but job search intensity will decrease to maintain this equality. Both of these responses will increase the expected duration of unemployment, and, when reservation wages decline with time, reduced job intensity increases the likelihood of being out of work when reservation wages are low. Thus, expansion of search models to allow for variable search intensity reinforces the prediction that an increase in UI will have a positive effect on expected duration and an ambiguous effect on expected post-unemployment wages.

There is an exception to the rule that all search models predict that an increase in UI increases the expected duration of unemployment and that exception is the reason that the effects of an increase in the *WBA* (a, b, c) were restricted to newly unemployed UI recipients. Most search models assume that once a job is accepted, it is kept until retirement or until a better job is located. Mortensen [20] has developed a model that includes the possibility of being laid off and this causes some new responses to UI. In Mortensen's model, workers who are not eligible for UI–new entrants, for example–may decrease their reservation wages and their expected durations when UI levels are increased because the value of working, which includes rights to UI payments, has increased. This same caveat applies to UI recipients who are near exhaustion: since future UI payments increase more than the nearly used up current payments, it becomes more attractive to return to work; consequently, reservation wages are lowered when the UI is increased.

[7]In Lippman and McCall [16] more job offers can be located by spending more money on search, and in Mortensen [19] or Burdett [1] by giving up leisure time.

3. Empirical results

The empirical results presented in this paper are based on administrative data from two state UI systems. The data are records of claimants who filed and were eligible for UI. Since the data come only from the UI-covered population and since every claimant had the same benefit amount over his entire spell of unemployment, the Mortensen caveat does not apply. Thus, an increase in UI should have a positive effect on expected durations, but the effect of UI on post-unemployment wages is ambiguous. There is a cautionary note that should be given about the correspondence between job search models and the empirical tests presented here. Job search models are a partial analysis with the wage offer distribution given exogenously. There is reason to believe that wages are not exogenous with respect to unemployment insurance. Since UI payments are part of the compensation package, an increase in UI could lead to a compensating reduction in wages. It may also be the case that employers view a lengthy spell of unemployment as a bad sign in judging the expected marginal product of a job applicant and thus, if UI increases the duration of unemployment, it may lower the distribution of wage offers facing a searcher. Equilibrium adjustments like these have not been tackled in search models and this should be kept in mind in evaluating the empirical work; the reported results may be due to UI-induced changes in wage offers as well as changes in the actions taken by job-seekers.

Whether or not the estimates of the effects of UI presented here are the result of the adjustment mechanisms described in any particular search model is not relevant to the issue of the relationship between UI and the unemployment rate. If an increase in UI always leads to an increase in the average duration of unemployment, without offsetting changes in the incidence of unemployment, then the unemployment rate will rise when benefit payments are liberalized.

3.1. The data

The data sets for this study come from two states: Arizona and Pennsylvania. They consist of quarterly earnings histories of individuals which were collected from employers to determine UI payroll taxes and benefit entitlement when a claim is filed. These quarterly tax records were merged with UI claim histories to form a longitudinal work and claim history for a random sample of UI claimants in both states.

The results reported in this paper are based on claims filed in the year before and the year after an increase in benefit entitlement that occurred in Pennsylvania on 1 January 1968 and in Arizona on 7 July 1968. This two-year period was chosen to avoid seasonal bias and to provide variation in benefit entitlement that is independent of previous earnings.

One major advantage of this data is that it contains the records of claimants who returned to work after filing a claim and before receiving any benefits. In many studies of the effects of UI, these claimants were either not included in the sample or were included with a weekly benefit entitlement equal to zero.[8] Both options are likely to introduce bias in the estimates of the effects of UI on duration and subsequent earnings. The data are also extremely accurate in comparison with the survey data used in many of the other studies. Measurement errors due to the inability or unwillingness of a survey respondent to recall such key variables as earnings or the weekly benefit amount are likely to be minimal in these samples.

Claim histories do have a major drawback. They record only the compensated weeks of unemployment, not total week of unemployment. The measured duration of unemployment for claimants who exhaust their benefits is truncated at the maximum number of weeks of eligibility. There is, however, a maximum likelihood technique (TOBIT) that is designed for this type of truncation problem. Both OLS and TOBIT results are reported.

3.2. *Methodological approaches to the data*

The empirical analysis in this paper consists of regression equations which relate: (i) the duration of unemployment, and (ii) post-unemployment earnings to levels of UI and other variables. All regressions are of the general form:

$$OUTCM = f(WBA, M, \bar{C}),$$

where *OUTCM* is one of the observable outcomes of the search strategy, either duration or post-unemployment earnings, *WBA* is the weekly benefit

[8]Estimates of the effect of UI on duration and/or earnings that are based on individual (as opposed to aggregate) data can be found in Lininger [15], Schmidt [25], Burgess and Kingston [2], Hills [10], Ehrenberg and Oaxaca [6], Holen [11] and Warner [28].

amount, M is the maximum potential duration of benefits (in weeks) and $\overline{C}$ is a vector of personal and labor market characteristics.

The duration and the earnings equations contain the same independent variables because post-unemployment earnings and expected durations are determined simultaneously; they are expected outcomes of an unobserved choice that a worker makes about the wages he will accept and how hard he will search. Anything that alters either of these elements of a worker's search strategy affects both the expected post-unemployment earnings and the expected duration of unemployment.

Independent variables, other than the two UI variables, were dictated by the data sets. Any variable that was in both data sets and was thought to reflect the wage offer distribution facing an individual or his search strategy was included in the regressions.[9] Sex and age are two demographic variables that were included in the regression both because they reflect individual choices (based on such factors as the value of time and discount rates) and because they may reflect differences in market opportunities for different ages and sexes.

Search models really don't have much to say about observable variables such as age and sex. Most of the variables in search models are unobservables, such as discount rates, the degree of risk aversion, and perceived offer distributions. In empirical work, observed variables are used as proxies for variables in search models. Most of the time, however, each variable in a data set reflects unobservable variables that influence both the offer distribution of wages and an individual's search strategy, almost always in ways that have an ambiguous effect on the duration of unemployment and post-unemployment earnings. Increased age, for instance, can reflect a shorter remaining working life, a lower discount rate, or a greater variance in the offer distribution because of increases in human capital. The theoretical upshot is ambiguous. Variables such as age are included in the regression not because their effects can be derived from search theory but because we know that these factors are influential in determining the outcome of the search process. Unemployment insurance is one of the few variables that is both observable and appears directly in search models, which is one reason that it is a particularly popular variable with search theorists.

Two measures of previous earnings have also been included in the regression. The first is earnings in the best quarter in the year before

[9]The Arizona data set had all the information that was included in the Pennsylvania data and much more. The additional variables in Arizona (e.g., occupation) did not affect the results reported here.

unemployment.[10] The second is the ratio of annual earnings to earnings in the best quarter, which is a measure of earnings stability that must lie between 1.0 (earnings only in one quarter) and 4.0 (constant earnings over the previous year). These measures should reflect differences in the offer distribution between individuals because of differences in human capital or firm-specific skill. Earnings stability also measures the seasonality of certain jobs and hence, to some extent, the correlation of unemployment spells over time.

Although it is certain that pre- and post-unemployment earnings will on average be positively related, the relationship between pre-unemployment earnings and the duration of unemployment is ambiguous. Higher potential earnings mean that the opportunity costs of being unemployed are higher and hence that the duration of unemployment should be shorter. But higher earnings could also reflect a wider range of alternatives (an offer distribution with a higher variance) and this effect works in the opposite direction–towards longer durations. As noted earlier, earnings instability reflects unemployment in the previous year so stability should be negatively related to the duration of unemployment. The relationship between earnings stability and post-unemployment earnings is not obvious, but a positive relationship between stability and the post-unemployment earnings measure used here (best quarter earnings after unemployment) seems likely because stable earners have more solid quarters of work from which to pick the best.

Industry dummies, which are based on the 2-digit SIC of the principal industry in the base year, are included in the regressions to measure demand conditions relative to the omitted class (wholesale–retail trade). There are also two cyclical variables in the regression equations. 'Year' measures the effect of differences in cyclical conditions between the two sample years. Since any cyclical effect could differ by skill level ('previous earnings'), a 'year–skill' interaction term was also included.

There are two UI variables in each regression: WBA and 'max weeks' (M). The weekly benefit amount (WBA) is determined by previous earnings and it can be collected for up to M in the 52-week period following the date that the claim is filed (the benefit year). In Pennsylvania, benefits can be collected for up to 30 weeks and in Arizona, for up to 26 weeks. Some claimants are not entitled to the maximum number of weeks because the total award in the benefit year is limited to a fraction of the earnings in

[10]In this paper the year before unemployment means the *base year* which is the first four of the last five calendar quarters preceding the date that the claim is filed.

the previous year. If more than one spell of unemployment occurs during the benefit year, the *WBA* remains unchanged. Since the legal parameters that determined *WBA* and *M* in the two states are referred to several times in the remainder of this paper, they are summarized in table 10.2.

One of the most difficult methodological issues in the empirical analysis reported here was determining the best functional form for the regression equations. The analytic solution to search models depends on such unobservable elements as the offer distribution of wages; but even if these unobservable elements were known, the resulting equations for reservation wages, expected durations, and expected post-unemployment wages usually have no explicit solution. Consequently, the results of several functional forms are reported in this paper. As it turns out, some results are robust with respect to functional form so that conclusions can be drawn despite the fact that the issue of functional form has not been dealt with directly.

Since the tactic of multiple approaches is used throughout the paper, there are many reported regression results. First, the total sample in each state is examined with different OLS functional forms; then, maximum likelihood regressions are used to remove the bias caused by the truncation of observed weeks of unemployment at the maximum weeks that benefits are available.

Following the regressions that combine both years of sample data, the results of regressions within a single year are presented. Within a single year there is an almost exact linear relationship between previous earnings and the *WBA* up to a maximum *WBA*. This relationship is used to fit a

Table 10.2. UI legal parameters,

	Pennsylvania (1967 and 1968)	Arizona (7 July 1967 to 7 July 1969)
Weekly benefit amount		
As a fraction of highest quarter earnings:	1/26	1/25
Maximum *WBA* if claim filed in:		
year 1:	\$45	\$43
year 2:	\$60	\$50
Maximum total award		
As a fraction of previous annual earnings	1/2	1/3
Maximum weeks of benefits	30	26

piecewise linear regression that eliminates the *WBA* since it has no independent variation within a single year. Up to the maximum benefit amount, both previous earnings and the *WBA* increase in step; after that, only earnings increase. The piecewise linear equation is allowed to break at the point where the *WBA* stops increasing. Then, inferences are drawn from the behavior of the equation at the break about the influences of both previous earnings and the *WBA* on the independent variables.

Finally, the regressions are repeated for those who returned to their pre-unemployment employer (recalls) and for those who did not to see if those waiting for recalls react differently to the incentives provided by unemployment insurance.

In general, the results of all the approaches lead to the same conclusion: UI has a significant effect on the duration of unemployment but little effect on post-unemployment earnings. Although each separate approach has its flaws, the concurring evidence provided by all the approaches is convincing.

3.3. The effects of UI on duration

In job search models, an increase in UI leads to an increase in the reservation wage, a possible decrease in search intensity, and, consequently, an increase in the expected duration of unemployment. The purpose of the empirical work presented in this section is to determine whether there is a positive relationship between the liberality of UI payments and the expected duration of unemployment.

The dependent variable in the duration equations is the number of compensated weeks of unemployment in the year following a claim for unemployment insurance. Table 10.3 lists the coefficients which result from three different specifications of the relationship between this measure of the duration of unemployment and the independent variables described above. The first column under each state lists the estimated coefficients from an OLS linear regression. The second column is coefficients from a regression in which all continuous variables were measured in natural logs. Several other functional forms were also estimated.[11]

[11]The other functional forms included log-linear equations and equations which included squared terms for the continuous independent variables. The age variable was also put into discrete classifications; 0–25, 26–40, 41–55, 55+. The age effect on duration appears to be linear.

Table 10.3. Duration regressions (dependent variable = weeks of compensated unemployment).

Independent variables (*t*-statistics in parenthesis)	Pennsylvania ($N=4240$) Coefficients			Arizona ($N=10.887$) Coefficients		
	Linear OLS	LN-LN OLS	TOBIT	Linear OLS	LN-LN OLS	TOBIT
WBA	0.11 (5.68)	1.03 (8.41)	0.12 (5.79)	0.12 (9.16)	0.84 (11.37)	0.14 (8.98)
Max weeks	0.19 (2.99)	1.09 (4.61)	0.07 (0.94)	0.23 (9.18)	0.58 (8.70)	0.12 (3.82)
Sex ($F=1$)	0.32 (0.88)	0.01 (0.28)	0.44 (1.11)	3.17 (16.26)	0.36 (12.66)	3.77 (16.29)
Age	19 (10.69)	0.46 (8.82)	0.12 (11.10)	0.13 (20.00)	0.72 (19.00)	0.15 (19.67)
Previous earnings	−0.002 (−5.94)	−0.60 (−7.28)	−0.002 (−5.76)	−0.001 (−8.57)	−0.47 (−10.70)	−0.001 (−8.12)
Earnings stab	3.07 (−10.83)	−1.32 (−12.36)	−3.13 (−10.05)	−1.25 (−8.76)	−0.65 (−11.92)	−1.30 (−7.77)
Industry dummies						
Agriculture	1.55 (1.05)	0.19 (0.94)	1.66 (1.02)	0.22 (0.17)	0.04 (0.19)	0.72 (0.43)
Mining	−2.19 (−1.99)	−0.25 (−1.68)	−2.45 (−2.04)	−2.26 (−6.34)	−0.41 (−7.91)	−2.70 (−5.23)
Construction	1.03 (1.92)	0.26 (3.61)	0.94 (1.61)	0.20 (0.74)	0.14 (3.56)	0.31 (0.97)
Nondurables	−2.68 (−6.45)	−0.33 (−5.83)	−2.97 (−6.55)	−0.17 (−0.48)	0.08 (1.62)	−0.14 (−0.33)
Durables	−0.53 (−1.18)	−0.09 (−1.55)	−0.61 (−1.25)	−0.02 (−0.06)	0.05 (1.28)	0.02 (0.07)
Transportation	−0.79 (−0.92)	−0.14 (−1.23)	−1.00 (−1.08)	−2.01 (−5.11)	−0.36 (−6.28)	−2.23 (−4.86)
Finance	3.50 (3.29)	0.31 (2.16)	4.14 (3.51)	−0.20 (−0.41)	−0.01 (−0.09)	−0.27 (−0.47)
Services	2.60 (4.18)	0.31 (3.61)	3.08 (4.49)	0.46 (1.61)	0.11 (2.63)	0.54 (1.61)
Public admin.[a]				−4.00 (−1.70)	−0.55 (−1.61)	−4.80 (−1.80)
SIC X[b]				1.26 (4.31)	0.25 (6.02)	1.50 (4.45)
Year (year 2 = 1)	−0.32 (−0.58)	1.07 (2.15)	−0.36 (−0.60)	−1.37 (−4.18)	−1.17 (−3.74)	−1.70 (−4.48)
Year–skill	−0.000 (−0.70)	−0.16 (2.34)	−0.000 (−0.77)	0.000 (2.49)	0.15 (3.42)	0.000 (2.62)
Constant	5.76	−1.97	8.94	−2.70	−2.10	−0.88
	$R^2=0.09$	$R^2=0.10$	$\chi^2=2534$	$R^2=0.09$	$R^2=0.10$	$\chi^2=10.037$
	$F=27.8$	$F=29.3$		$F=58.6$	$F=67.5$	

[a]Public administration employees are covered under the Unemployment Compensation for Federal Employees (UCFE) program. This program was not included in the Pennsylvania sample.
[b]Means that the field was blank. Almost exclusively in records of claimants from the military or the federal civilian government.

All OLS regressions produced positive and significant estimates of the *WBA* and *M* coefficients. The two reported functional forms are a very good indication of the range of estimated *WBA* elasticities for all OLS equations. The elasticities at the mean for the linear equations are 0.60 and 0.61 for Pennsylvania and Arizona respectively. The elasticities for the natural log equations are the coefficients. These elasticities imply that, at the mean of the duration and *WBA* variables, a 1 per cent increase in weekly benefits leads to between a 0.6 per cent and a 1 per cent increase in duration.

In the OLS equations, compensated unemployment is used as a surrogate for the more interesting and relevant variable–total weeks of unemployment. Any OLS estimate of the effects of *WBA* on compensated duration may not be an unbiased estimate of the effects of *WBA* on total duration. If an increase in *WBA* increases the probability of exhausting benefits, then there is an unmeasured increase in total duration that is not included in the OLS estimates. The distinction between total duration and compensated duration is even more important in the case of the *M* variable. The coefficient of *M* was positive and significant in all the OLS regressions. The positive coefficients do not necessarily imply that an increase in *M* results in an increase in the total duration of unemployment. Even if *M* had no effect on total duration, there would still be a positive relationship between *M* and compensated duration (*CD*) because an increase in *M* increases the observable range of compensated duration.

If the relationship between total duration (*TD*) and the vector of all independent variables is linear, then

$$TD_i = \beta' \overline{X}_i + \mu_i, \tag{8}$$

$$CD_i = \begin{cases} TD_i & \text{if} \quad TD_i < M_i, & (9) \\ \text{M} & \text{if} \quad TD_i \geqslant M_i & (10) \end{cases}$$

OLS estimates that are based only on compensated duration ($CD_i = TD_i$ for all i) will consistently underestimate *TD* for exhaustees.[12] This implies a systematic relationship between the error term and the exogenous variables. The OLS estimates are not, therefore, unbiased estimates of β'. A maximum likelihood, variable limit, TOBIT equation was estimated to obtain efficient and consistent estimates of β'.[13] The third column under

[12]Exhaustees accounted for 8 per cent of the sample from Pennsylvania and 14 per cent of the sample from Arizona.

[13]See Tobin [27] and Nelson [22].

each state in table 10.3 lists the TOBIT estimates of a linear duration equation. The major difference between OLS results and the TOBIT results is in the coefficient of M. (Compare the first and third columns under each state in table 10.3.) Although the coefficient of M is positive for both states, it is considerably lower than the OLS estimates and not significant for Pennsylvania. The lower estimates using the maximum likelihood technique are not surprising since the TOBIT equations provide estimates of $\partial TD/\partial M$ and TD is not constrained by M. As expected, the TOBIT estimates of the WBA coefficients are slightly higher for both states. The coefficients of WBA for other functional forms of the TOBIT equations can be predicted very accurately by examining the pattern in table 10.3. Although always positive, the M coefficients did not exhibit the same predictability. The strong correlation between M and earnings stability together with the pronounced effect of earnings stability on duration results in estimates that are sensitive to functional form. These results support the hypothesis that an increase in M increases the duration of unemployment but little confidence can be placed in any estimated range of the magnitude of this effect.

The apparent robustness of the significant and positive relationship between duration and WBA can be pursued further. The two year period for each sample was chosen to include a change in WBA that was independent of previous earnings, but the variation of WBA that occurs within years can also be used to provide striking evidence that the level of the weekly benefit payment has a strong effect on the duration of unemployment.[14] If claimants are separated into year 1 claimants and year 2 claimants, then there is a known precise relationship between WBA and PE. Within each sample year, the weekly benefit amount is a constant fraction (α) of previous earnings (PE) up to the maximum weekly benefit amount (K):

$$WBA = \begin{cases} \alpha PE & \text{if} \quad PE < \dfrac{K}{\alpha}, \\ K & \text{if} \quad PE \geqslant \dfrac{K}{\alpha}. \end{cases} \tag{11a}$$

In addition, assume that duration (D) is a linear function of the independent variables, that is

$$D = b_0 + b_1 WBA + b_2 PE + \Sigma b_i X_i. \tag{11b}$$

[14]This test was suggested by Welch [29] in comments made on an earlier paper by Classen [3].

Combining (11a) and (11b) yields:

$$D = b_0 + \gamma_1 PE + \gamma_2 \left[PE - \frac{K}{\alpha} \right] z + \Sigma b_i X, \tag{12}$$

where

$$z = 1 \quad \text{if} \quad PE > \frac{K}{\alpha}, \quad \text{and} \quad 0 \text{ otherwise,}$$

$$\gamma_1 = \alpha b_1 + b_2,$$

$$\gamma_2 = -\alpha b_1.$$

Equation (12) is a piecewise, linear equation that allows the relationship (slope) between previous earnings and duration to change at K/α. Equation (12) does not contain an explicit term for the weekly benefit amount because there is no independent variation in this variable. Between 0 and K/α the *WBA* increases by α for every one dollar increase in *PE* and after K/α the *WBA* equals *K*. Thus, within a single year, we can capture the full effect of both previous earnings and the weekly benefit amount on duration by looking only at previous earnings. According to the OLS linear equation in table 10.3, the piecewise linear equation that fits duration to previous earnings should look like figure 10.1. Up to K/α there are two effects of increased earnings: the negative effect of higher earnings and the positive effect of the higher weekly benefit amount. The linear OLS equation in table 10.3 asserts that the relationship between previous earnings and duration up to K/α should be positive because the positive *WBA* effect (equal to α times the *WBA* coefficient for every one dollar increase in previous earnings) is greater than the negative earnings effect. After K/α only earnings increase, hence, the slope is negative because the *WBA* effect is zero in that region.

The change in the law that occurred in each state provides a natural experiment that can be exploited with piecewise linear regressions. If the

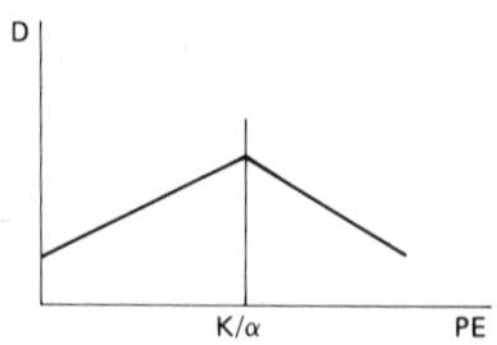

Figure 10.1

relationship between duration and previous earnings is linear and the *WBA* effect is positive, then the piecewise regression should show a change in slope at K/α and only at K/α. The two states, each with a change in the law, give us four tests with four different K/α's. A piecewise linear regression was run for each state in each year. Each equation was allowed to change slope or break at the relevant K/α. In addition, each equation was allowed to break at another point to test the assumption of linearity in the relationship between duration and previous earnings. Both a nonlinear relationship between duration and earnings and a positive *WBA* effect on duration could produce a break at K/α. An extraneous break was added to distinguish between these two cases. Each state has two K/α's, one in year 1 (K_1/α) and another in year 2 (K_2/α). In order to make the computations somewhat simpler, the extraneous break point for year 1 was set equal to K_2/α and the extraneous break point for year 2 was set equal to K_1/α. This leads to the following estimation equation:

$$D=\gamma_0+\gamma_1 PE+\gamma_2\left[PE-\frac{K_1}{\alpha}\right]Z_1+\gamma_3\left[PE-\frac{K_2}{\alpha}\right]Z_2+\Sigma b_i X_i \tag{13}$$

where

$$Z_1=1 \text{ if } PE>\frac{K_1}{\alpha}, \quad \text{and} \quad 0 \text{ otherwise},$$

$$Z_2=1 \text{ if } PE>\frac{K_2}{\alpha}, \quad \text{and} \quad 0 \text{ otherwise},$$

$\alpha=1/26$ for Penn., $1/25$ for Ariz.,

$K_1=\$45$ for Penn., 43 for Ariz.,

$K_2=\$60$ for Penn., 50 for Ariz..

The four piecewise linear equations included all the independent variables (X_i) listed in table 10.3 with the exception of year, year-skill and *WBA*. The OLS estimates of γ_1, γ_2 and γ_3 are presented in table 10.4.

Note that the only significant negative coefficients appear at the relevant break points. This means that the relationship between earnings and duration bends down sharply as soon as the *WBA* stops increasing with earnings; equivalently, increased benefits have a positive effect on duration. Note also that the equations do not bend down at the extraneous break points, neither after the relevant break point, as in the case of year 1, nor before as in the case of year 2.

Table 10.4. Piecewise linear duration equations (dependent variable = weeks of compensated unemployment (t-statistics in parentheses)).[a]

	Pennsylvania Year 1	Pennsylvania Year 2	Arizona Year 1	Arizona Year 2
Estimate of γ_1 = slope up to K_1/α	0.002 (2.10)	−0.000 (−0.14)	0.003 (4.20)	0.004 (3.92)
Estimate of γ_2	[−0.006 (−2.17)]	0.005* (1.75)	[−0.008 (−2.88)]	0.002* (0.64)
Slope between K_1/α and $K_2/\alpha = (\gamma_1+\gamma_2)$	−0.004	0.005	−0.005	0.006
Estimate of γ_3	0.001* (0.57)	[−0.006 (−3.03)]	0.003* (1.50)	[−0.006 (−2.56)]
Slope after $K_2/\alpha = (\gamma_1+\gamma_2+\gamma_3)$	−0.003	0.001	−0.002	0.000

[a]Relevant break points are in boxes. *Indicates extraneous break point

This is an important piece of information; a negative coefficient at the extraneous break point would mean that the equations bent down because duration was a concave function of previous earnings holding benefits constant. This concave relationship would cause the equation to bend down (have a negative coefficient) at the relevant break point. If anything, it appears that duration is a convex function of previous earnings, holding benefits constant; therefore, the negative coefficient at the relevant break point is very strong evidence that benefits increase duration.

The piecewise linear equations give very strong evidence that higher benefits increase the duration of unemployment; but by how much? The relationships expressed in (11a), (11b) and (12) can be used to answer this question. In the year 1 Pennsylvania equation,

$$\gamma_2 = -\alpha b_1 = -0.006.$$

Since $\alpha = 1/26$, the year 1 Pennsylvania equation implies that

$$b_1 = 0.156 = \partial D/\partial WBA.$$

Similar estimates for the other equations can be obtained by multiplying the number in the boxes by 26 in the case of Pennsylvania and 25 in the case of Arizona. These are all larger estimates than produced by the OLS linear equation in table 10.3 because the equation in table 10.3 is equivalent to a piecewise linear spline with only one break point. A single break point assigns all changes in the slope to the *WBA* coefficient and since it appears that the slope is increasing with increased previous earnings (convexity), this assignment dampens the estimate of the *WBA* effect. Thus, the piecewise linear method gives us some insight into why the linear OLS estimates of the *WBA* effect are lower than non-linear estimates.

3.4. Recalls vs. job-changers

Another tactic that was used to investigate the effect of UI benefits on the duration of unemployment was to divide the sample into those who had returned to their pre-unemployment jobs (recalls) and those who did not (job changers). It would seem that since the recall date is largely determined by employer demand conditions rather than employee decisions, the duration for recalls should be less sensitive to *WBA* levels.

Other studies of the incentive effects of UI have eliminated recalls from the sample because they were thought to be nonsearchers. Most of the empirical work reported here includes recalls for two reasons: First, UI levels may affect the decision to wait for recall. If an increase in UI induced some unemployed individuals to wait a few more weeks to be recalled, rather than look for or accept another job, empirical results based on only job changers would not pick this effect. Second, employers may postpone recall dates when UI levels increase because of the tax incentives that Feldstein [7] discusses or because higher UI levels increase the probability that a skilled worker will be available to be recalled.[15] In short, there are many channels through which UI can increase the duration of unemployment, and although not all of them show up in search models, they can all increase the unemployment rate. Including as many people as possible in the sample is the best way to find out how UI affects the unemployment rate through changes in duration.

Neither data set provides any direct information on whether a claimant was recalled. In both states, recalls were identified by indirect means. In Pennsylvania, if someone was reported to have only one employer in a

[15]There are two tax incentives. First, benefits are not taxed as income. Second, the tax system that raises UI funds creates a subsidy to unstable firms. Both of these create incentives that increase the duration of layoffs.

Table 10.5. *WBA* coefficient for recalls and nonrecalls in duration equations (OLS = linear regression (t-statistics in parentheses)).

	Pennsylvania		Arizona	
Recalls	0.08 (1.70)	$N=720$	0.07 (2.66)	$N=2810$
Nonrecalls	0.23 (4.07)	$N=440$	0.14 (8.54)	$N=8080$

calendar year and he was employed before and after his spell of unemployment in the same calendar year, he was identified as a recall. Recalls and nonrecalls do not add up to the total sample size in Pennsylvania because all claimants whose unemployment spanned two calendar years were not included in either group.

In Arizona, identification of recalls was based on employer identification numbers that were not available in Pennsylvania. Each claim history contained the identification number of all employers in the previous year but not in chronological order. The work histories also listed employer numbers, but again, not chronologically. Any claimant whose principal employer in the year after unemployment was the same as any employer in the year before unemployment was marked as a recall. All others were marked as nonrecalls.

Neither method for identifying recalls is perfect, but each produces groups that are largely recall or largely nonrecall. Table 10.5 lists the *WBA* coefficients for recalls and nonrecalls. The independent variables were the same as those listed in table 10.3. There is a difference between the *WBA* coefficients for the two groups and, as expected, the *WBA* coefficient is larger for nonrecalls than for recalls. The positive coefficient for nonrecalls could reflect either the effects of UI or misclassification of the observations. The *M* coefficients were nearly identical for the two groups in both states. This equality implies that most of the positive coefficient produced by OLS estimates is due to the truncation bias discussed earlier. Maximum likelihood techniques do not work very well here because most of the claimants are entitled to the maximum weeks of eligibility. Even the piecewise linear splines do not give much information because there was no change in the *M* law that made the *WBA* analysis so convincing. More independent variation is needed in the *M* variable to get a good estimate of its effects on the duration of unemployment.[16]

[16]Holen [11] presents some convincing evidence based on a cross state comparison that longer benefits do increase actual duration. See Hanna, Butler and Steinman [9] and Dillon and Nicholson [5] for estimates of the effects of the extended benefit programs.

3.5. The effects of UI on earnings

The purpose of the empirical work presented in this section is to determine the effect of UI on the jobs eventually accepted by claimants. The empirical work was designed to determine whether an increase in UI leads, on average, to the generation and acceptance of a better job offer. There are, of course, many attributes of a job that are important to job searchers. The job attribute that is used in this paper to measure the effects of UI on the outcome of the job search process is quarterly earnings. It is assumed that if an increase in UI leads to the acceptance and generation of a better job offer, then this effect of UI will show up in quarterly earnings. This assumption is warranted if: (i) most workers do not search for a set of other job attributes at the expense of wages, and (ii) an increase in wages implies an increase in quarterly earnings. We would not expect all searchers to accept better jobs that had less pay because this would imply some disequilibrium in the market determination of the employee renumeration package: a better job at lower pay means that the searcher must have traded nonpecuniary for pecuniary benefits at an exchange that was better than he could get by taking higher pay and buying the benefits outright. This kind of profitable exchange should not exist in equilibrium.

The second assumption is not particularly stringent either. Someone might work less hours when he is offered higher wages per hour, but he will not have lower earnings (wages times hours) unless leisure is an inferior good–which seems unlikely.

The regression results for two forms of the earnings equation are reported in table 10.6. The dependent variable is earnings in the best quarter in the year following unemployment.[17] Claimants who had no earnings records in the year following unemployment were not included in the regressions.[18]

The regression results do not support the hypothesis that an increase in UI leads to the generation and acceptance of better job offers. The results are, in fact, quite mixed in the case of both UI variables. The regression coefficients of the UI variables for both the recall and nonrecall groups were also mixed and sensitive to functional form. A comparison of the same functional form for recalls and nonrecalls did not indicate any significant, consistent difference between the two groups.

[17]When earnings for a longer period were used as the dependent variable, the results were the same, although the R^2's were lower.

[18]The effect of excluding these claimants on the estimated UI coefficients is discussed in [4]. The bias caused by this exclusion is small.

Table 10.6. Earnings regressions (dependent variable = earnings in the best quarter of the year following unemployment).

Independent variables (*t*-statistics in parentheses)	Pennsylvania ($N=3715$) Coefficients				Arizona ($N=7592$) Coefficients			
	Linear		LN-LN		Linear		LN-LN	
WBA	1.67	(1.28)	−0.10	(−1.59)	−0.27	(−0.17)	−0.30	(−5.36)
Max weeks	−8.28	(−1.83)	−0.13	(−1.03)	11.92	(3.84)	0.06	(1.15)
Sex ($F=1$)	−216.94	(−8.47)	−0.13	(−4.70)	−387.03	(−15.91)	−0.21	(−9.55)
Age	−3.15	(−4.49)	−0.09	(−3.31)	−4.02	(−5.03)	−0.13	(−4.38)
Previous earnings	0.66	(31.60)	0.77	(17.93)	0.42	(28.92)	0.69	(21.79)
Earnings stab	81.35	(4.15)	0.17	(3.02)	62.45	(3.65)	0.15	(3.63)
Industry dummies								
Agriculture	92.85	(0.88)	0.22	(1.97)	42.39	(0.25)	0.18	(1.46)
Mining	182.00	(2.43)	0.16	(2.00)	449.62	(11.22)	0.26	(2.09)
Construction	273.87	(7.40)	0.19	(4.95)	625.76	(19.58)	0.32	(11.02)
Nondurables	39.89	(1.38)	0.13	(4.40)	3.10	(0.07)	0.05	(1.36)
Durables	141.44	(4.55)	0.12	(3.70)	182.34	(5.31)	0.13	(4.27)
Transportation	277.84	(4.73)	0.19	(3.13)	343.15	(7.71)	0.21	(5.28)
Finance	−89.39	(−1.12)	0.05	(0.63)	−39.81	(−0.64)	−0.02	(−0.32)
Services	−89.78	(−2.02)	−0.02	(−0.42)	−61.72	(−1.75)	−0.06	(−1.93)
Public Admin.					126.95	(0.42)	0.31	(1.13)
SIC X					−163.55	(−4.22)	−0.18	(−5.19)
Year	−4.86	(−0.13)	−0.42	(−1.57)	−201.57	(−5.05)	−0.16	(−0.67)
Year–skill	0.05	(2.13)	0.07	(1.80)	0.13	(6.47)	0.03	(0.24)
Constant	620.317		2.52		1033.22		3.52	
	$R^2=0.60$		$R^2=0.39$		$R^2=0.47$		$R^2=0.32$	

One reason why the results of the earnings equations are mixed is that it is very difficult to disentangle the separate effects of previous earnings and benefits on post-umemployment earnings. Previous earnings has a positive effect on post-unemployment earnings, making it difficult to detect the positive effect of the highly collinear *WBA* variable. Since previous earnings had a negative effect on duration, it is much easier to assign the separate effects of the two variables and thus, the duration results are not as sensitive to the choice of functional form.

Some insight into the true relationship between post-unemployment earnings and pre-unemployment earnings can be gained by using piecewise linear regressions. By allowing breaks in the relationship between pre- and post-unemployment earnings after benefits have stopped increasing with earnings (K/α), we can see whether the relationship in that range is linear, concave, or convex. If we assign the same shape to the relationship prior to K/α, the remaining movements in the relationship between pre- and post-unemployment earnings between 0 and K/α can be assigned to the effects of increased benefits.

As in the case of the duration equations, the spline equations should also indicate breaks in the relationship between pre- and post-unemployment earnings at K/α if the level of the weekly benefit amount does have an independent effect on post-unemployment earnings. If *WBA* has an independent positive effect on post-unemployment earnings, then the relationship between pre- and post-unemployment earnings should become flatter at the point where benefits no longer vary with earnings.

Table 10.7 reports the previous earnings coefficients from the following regression:

$$Y_Q = \theta_0 + \theta_1 PE + \theta_2 \left[PE - \frac{K_1}{\alpha} \right] Z_1 + \theta_3 \left[PE - \frac{K_2}{\alpha} \right] Z_2 + \Sigma c_i X_i, \tag{14}$$

where Y_Q is the earnings in highest quarter in the year following unemployment and the other variables are the same as those in (13).

The year 1 coefficient θ_3 indicates that Y_Q is a nonlinear function of *PE* when benefits are held constant because the slope of the relationship becomes flatter *after* *WBA* has stopped increasing. The negative θ_3 coefficient for year 1 implies that when $PE > K_1/\alpha$, Y_Q is a concave function of *PE*. If we assume that the concavity holds throughout, then the relevant break coefficient (θ_2) will surely be negative if the *WBA* effect is positive since both the concavity and the positive *WBA* effect will flatten out the relationship between Y_Q and *PE*. Since the relevant break

Table 10.7. Piecewise linear earnings equations (dependent variable = best quarterly earnings in the year following unemployment (t-statistics in parentheses)).[a]

	Pennsylvania		Arizona	
	Year 1	Year 2	Year 1	Year 2
Estimate of θ_1 = slope up to K_1/α	0.58 (7.11)	0.61 (6.49)	0.25 (2.42)	0.44 (3.22)
Estimate of θ_2 =	0.51 (2.86)	0.31* (1.63)	1.57 (4.74)	0.12* (0.27)
Slope between K_1/α and $K_2/\alpha = (\theta_1 + \theta_2)$	1.09	0.92	1.82	0.56
Estimate of θ_2	−0.47* (−3.35)	−0.21 (−1.45)	1.44* (−5.39)	0.04 (0.12)
Slope after $K_2/\alpha = (\theta_1 + \theta_2 + \theta_3)$	0.62	0.71	0.38	0.60

[a]Relevant break points are in boxes. *Indicates extraneous break point.

coefficient (θ_2) is actually positive for year 1, either the concavity assumption and/or the hypothesis that the *WBA* effect is positive must be rejected. A comparison of the θ_2 coefficients across years indicates that a positive *WBA* effect is the most likely candidate for rejection. If higher benefits do increase post-unemployment earnings, then θ_2 for year 1 should be less than θ_2 for year 2 because *WBA* is still increasing in year 2 up to K_2/α, and there can be no *WBA* effect between K_1/α and K_2/α in year 1.[19] The actual result is just the opposite. If anything, the spline results indicate that weekly benefits have a negative effect on post-unemployment earnings.

4. Conclusion

The empirical results presented in this paper provide very strong evidence that an increase in the weekly benefit amount leads to an increase in the average duration of unemployment. Even small increases in the average

[19]An equivalent way of looking at this is to see whether the slope between K_1/α and K_2/α is greater in year 2 than year 1. It should be if the *WBA* has a positive effect on earnings.

duration of unemployment can result in significant increases in the unemployment rate. Thus, when benefits are liberalized, as they have been recently, the resulting increase in the unemployment rate should not be interpreted as a sign that the economy is suffering from some ailment that can easily be cured by aggregate demand policies.

Just how much the unemployment rate will increase when UI increases depends on many factors. Only one of them–the increase in the average duration for covered workers–has been addressed in this paper. UI may also affect the average duration of unemployment for the unemployed who are not covered by UI, and the incidence of unemployment in both the covered and noncovered sectors. Another potentially important factor that has not been addressed here is the possibility that UI has differential effects on duration over the cycle. The analysis presented here covers a period of peak economic activity in both Pennsylvania and Arizona. It is not clear whether the effect of UI on duration should be positively or negatively related to the level of economic activity; only additional empirical research can resolve this issue. It is clear, however, that holding the effect of UI on duration constant, UI has a bigger effect on the unemployment rate the greater the number of people who become unemployed (the higher the incidence).[20] Thus, an increase in UI can have a larger impact on the unemployment rate in a recession, even though its effect on duration is smaller in a recession.

The hypothesis that UI increases subsequent earnings was a direct result of the literature on optimal job search. In fact, an unambiguous positive effect of UI on post-unemployment earnings can be derived only from a very limited class of infinite horizon search models in which the reservation wage is nondecreasing over the period of unemployment. When reservation wages decline over the period of unemployment, the relationship between UI and post-unemployment earnings is ambiguous. The empirical results presented here indicate that the relationship between the level of the weekly benefit payment and post-unemployment earnings is not positive and it may very well be negative. This result disagrees with other studies that have found that UI has a positive effect on the pecuniary returns to jobs subsequent to unemployment.[21] Does this mean that further research on the UI-earnings relationship issue is required? Certainly the issue is empirically and theoretically interesting. It is not, as is often

[20]If U is the average yearly rate of unemployment and AD is the average duration of unemployment and I *is* the incidence of unemployment, then $U=(AD\cdot \mathrm{I})/52$ and $\mathrm{d}U/\mathrm{d}AD=I/52$.

[21]See Burgess and Kingston [2], Ehrenberg and Oaxaca [6] and Holen [11].

claimed, a central or even necessarily relevant issue in evaluating the merits of the UI program. There is a disturbing tendency to label the impacts of UI on duration as adverse incentives and to label any positive effect of UI on earnings as beneficial incentives. The implication is that beneficial incentives counteract the adverse incentives and that given any impact of UI on duration, the UI system should receive higher marks in efficiency, the more potent is its positive effects on subsequent earnings. This kind of argument ignores the fact that UI payments are a real resource cost that is not borne by the searcher. Since UI payments reduce the private cost of search below the social cost of search, they may result in a socially inefficient amount of search.

There is growing evidence that UI increases the duration of unemployment. This does not necessarily mean that the optimal level of UI is zero. UI redistributes income and risk. It also provides a way of pumping money into the economy during downturns. The UI program should be justified on these grounds, not on the basis of UI-induced earnings gains.

References

[1] Burdett, K., "Unemployment insurance payments as a search subsidy," Institute for Research on Poverty, University of Wisconsin, 1977.

[2] Burgess, P. L., and Kingston, J. L., "Impact of unemployment insurance benefits on reemployment success," *Industrial and Labor Relations Review*, 30 (1976), 25–31.

[3] Classen, K. P., "The effect of unemployment insurance on the duration of unemployment and subsequent earnings," *Industrial and Labor Relations Review*, 30 (1977), 438–444.

[4] Classen, K. P., "Unemployment insurance, the duration of unemployment and post-unemployment earnings," PhD Dissertation, UCLA, 1978.

[5] Dillon, A., and Nicholson, W., "A job search model of the effect of extended unemployment insurance benefits on re-employment," Amherst College, 1976.

[6] Ehrenberg, R. G., and Oaxaca, R. L., "Unemployment insurance, duration of unemployment, and subsequent wage gain," *American Economic Review*, 66 (1976), 754–766.

[7] Feldstein, M., "Temporary layoffs in the theory of unemployment," *Journal of Political Economy*, 84 (1976), 937–957.

[8] Hall, J. R., Lippman, S. A., and McCall, J. J., "Expected utility maximizing job search," see this volume, pages 133–155.

[9] Hanna, J. S., Butler, R. T., and Steinman, J. P., "The socio-economic impact of extended benefits," Nevada Employment Security Department, 1975.

[10] Hills, S. M., "Unemployment insurance, job search, and the duration of unemployment," PhD Dissertation, University of Wisconsin, 1975.

[11] Holen, A., "Effects of unemployment insurance entitlement on duration and job search outcome," *Industrial and Labor Relations Review*, 30 (1977), 445–450.

[12] Hosek, J., "Unemployment patterns among individuals," The Rand Corporation, 1975.

[13] Kasper, H., "The asking price of labor and the duration of unemployment," *Review of Economics and Statistics*, 49 (1967), 165–172.

[14] Katz, A., "Acceptance wages of the longer term unemployed". University of Pittsburgh, 1974.

[15] Lininger, C. A., "Unemployment benefits and duration," Institute for Social Research, University of Michigan, 1963.

[16] Lippman, S. A., and McCall, J. J., "The economics of job search: a survey," *Economic Inquiry*, 14 (1976), 155–189 and 347–368.

[17] Lippman, S. A., and McCall, J. J., "Job search in a dynamic economy," *Journal of Economic Theory* 12 (1976), 365–390.

[18] McCall, J. J., "Economics of information and job search," *Quarterly Journal of Economics*, 84 (1970), 113–126.

[19] Mortensen, D. T., "Job search, the duration of unemployment, and the Phillips curve," *American Economic Review*, 60 (1970), 847–862.

[20] Mortensen, D. T., "Unemployment insurance and job search decisions," *Industrial and Labor Relations Review*, 30 (1977), 505–517.

[21] Nachman, D. C., "Risk aversion, impatience and optimal timing decisions," *Journal of Economic Theory*, 11 (1975), 196–246.

[22] Nelson, F. D., "On a general computer algorithm for the analysis of models with limited dependent variables," National Bureau of Economic Research, 1974.

[23] Rothschild, M., "Searching for the lowest price when the distribution of prices is unknown," *Journal of Political Economy*, 82 (1974), 689–712.

[24] Salop, S. E., "Systematic job search and unemployment," *Review of Economic Studies*, 40 (1973), 191–202.

[25] Schmidt, R. M., "Determinants of search behavior and the value of additional unemployment," Graduate School of Management, University of Rochester, 1974.

[26] Stigler, G. J., "Information in the labor market," *Journal of Political Economy*, 70 (1962), 94–104.

[27] Tobin, J., "Estimation of relationships for limited dependent variables," *Econometrica*, 26,(1958), 24–36.

[28] Warner, J. T., "Empirical tests of job search hypotheses: the generation and acceptance of job offers," PhD Dissertation, North Carolina State University, 1976.

[29] Welch, F., "What have we learned from empirical studies of unemployment insurance?," *Industrial and Labor Relations Review*, 30 (1977), 451–461.

Biographical information about authors

Kenneth Burdett

Assistant Professor, Department of Economics, University of Wisconsin-Madison, Madison, Wisconsin 53706, and Research Associate, Institute for Research on Poverty, University of Wisconsin-Madison, Madison, Wisconsin 53706. Professor Burdett obtained his first two degrees in England, both in Economics. After receiving his MSc degree with distinction from the University of London, he studied under Dale T. Mortensen at Northwestern University. In 1973 he went to teach at the University of Essex, and in 1976 he returned to the United States, completed his PhD, and took a position at the University of Wisconsin-Madison. His major research interest is economic theory, especially markets with imperfect information. He has several publications including articles in *American Economic Review* and the *Journal of Public Economics*. At present he is engaged in a large project on matching in the labor market with Dale T. Mortensen.

Kathleen P. Classen

Economist, Center for Naval Analyses, 1401 Wilson Blvd., Arlington, Virginia 22209. Kathleen Classen received a BA degree in Economics from California State College, Northridge in 1970 and a PhD from UCLA in 1978. Her dissertation, an empirical study of the effect of unemployment insurance, was written under John McCall. Since 1974 she has been at CNA where she has worked on labor market problems including unemployment, military retirement, and military recruiting. Some of her work on unemployment insurance appeared in the *Industrial and Labor Relations Review*.

John P. Danforth

Assistant Professor, Department of Economics, University of Minnesota, Minneapolis, Minnesota 55455. Professor Danforth received his AB in Economics from UC Santa Barbara with high honors in 1968. He pursued graduate study in Economics at Northwestern University. There he obtained an MA in 1970 and a PhD in 1974, with supervision provided by Bernt P. Stigum. Professor Danforth's past research interests in the theory of individual attitudes toward risk have led to publications in the *Journal of Economic Theory*. His recent interests center on the application of probabilistic microeconomic theory to the agricultural sector. Except for being on leave in 1977–1978 to the Federal Reserve Bank of Minneapolis, Professor Danforth has been at the University of Minnesota since 1972.

Jeffrey R. Hall

Assistant Professor, University of Santa Clara, Santa Clara, California 95053. Professor Hall received his AB degree in Economics from Northwestern University. He was awarded a PhD in Economics from UCLA in 1975 under the direction of John J. McCall. Lamentably, Dr. Hall perished in a mountaineering accident in 1977.

Nicholas Kiefer

Assistant Professor, Department of Economics, University of Chicago, 1126 East 59th Street, Chicago, Illinois 60637. Professor Kiefer received his AB degree in Economics from Florida State University in 1972. He continued his studies at Princeton University where he was awarded an MS and PhD in Economics under the direction of Orley Ashenfelter and Richard Quandt in 1976. His research has appeared in several economics journals and in a collection of essays edited by Goldfeld and Quandt, *Studies in Nonlinear Estimation*, Ballinger, 1976. Professor Kiefer's research interests have focused on econometric issues in estimating the effects of government training programs and, more recently, on the specification and estimation of switching regression models. He has been a reviewer for several journals and a member of the Department of Economics at Chicago since 1976.

Roger C. Kormendi

Assistant Professor, Graduate School of Business, University of Chicago, Chicago, Illinois 60637. Professor Kormendi began his studies in Economics at the University of Virginia and received the AB degree in 1971. He undertook graduate studies at UCLA; there he received the PhD degree in 1977 under the supervision of Robert W. Clower. Prior to joining the faculty at Chicago in 1975, he served as Assistant Editor for *Economic Inquiry* from 1973 until 1975. His interests in the economics of information, industrial organization, law and economics, and economic theory have resulted in several publications, including a piece in the *Journal of Law and Economics*.

Steven A. Lippman

Professor, Graduate School of Management, UCLA, Los Angeles, California 90024. Professor Lippman, coeditor of this volume, received his AB degree Phi Beta Kappa in Economics and Statistics at UC Berkeley. He continued his education at Stanford University; there he was awarded an MS degree in Statistics and a PhD in Operations Research under the direction of Arthur F. Veinott Jr. in 1968. His research, which includes nearly two dozen published articles as well as an introductory textbook *Elements of Probability and Statistics*, has appeared in applied mathematics and operations research journals as well as *Journal of Economic Theory* and *Economic Inquiry*. His research interests began with inventory theory and dynamic programming and then shifted to applied probability and the optimization of queueing reward systems. His most recent work focuses on the economics of search and probabilistic microeconomics. Professor Lippman has been at UCLA's Graduate School of Management since 1967, having served as Vice-Chairman of the Department and Assistant Dean, Doctoral Program for the last three years. He has been a reviewer for numerous journals and Associate Editor of *Management Science* since 1971.

John J. McCall

Professor, Department of Economics, UCLA, Los Angeles, California 90024. Professor McCall, coeditor of this volume, received his AB degree in Philosophy and Physics from the University of Notre Dame. His PhD was obtained in 1959 at the University of Chicago with Milton Friedman his major advisor. Publications include two books, *Optimal Replacement Policy* (with Jorgenson and Radner) and *Income Mobility, Racial Discrimination and Economic Growth* and numerous articles in journals that include *American Economic Review, Bell Journal, Economic Inquiry, Management Science, Journal of Economic Theory, Journal of Political Economy, Journal of Business, Journal of Human Resources, Journal of American Statistical Association, Quarterly Journal of Economics* and *Review of Economic Studies*. His primary research interest is probabilistic economics. He is a consultant to the RAND Corporation.

George R. Neumann

Assistant Professor, Graduate School of Business, University of Chicago, 5836 Greenwood Avenue, Chicago, Illinois 60637. Professor Neumann received his AB degree in Economics from LeMoyne College in 1968. His graduate studies were undertaken at Northwestern University where he was awarded an MS in Economics in 1969, and a PhD in Economics under the direction of Dale T. Mortensen in 1974. His publications have appeared in several economics journals as well as in several edited volumes. Professor Neumann's research activity has been in the field of labor economics, particularly the impact of government transfer programs. His recent work focuses on the econometric modelling of discrete choice problems in job search and union membership. Prior to joining the faculty at Chicago, he was Assistant Professor of Economics at The Pennsylvania State University from 1972 to 1975.

Charles Stuart

Assistant Professor, Department of Economics, University of Western Ontario, London, Ontario, N6A 5C2, Canada. Professor Stuart received his AB degree in Economics from UCLA and continued his studies there until receiving his MA in 1972. His graduate work culminated in 1975 with the PhD at the University of Lund in Sweden, with Ingemar Stahl his major advisor. Professor Stuart's research interests have included search theory and the economics of traffic accidents and, more recently, information and product quality as well as the economics of property rights.

Joseph Brooke Wharton

Research Economist, Southern California Edison Company, Rosemead, California 91770. Dr. Wharton attended Occidental College and was awarded his AB degree in Economics in 1966. He continued his education at UCLA where he received an MA in 1968 and a PhD in 1976 under the direction of John J. McCall. All three of his degrees are in Economics. Dr. Wharton has worked for The RAND Corporation; the Governor's Office of Planning and Research, State of California; National Economic Research Associates; and currently for Southern California Edison. His research interests include unauctioneered markets, econometric models of energy demands, and the economics of peak-load pricing and energy conservation.

Louis L. Wilde

Assistant Professor of Economics, Division of the Humanities and Social Sciences, California Institute of Technology, Pasadena, California 91125. Professor Wilde received a Bachelor's Degree in Mathematics from the University of Iowa in 1972. He then entered the University of Rochester where he received an MS in Economics in 1975 and a PhD in Economics in 1977 under the direction of Sherwin Rosen. Professor Wilde spent the final year of his graduate program in residence at the University of Chicago under the sponsorship of Professor Gary Becker. During this time he studied under a Grant in Support of Doctoral Dissertation from the US Department of Labor. At the University of Rochester, Professor Wilde specialized in General Equilibrium Theory and Labor Economics. His dissertation, *Labor Market Equilibrium Under Imperfect Information* drew from both of these areas. His current research involves extensions of this dissertation (forthcoming in *Journal of Economic Theory*), further studies in the theory of search, and applications of search theory to information problems in consumer product and financial markets. Professor Wilde has been at the California Institute of Technology since 1976.